Fernando Wood

BIOGRAPHY

OF

HON. FERNANDO WOOD,

MAYOR OF THE CITY OF NEW-YORK.

BY DONALD MAC LEOD,

AUTHOR OF "PYNNSHURST," "BLOODSTONE," "LIFE OF SIR WALTER SCOTT," ETC.

NEW-YORK:
O. F. PARSONS, PUBLISHER, 140 NASSAU ST.
BOSTON: FETRIDGE & CO.
PHILADELPHIA: J. B. LIPPINCOTT & CO.
1856.

JOHN A. GRAY,
PRINTER AND STEREOTYPER,
95 and 97 Cliff st., N. Y.

TO THE

HON. EDWARD EVERETT,

THE

ILLUSTRIOUS SCHOLAR AND STATESMAN,

THIS WORK,

BY HIS PERMISSION,

IS MOST RESPECTFULLY INSCRIBED.

CONTENTS.

CHAPTER I.

CHAPTER II

CHAPTER III.

CHAPTER IV.

CHAPTER XIII.

CHAPTER XIV.

CHAPTER XV.

CHAPTER XVI.

CHAPTER XVII.

APPENDIX.

CHAPTER I.

NATIONAL AND MUNICIPAL GOVERNMENT—PECULIARITIES OF GOVERNMENT IN THE UNITED STATES—PECULIAR CONDITION AND WANTS OF NEW-YORK CITY.

EVER since men stood in need of a government, they have disputed as to what was the best form and principle for it. Monarchy, absolute and limited, hereditary and elective; Empire; Aristocracy; Representative Republicanism; and Absolute Democracy, have all been tried—all had their merits and their difficulties; all produced loyalists and malcontents; all have been overthrown and reëstablished; all have their opponents and their votaries; and each will have its respective enemies and defenders while this earth of ours shall exist.

We, the people of the United States, have decided that the best government for us is Representative Republicanism.

Every country has national or general and municipal or city government; and in no country in the world are these two so distinct. Nay, we add even a third kind, State government, which is independent, and bears no resemblance to European provincial government. With this last, however, we have at present nothing to do. Our national government is limited in its powers to the great *general* rule of the nineteen or twenty millions, who form the population of the States—to that and only that which concerns Maine and Louisiana, Pennsylvania and Oregon alike. But municipal governments apply particularly and individually, deal with you and with me personally, as private citizens, as householders, as professional men. There is no centralization—no capital of the land, in the European sense. Paris is France; Berlin is Prussia; Vienna is Austria; the judiciary, the bar, the police, the military, the license-laws, all issue from the capital, and pass through the entire realm; but Washington has none of these powers out of the boundaries of the small District of Columbia. That city is not the United States in this sense; for, with few exceptions, each State is an independent sovereignty; and even cities are sometimes independent of the States in matters of police and finance, although that may be changed by alteration of charter.

See, then, how widely distinct are our national and municipal governments, and it is well so. This republicanism, with the powers of its representatives so limited, is found the most admirable general system for the nation; but when you take into consideration the fabulous extent of territory, the extraordinary diversity of interests, the singular composition of the populace, Anglo-Saxon, Celtic, Norse, Teutonic, Gallic, etc., you will see how utterly impossible a thing it is for a central, unique capital to rule it intimately and well.

Municipal government requires a certain local, independent power, so that its action may be instant, and its authority in particular points almost irresponsible, inasmuch as none can see its necessities and its difficulties except those who live daily and hourly exposed to them.

No man but a New-Yorker can imagine the difficulty of governing this city. He can not guess at it. Its population of nearly three-quarters of a million occupies an area of twenty-two square miles, and is infinitely various in character, language, and ideas. Properly-called New-Yorkers—that is, natives of two or three descents—are almost extinct; their number would scarcely reach a dozen of thousands. Of the old Dutch and English families very few remain; the immigration from the Eastern States alone would out-number them; and the overwhelming influx of Europeans of late years, while it has caused the unprecedented growth of the city, has helped still more to divide and subdivide the classes of inhabitants. There are thousands of Spaniards, and Frenchmen, and Italians; there are hundreds of thousands of Irish and Germans; there are quarters in the city populated by eighteen or twenty thousand souls, who speak no English; the Saxon, Celt, Teuton, and Gaul are heaped together in the mighty town. And all these have different ideas of government, of the meaning of the word "liberty;" have different rules of action, different manners of thinking, different habits of life.

They have national and natural antipathies for each other; each race is jealous of the advance to power of the others; each believes the other ambitious of influence and capable of abusing that influence to the detriment of all not belonging to itself. Again, New-York is the basket at the hospital-gate for European foundlings. Wild, rough, ignorant of the language, customs, and requirements of the city, they are set upon our wharves by thousands to linger listlessly about the boarding-houses and emigration-offices; or to walk the streets with gaunt eyes wondering at the din and bustle, or with pale faces and outstretched hands soliciting charity from the stranger, upon whose pity they have wandered here to throw themselves.

Now, how to govern so huge, so densely packed a mass; how to unite or at least keep harmonious, so many, so powerful discordant elements; how to reconcile their antipathies, subdue their jealousies; how to manage the newly-landed hordes of poor; how to please all, or at least to keep all quiet—these present a complicated problem, the solution of which requires a wise man. Where such a diversity of thought, language, rule of action, habit of judgment, predisposition, and effect of education exist, there is no such thing as *one* public mind; where there is not *one*, a *single* public mind, it is almost impossible that the decrees or wishes of the government can be generally understood or made acceptable. Therefore, in order well to rule such a city, the government must have power commensurate with its necessities. If one State go wrong there are the other thirty to bring it back, because the nation has a common public mind. But there being no such thing in New-York, city government becomes more difficult and requires more precise, more unquestionable power.

Men in huge cities are careless about the ordinary

events that occur daily in their midst; commercial New-York, so busy, so headlong, has no time to give to the study of its own individual peculiarities. Our citizens are satisfied with a general knowledge of what the *nation* is doing and wanting, without troubling their heads about what is going on next door, or at the end of the block, or in the quarter where they do not reside. If they happen to *see* a man knocked down and robbed, they say: "Ah! what are our governors about? there is a screw loose somewhere." They explain the matter philosophically to their wives, and at 12 M. next day, they have forgotten it.

They have also the national defiance of intrusting their rulers at Washington, the President and the Congress, with power; they have the same fear of intrusting their municipal rulers with power. Because they do not see the precise condition of the populace here, the absolute need of additional, positive authority; because they do not reflect that no other such city, no city with such peculiarities, difficulties, and necessities exists here, or, indeed, upon the face of the whole earth.

Because of this lack of observation and reflection, a demand for more power would probably be unpopular. Therefore it is a brave thing to demand it, and patiently to set to work to prove that it is needed. The man who demands it is brave; the man who obtains it is *capable*, and if capable, a fit ruler for you and for me.

To write the life and career of such an one is an honorable task for the man of letters; is a good deed done for the people.

CHAPTER II.

HENRY WOOD, THE FOUNDER OF THE FAMILY—RELIGIOUS PERSECUTION IN NEW-ENGLAND—FLIGHT FROM NEWPORT AND SETTLEMENT ON THE DELAWARE.

THE history of this country's original settlement is the history of religious persecution. The Puritans, self-exiled for conscience' sake to New-England, were more fiercely and implacably intolerant than their Episcopalian foes in England had been. Roger Williams, the Baptist, was driven to and colonized Providence, Rhode-Island; and Henry Wood, a Quaker, who had emigrated from Wales about 1650, was further compelled to leave Massachusetts, to save life and property.

He, the first of the family in America, was born in 1616; but the stern period of the Protectorate rendered a stay in his native country impossible. He fled to New-England, but only to discover that the Puritans in their new home were more bitterly severe than in the old land of their nativity. Their only idea of religious liberty was that others were free to believe their sour dogmas, and no other thing. They were particularly violent against the Quaker. The Blue-Laws forbade him food or lodging, and the laws of the Plymouth Colony were still more severe. In one case the court decided, "that in case any shall bring in any Quaker, Rantor, or other notorious heretique, either by lande or water, into any parte of this government," he shall be condemned to pay twenty-five shillings a week penalty, or take the said "heretique" away.

October 6, 1657, however, witnessed the passing of the crowning glory of Pilgrim-paternal legislation: "As an addition to the late order in reference to the coming or bringing in of the cursed sect of Quakers into this jurisdiction, it is ordered, that whosoever shall henceforth bring or cause to be brought, directly or indirectly, any known Quaker or Quakers, or other blasphemous heretiques, into this jurisdiction, every such person shall forfeit the sum of one hundred pounds to the country, and shall by warrant from any magistrate, be committed to prison, there to remain until the penalty be satisfied and paid. And if any person or persons within this jurisdiction shall henceforth entertain or conceal any such Quaker or Quakers, or other blasphemous heretiques, knowing them to be so, every such person shall forfeit to the country forty shillings for such entertainment of any Quaker or Quakers, as aforesaid, and shall be committed to prison, as aforesaid, until the forfeiture be fully satisfied and paid: and it is further ordered, that if any Quaker or Quakers shall presume, after they have once suffered what the law requireth, to come into this jurisdiction, every such male Quaker shall for his first offense have one of his ears cut off, and be kept at work att the house of correction until he can be sent away att his own charge: and for the second offense, he shall have the other ear cut off, and be kept at the house of correction as aforesaid. And every woman Quaker that hath suffered the law here, and hath presumed to come into this jurisdiction, shall be severely whipt and kept at the house of correction until, etc. And for every Quaker, he or she, that shall a third time herein again offend, they shall have their tongues bored through with a hot iron and be kept, etc."

Where such laws were in fashion, it is not at all astonishing that ship-builder Henry Wood, an energetic man, should soon find himself in collision with the authorities, and find that his only safety lay in flight. He took a sloop which he owned, perhaps which he had builded, put his wife, his sons—clever, well-grown boys—and his other valuables, aboard, or at least such as he could lay hands on at short notice, and so put forth from intolerant New-England. By way of help on the voyage, he took with him a very limited general knowledge of navigation, a fine, persistent will, some trust in God, and a wife who helped him navigate and stood her watch at the wheel or tiller like a staunch sailor.

This brave Quaker, Henry Wood, steered south-west, probably because pleasant winds came from that direction, and he fancied that sweet winds come from pleasant places. Anyhow, he steered south-westwardly, and by the blessing of Heaven, he made Cape May one morning. He did not know where he was precisely; but as there was rather a nice inlet and a fine bay, he put his helm up, and ran with such breeze as he could get, up the Delaware River. Forests and plains, sunny slopes of upland, pleasant valleys, and a hill or so, he doubtless saw: but for the first thirty miles, nothing that looked like humanity, far less like civilized humanity. But, so much of the voyage accomplished, he came upon certain huts, built there in 1643 by adventurous Swedes, and now in 1855 called by us moderns Newcastle.

The Swedes had been in the neighborhood since 1637, purchasing at that time from the Indians the whole district of country up the Delaware from the Capes to Trenton, some thirty miles or so above the present site of Philadelphia. They called these lands New-Sweden. It was from these settlers that Penn bought the site of Philadelphia and of other portions of the country. The seller's name was Sven, which was corrupted into Swan; and Sven's sæner, or the sons of Sven, have their name still commemorated by Swanson street in Southwark.

This Swedish settlement was, in 1655, conquered by our own doughty Petrus Stuyvesant, hard kœpig Piet, who, with many voluminously-breeched Dutchmen, and with his brave trumpeter Anthony doubtless, came valiantly up the Delaware, and did then and there manfully set upon and conquer those pestilent Swedes. After which important event, the colony became Dutch in ownership and government, but remained purely Swedish in populace. They were good people, these Swedes, kind and just to the Indians, and therefore trusted and beloved by those red people, with whom they lived in friendship and mutual kind feeling, when our adventurer sailed up the Delaware.

But Swedes are not Quakers, and his late experiences had induced him to prefer communication with the members of that sect rather than with any other people. So he would not stop, nor hold communication with those blonde-haired men, nor let them come aboard, but drove right on until his eye fell upon a spot where he fancied he might live in peace, although such peace might include considerable isolation.

I don't know that he beached the sloop, but I rather fancy he did; and then, like Noah, he and his wife and his sons came out of their ark, and went bravely up into the forest, to make for themselves what manner of home their own stout hearts and arms could accomplish. Sharp axes and some physical strength were needed in those rough days of America, when thirty miles up the Delaware was backwoods, and we presume that Henry Wood was provided with both; for the kingly trees were felled, a clearing made, a cabin built, as nicely as could be managed at the time, and Henry and his wife and boys entered therein and dwelt there.

Doubtless there were seeds of maize, and wheat, and oats among the sloop's stores, which he and the boys planted as best they might. At least he and they might live there and preach, if it pleased them, without having their "tongues bored through with a hot iron." Relatively speaking, even this cabin in the forest was a change for the better. When the smoke came out of the chimneys or the crannies in the logs, as the case may have been, it rose up and floated over lands which lie just now some five miles above Camden; that is, opposite to the pleasant though rectangular city of Philadelphia.

His Majesty James Stuart, Seventh of Scotland, and Second of England, was the kind friend and generous protector of the peaceful though much-persecuted

Quakers. Shortly after his accession to the throne, more than four hundred of those religionists were released from prison at one time. William Penn was the personal and familiar friend of the king, passed much of his time at court, and was supposed to have more influence than any other person there. It was in payment of an old debt due from the crown, that the grant of the American province was made to him; and when, in the year of our Lord sixteen hundred and eighty-three, he came with his colonists to found Philadelphia, he was met by Henry Wood, who had lived alone in the forest there on the banks of the Delaware, with his stout-hearted wife and sons, his broad-brimmed principles, and his absolute determination to keep his conscience free.

Wood was the first white man to mount the quarter-deck of the owner and lord of Pennsylvania; and it is said, that when he saw his brethren in the faith, he, like the patriarch of old, lifted up his voice and wept for joy that his twenty-seven years of isolation were at an end.

He had settled, as we have seen, in the vicinity of Camden; indeed his tract comprehended the site of that city; settling first, as men did in those days, without troubling himself about the ownership of the place, but afterwards, like a just man, purchasing fairly from the Indians the huge property. The savage called the eastern lands of the Delaware, where now are the counties of Burlington, Gloucester, and Camden, Arwowmosse, and hereabout Wood added to his vast estate, by purchase from one Samuel Cole, several hundred acres more of lands. The deed is old and quaint, and it may gratify some readers' curiosity to see how conveyancing was accomplished in those primitive times of America.

THE DEED.

This Indenture made the fifth day of September in the yeare of our Lord according to English Accompt. one Thousand Six Hundred Eighty and Two Betweene Samuell Cole of Arwawmosse in the Province of West Jersey, Yeoman and Elizabeth his Wife of the One part, and Henry Wood now or late of Newport upon Road Island in new England Carpenter of the other part Witnesseth, that the said Samuell Cole for & in consideration of the Sum of fifty three pounds of Current money (that is to say) fifteene pounds (part thereof) of lawful English money and Thirty and eight pounds (the remainder thereof) of Currant Boston money of new England to him the said Samuell Cole in hand paid & secured. to bee paid by the said Henry Wood at or before the sealeing and delivery of these prsents the receipt whereof Hee the said Samuell Cole doth hereby acknowledge and thereof and of every part and parcell thereoff doth acquit Exonorate Deliver and Discharge the said Henry Wood his heires Executors & Administrators and every of them for ever by these prsents. And the rather for that it stands with the good will & knowing of the said Elizabeth the wife of the said Samuell and by her consent and appointm't certifyed by her being a party to these prsents and putting her hand and seale hereunto. Hath Granted Bargained and Sold Assigned Enfeoffed Released and Confirmed. And by the these prsents doth fully, clearly and absolutely Grant Bargain & sell Assign Enfeoffe Release and Confirm unto the said Henry Wood his Heires and Assignes for ever (in his Actual possession now being by virtue of a Bargaine & Sale for one whole yeare to him thereof made by Indenture hereupon endorsed bearing date the day before the date of these prsents and of the Statute for transferring uses in possession) one twentieth prte (in Twenty prts divided or to be divided) of that Propriety or tract of Land in West new Jersey aforesaid purchased by him the said Samuell Cole, and Benjamin Bartlett of William Penn, Gawen Lawey Nicholas Lucas and Edward Billings by Indenture of Lease and Release beareing date the first & second days of March in the yeare of our Lord 1676. And alsoe all that the Dwelling House or Tenement of him the said Samuell Cole situate standing or being at Arwawmosse aforesaid wherein hee the said Samuell Cole now inhabitteth, with all and singular the outhousing and appurtenances thereunto belonging. And also one hundred Acres of Land now being the plantation of him the said Samuell Cole whereon the said dwelling house stands with all and every the foulds yards backsides orchards gardens floures walls wayes waters & pitts commodities & improvements to the said one hundred Acres or Plantation belonging or appertaining with all and every the mines minerals woods fishings hawkings huntings & fowlings and all other pitts and commodities Hereditam[ts] and Appurtances to the said Granted premises or any prte or drcll thereoff belonging or appertaining (except & reserved foth of this Grant unto the said Samuell Cole his Heires & Assigns for ever one Cow House belonging to the said Dwelling House) And all the Estate Right Tytle Interest and possession property clayme and demand whatsoever of him the said Samuell Cole or Elizabeth his Wife or either of them of, in or unto the same or any prte or prcll thereof. And the Reversion & Reversions Remainder or Remainders of the same. And all deeds evidences and writings concerning the said Granted p[r]misses onely or onely any pte or prcll thereof and true coppies of such other deeds evidences and writings as are in the Custody or possession of the said Samuell Cole which concerne the said Granted premises joyntly with other lands, such said copies to bee made out and written at the pper costs and charges of the said Henry Wood his heires or assigns To HAVE AND TO HOLD the said granted premises or herein and hereby mentioned or intended to bee granted bargained or sold with their or every of their Appurtenances (except before excepted) unto the said Henry Wood his heires and assigns for ever to the only proper use and behoof of him the said Henry Wood his heires and assigns for evermore. And the saide Samuell Cole, for himselfe his heires, executors and Admtrs. do covenant devise and grant to and with the said Henry Wood, his heires and assignes by the s[d] presents and it shall and may bee lawful to and for the said Henry Wood his heires and assignes for ever hereafter peaceably and quietly to have, hold, use occupie possesse and enjoy the said granted premises and every pts and prcls, thereof with theire appurtn^{s}, without any law let suits trouble dangers, eviction, ejection or disturbance of him the said Samuel Cole and Elizabeth his wife or either of them their or either of their heires or assignes or of any other psons, their assignes or any other prsons lawfully clayming or to to be claymed in, by, from, or under them or either or any of them, freed, discharged of and from all other estates tytles, dower, tytle of dower troubles charges, burthens, and incumbrances whatsoever had made, done, committed or suffered or hereafter to be had made, done, committed suffered or * * * * * by the said Samuel Cole and Elizabeth his wife or either of them their or either of their heirs or assignes, or by any other pson or psons clayming or to be claymed by — * * * [Here follows a line illegible because of the dilapidations of this quaint old deed] forth of the said granted premises unto James Duke of Yorke his heires and assignes excepted and foreprized and further that the said Samuel Cole and Elizabeth his wife and their heires shall and will, at the request, cost and charges of the said Henry Wood, his heires executors and assignes at all or any tyme or tymes, dureing the terme and space of seven yeares next ensueing the date hereof, make, doe, execute and suffer or cause to be made done executed and suffered, all or any such other acte or acts, thing or things conveyance or assurance or by the same Henry Wood, his heirs or assignes shall be reasonably and lawfully required for the further better and more perfecte conveying and assuring the said granted premises and every prt and prcl of the said premises unto the said Henry Wood his heires and assignes forever according to the purport, true intent and meaning of these prsts, soe as that for the doeing and executing thereof, the said prties, who shall bee required to make such further assurance bee not bee compelled or compellable to travel further than the space of twelve miles from his or their place of aboad at the tyme of such request to be made and soe as such further conveyance or assurance containe noe further or larger warrantee than as aforesaide.

In Witness whereof the said prties to these prsnts; interchangeably have sette theire hands and seales, the day and yeares above written 1682.

Here follows the confirmation of the above deed by Wm. Penn or others associated with him in the commission which contained his grant of Pennsylvania.

THIS INDENTURE made the fowreth, 4th, day of September in the yeare off our Lord according to English accompts one thousand six hundred and eighty and two, betweene Samuel Cole of Arwawmosse in the province of West Jersey Yeoman of the one pte and Henry Wood now or late of Newport, Road Island in New England, Carpenter of the other part Witnesseth, that the said Samuel Cole for and in consideration of Five shillings of Currant English money to him in hand by the said Henry Wood at and before the sealing and delivery of these presents whereof and wherewith hee the said Samuel Cole doth hereby acknowledge himselfe fully satisfyed contented and paid hath devised granted bargained and sold And by these psnts doth demise grant bargain and sell unto the said Henry Wood his Exrs Admtrs and assignes one twentieth pt (in twenty pts divided or to be divided) of that portion or tract of land in West New Jersey aforesaid purchased by the said Samuel Cole & Benjamin Bartlett of William Penn Gawen Lowrey and Nicholas Lucas and Edward Billings by indenture of lease and release bearing date the first and second dayes of March in the year of o^{r} Lord 1676 and alsoe all that the dwelling house or tenem^{t} of him the said Samuel Cole situate standing or being at Arwawmosse aforesaid wherein hee the said Samuell inhabitteth with all and singular the outhouses and appurtenances thereunto belonging and also one hundred acres of land more being the plantation of him the said Samuell Cole whereon the said dwelling house stands with all and every the ffoulds yards backsides orchards gardens flowers walls ways waters prfitts commodities improvements to the said one hundred acres or plantation belonging or appertayning with all and every the mines mineralls woods ffishing hawkings huntings and ffowlings and all other prfitts commodities hereditam^{ts} and appurtenances to the said granted p^{r}misses or any pt or prcell thereof belonging or appertayning except reserved forth of this devise grant unto the said Samuell Cole his heires and assignes forever one cowhouse belonging to the said dwelling house TO HAVE AND TO HOLD the said devised and granted p^{r}misses and every p^{t} and p^{r}cell thereof with their and every of their appurtenances (except before excepted) unto the said Henry Wood his Exrs Admrs and assignes from the day before the date hereof for and during one whole yeare from thence next ensuing fully to be compleat and ended to the intent that by vertue of these p^{r}sents and for the statute for transferring uses into possession he the said Henry Wood may be actuall possessor of the said p^{r}misses and may be enabled to accept and take a grant of the revision of the p^{r}misses to the uses thereof to be declared.

IN WITNESSE whereof the said prties to these p^{r}sent Indentures Interchangeably hav sett their hands and seales the day and yeare first above written 1682.

The above deed and confirmation appear to have been duly acknowledged before Elias Farr and James Devenport in the presence of Samuel Lorings, Robert Wade, Thos. Revell.

Endorsed on the Parchment appears as follows:

"Entered into the Records of the Province above sd in the 66 & 67 pages of book B. by me Tho Revell, Record^{t}.

Also:

"Aprill ye 12th Acpp^{t} 1689.

"Granted that a warrant to Henry Wood for ye survey of sd second of the within Granted premises be issued promptly per me. JOHN REDDING.

CHAPTER III.

PEASHORE, AND THE FAMILY THERE—PENN AND THE QUAKERS—THE PATRIARCH'S DEATH, AND HIS SUCCESSORS.

THE precise spot on which the worthy Friend builded his house and dwelt, he called Peashore, because of the abundant crops of that delicious esculent produced by the seeds which came in the sloop from Newport, and Peashore has been the family homestead ever since. Here were born and lived the ancestors of the Mayor of this our Empire City, and not far off is the burial-ground where, one by one, as they grew old and weary, they were carried and laid down to rest.

Henry and Benjamin were the names of the two sons, of whom the former died soon after the new settlement, and of whom nothing is recorded save that he lived and helped his father, and died in the midst of his youth. But Benjamin, who was born in England in 1649, lived stoutly, and when he grew old enough was endowed by his father with an estate of seven hundred and eighty-four acres, whereof the record may be seen to this day in Book M. S. B., pp. 162 to 164, at the Register's office in Burlington, New-Jersey. It seems that they were carried there when the record-office of Gloucester county was destroyed, during the stormy times of the War of Independence.

Armed with the royal grant, William Penn went resolutely to work to establish his new colony on a firm basis. He made his famous treaty with the Indians, shaming, by its moderation and kind integrity, the cruel and unjust way of dealing which was generally adopted by other white settlers in this country.

There was much to do. A constitution was to be formed, a legislative assembly and supreme council to be chosen. All were free to believe as they pleased, and go to what church they liked, provided only that they did not believe in the innocence of stage-plays, or pledging of healths. Then there were quarrels with Lord Baltimore about the boundary line between Penn's grant and Maryland, which doubtless vexed the worthy Quaker's soul. There were also the Swedes and Hollanders to be naturalized, and taxes and imposts to be regulated, and their collection to be provided for.

But at last all this work was accomplished, and the "Governor and proprietary" of the Province saw his colony in a condition prosperous and likely to prosper.

No one enjoyed a closer intimacy with Penn than Henry Wood. From his long residence in the country before the arrival of the great Quaker, he was familiarly known to and trusted by the natives. Consequently, he was employed as arbiter and regulator of disputes, which might arise between the whites and Indians. His reputation as pioneer, and the long experience which he had enjoyed, made him naturally the counsellor and protector of the young colony, and his many and important services were rewarded by Penn with a confirmation of title to the property which he already held by purchase from the Indians.

So at last the end came. The snows of seventy-eight winters were white upon the staunch old Quaker's head; the tall, powerful frame was beginning to bow and grow feeble, and at last, in 1694, he put off the robes of this mortality, and lay down in the burial-ground at Peashore beside his first-born son.

Thirty-eight years before, he had settled where his dust reposes now, coming out of his sloop and planting his dried peas. Persecution drove him from his native land, and followed him to that which he adopted. For him there was no religious peace nor freedom to worship God either in Old or New-England. The civilized, the learned, the Christian populations had no charity for him or for his creed, and so he took refuge in the wild forest among the dusky savage tribes, and the savage gave him hospitality and liberty of conscience; learned to respect and confide in him; gave him a share of their lands, and bade him stay there and be happy, without fear of prison, or stocks, or whipping, or of having his tongue bored through with a red-hot iron for speaking, when the Spirit moved him, the words which such Spirit incited him to say.

Benjamin Wood succeeded to the large property left by his father, as well as to the indomitable energy and excellent characteristics of the old man. He continued the clearing of the forest and the cultivation of the land, and added thereto another source of wealth. He embarked largely in the Delaware fisheries, which were excellent particularly, as at this day, for shad, and supplied the new colony of Philadelphia and its broad-brimmed inhabitants with that delicate fish. And so his wealth increased, and would have been enormous but for a great good-nature and perhaps over-generous temperament.

People were settling now along the opposite shores of the Delaware, and he was always ready to assist them with money or a bit of land, as the case might be. At last he managed to pass away the whole of his immense estate, except the old house, the burial-ground, and about a thousand acres more. Tradition tells the story on this wise: That Mr. Wood had long been urged to sell, but had an unconquerable dislike to do so. A friend of his, however, living in Camden and Philadelphia, induced him to grant a lease of his estate for ninety-nine years; and Wood, persuaded that the fisheries were less laborious than farming, and far more profitable, agreed, and signed the instrument. All was conveyed, but what we have excepted, for several miles along the river, including the site of Camden, a property now worth many millions.

Well, this lease has disappeared; lost, stolen, or destroyed, no one knows what, but at any rate gone from human sight altogether. The older members of the family have employed lawyers and antiquarians, have instituted careful researches, but without effect, and in spite of the belief of all the descendants of Henry Wood, that the paper was a lease and no other thing, the splendid property is lost to them for want of written evidence, and must remain in the hands of those who hold it now.

So Benjamin Wood went on driving his trade in fish with his Philadelphian brethren, and cultivating his thousand acres at Peashore until, in 1713, he was peaceably gathered to his fathers.

Three sons outlived him—Henry, Benjamin, and Isaac, of whom the second died in youth and childless. Isaac moved nine miles down the river, and founded there a little separate colony, which soon became a town, and which commemorates his enterprise and bears his name to this day—it is the town of Woodbury, in New-Jersey, although then it formed a portion of the Pennsylvanian grant.

Isaac, too, died childless, for his two sons preceded him in death, and Henry was left to perpetuate the family and keep the name of the old pioneer in the memories of men. He did both admirably, for he had seven children and his grandsire's character.

He was a quiet, placid man, an inveterate, calm, obstinate disciple of George Fox, a Quaker according to the strictest sect of that peculiar religion; stuck to broad skirts and brims; combed the curls out of his hair; used the second person singular in conversation, instead of following the example of what is called polite society; was benevolent, and good, and kind, and probably, as is the wont of that sect to-day, had his plain coat made of the finest possible cloth, of the most exquisite possible shade. He lived at Peashore, wore his distinctive garments, was gentle and friendly to all his neighbors, did his duty, never had his tongue bored through with a hot iron, and went away finally about the year of God seventeen-seventy, to receive such reward as his Maker had in store for him.

CHAPTER IV.

THE WAR OF INDEPENDENCE—FIGHTING QUAKERS—MATERNAL ANCESTRY —IMMEDIATE FAMILY OF FERNANDO WOOD.

THEN Henry, his son, succeeded him. And he, too, cultivated Peashore and went in the way of his fathers—at least, in all points but one. Although a Quaker, and having by inheritance and conviction the horror of warfare for which that sect is distinguished, yet when, in 1775, the country was aroused to assert its independence of Great Britain, he did as others of his co-religionists did, girded his loins and went out as a man of war. Doubtless he remembered the wrongs which his people had suffered from persecuting England, his great-grandfather's exile and long, lonely sojourn in the western wilderness; doubtless, too, a pure patriotism was his chief influence and inducement; and perhaps we may venture to suggest that under that plain drab coat there lingered still a little of the old Adam.

There was room enough in him to hold all these motives, for though only eighteen years old, he held his stalwart figure erect, was over six feet in height, and weighed two hundred pounds. An ugly customer to

2*

cross, with that inherited persistent will of his, Quaker though he were.

There were giants on the earth in those days, for in the whole troop which he raised and commanded, no soldier was under six feet. So, with these stout fellows behind him, Henry Wood set up for a soldier, keeping at first about the neighborhood of his home. At last came the battle of Germantown, fought in that suburb, on the 4th day of October, 1777, whereat our young captain, riding at the head of his men, received a severe wound, which did not, however, disable him from further warfare; but he went on fighting for his native land, and was turned out of meeting by his brethren in consequence.

His elder brother, Isaac, participated in the general feeling, and helped the cause of independence forward, both with tongue and purse, rousing the farmers with one, and supplying the sinews of war with the other. The other children were then too young for such service.

But if the long war of the Revolution resulted in the complete independence of the colonies and the formation of the United States, it also brought Henry Wood to the verge of pecuniary ruin. His constant martial activity of course prevented him from giving proper attention to his farm: his family was very large, eight boys and three girls, to be provided for, so that with much going out, and nothing coming in, debts began to accumulate and creditors to press for payment. Bit after bit of the lands of Peashore had to be sold to satisfy these demands; and at the beginning of the present century, there was little left to Henry Wood but the old God's acre, where he too expected to be one day quietly at rest.

Of his large family, we have little to say. Two sons, Joseph and Henry, men of wealth and high respectability, still live at Trenton, in New-Jersey; the daughters married well, and all appear to have maintained the worthy and firm character derived from the old man, whose sloop first came to Peashore. Only of one have we something more particular to say.

Benjamin Wood, father of the present Mayor, was born on the 15th of February, 1784, and at an early age quitted the Delaware home, at Peashore, to go and learn how to be a wholesale dry-goods merchant, in the city of brotherly love. We dare say he acquitted himself as well in this peaceable calling, as his father had in battling; at any rate, he took to early independence, and at the age of twenty-two, with the aid of such capital as the old soldier could give him—not much, we suppose—he started in trade for himself; his father, however, retaining some interest in the business.

Next year, on January 6, the young man married, and five years afterwards, Fernando was born. The father continued business in Philadelphia, subject to the varied chances of trade. During the war of 1812 to 1815 his success was brilliantly steadfast, but peace, that brought good to all others, brought distress to him. A very large stock of goods, then in his store, depreciated very much and suddenly in value, and the result was bankruptcy.

However, he cleared away the wreck as best he might,

and, though his health was broken and his strength impaired, he hoped, and waited, and showed the onward determined will which characterized his family. His health demanded an absolute change of climate, and so he took his wife and little ones, six in number at the time, and started on a southern tour. First to Kentucky, and then down the Ohio and the turbulent, huge Mississippi to New-Orleans. From New-Orleans he went to the Havana, and thence, with recruited energies, back northward to settle permanently, in 1821, in this city of New-York, and re-commence business as a merchant.

We have seen the warlike Quaker father expelled from that peaceable sect for his martial tendencies, and the children, it would appear, have not returned to its communion. Mr. Benjamin Wood was an elder, with Colonel Rutgers and William B. Crosby, in the Market-street Presbyterian Church, and so remained until the extreme severity of the winter of 1832 drove him southward in search of a more genial climate. He found it at Charleston, South-Carolina, but it could not restore him to health. He lingered there till the month of November, and then died.

Old residents of New-York remember him well, and speak freely of his virtues, and of certain characteristics of his, the development of which in the Mayor of New-York have much interested the public. They speak of his kindness of heart; his integrity in business; his absolute onward-going where duty or supposed duty called him; his self-reliance; his steadfast will; his great industry, and immense endurance.

We have done now with Mr. Wood's paternal ancestry, and have a word or two to say of his excellent mother, who now lives in good health with her distinguished son. Her grandfather, General Lehman, was a gallant officer of the famous ten years' war in Germany, where he served from 1740 to 1750, with distinction. The son of this gentleman, Henry Lehman, was born in the free town of Hamburgh, 1745, immigrated to America before the war of the Revolution, and settled in Gloucester county, a few miles below Woodbury.

Oddly enough, here was another warlike Quaker, who did precisely as Henry Wood had done; took off the drab coat, and put on the gold-laced blue; served through the whole war, got turned out of meeting, was an officer in the same battle of Germantown, and got shot through both cheeks by a British bullet, which cut off a slice of his tongue, and carried away several of his teeth on its swift road through.

Rebecca, his daughter, had been a schoolmate of young Benjamin Wood, had grown up with him, was his child sweetheart in their earlier days, and the faithful, affectionate wife of his manhood. There was good soldier blood in her too. She could follow her husband cheerfully through Kentucky, Louisiana, and Havana, and when the time came for showing more absolute, personal, and, in a woman, unexpected courage, she was not found wanting.

Some time before her husband's death, during his absence from the house, Mrs. Wood had gone into her next door neighbor's for some purpose, leaving a servant sitting at the open door. But while the mistress was absent, the servant disappeared, and, the door being left invitingly open, a big negro walked in and began to investigate the contents of the house with an ultimate view to the personal appropriation of any portable articles of value that he might discover.

On her return, the lady found no servant, but the door still open, and the hall lamp extinguished. Her children, sleeping above, first occupied her, and she moved upstairwards, until she found her path obstructed by the said big negro. To her demand of what he wanted there, he made no answer, but only tried to push past her. She seized the fellow, uttering this gentle admonition: "If you move an inch, I'll blow your brains out!" and called for lights. The servant came from below stairs with a candle, and discovered the darkey with his arms full of property. Her cries brought the watch, and Sambo, stripped of his ill-gotten goods, was hospitably entertained by the municipal government. Mrs. Wood of course had no pistol wherewith to accomplish her threat, and one blow from the fellow's fist would have stunned her.

But she could do more than this if it were needed: she could and did *fight* side by side with her husband. They were at Edenton, North-Carolina, in the year 1811, during an insurrection of the slaves there. The proprietor of the house in which they were staying was obnoxious to the negroes, and they had determined to destroy him and all the inmates of the house. But these latter were prepared, and at the first noise near their room, Mr. Wood, well armed, came out, followed by his wife, also armed. They were instantly attacked by four negroes, with clubs, but the battle was short, for Mr. Wood shot two of the assassins, while his wife felled the others to the ground.

In her twenty-five years of wedlock, Mrs. Wood remained the friend, consoler, companion of her husband. She bore him seven children—five sons and two daughters—and now resides with her son Fernando, vigorous in body and in mind.

The eldest son, Maundred, went early in life to Texas, while that State was still a province of the Mexican Republic. He took part in the revolution there, and was present at the storming of the Alamo, and with General Houston at the battle of San Jacinto. After the independence of Texas was established, he served in several positions of distinction, and died there. The other children reside in New-York city, except Adolphus, a physician of some distinction, living in Missouri.

CHAPTER V.

BIRTH AND CHILDHOOD OF THE MAYOR—EARLY INDEPENDENCE AND ENERGY—ADVENTURES AND ANECDOTES.

FROM such a stock there is descended the subject of these memoirs, Fernando Wood, now Mayor of the City of New-York. In his veins flows the blood of the peaceful yet sturdy Quaker, who could suffer for conscience' sake with fortitude, but could not renounce his faith; at once a non-combatant Friend and a stalwart pioneer in the wilderness of the Delaware. In the same veins flows the blood of that Newport exile's peaceful descendants, whose calm agricultural lives passed away tranquilly at Peashore; the blood of the patriot soldier who disobeyed his religion for his country; the blood of the stout comrade of Tilly or Wallenstein; and of the two who, leading tranquil burgess lives, showed, when occasion required, the personal courage, the onwardness, the firm perseverant will and powers of endurance which render their son so eminent.

Fernando Wood was born in the city of Philadelphia, on the 14th day of June, 1812, the day upon which the cabinet council decided to declare war against Great

Britain for the second time. It is said that he took this first important step somewhat as General Jackson removed the deposites of the United States Bank—on his own responsibility; for the accoucheur who was sent for found upon his arrival that his services were no longer required, his client having entered the world without his assistance and in promising health.

It is recorded that when he had reached the age of twelve months he was visited with a severe illness. The father, whose own parents had renounced Quakerism, had as yet professed no other creed. But when the physicians told him that the limits of their skill had been obtained, and that they could do no more, he fell upon his knees, and with tears plead to God for the life of his child. And God heard his prayer, and in His pity granted it.

Henry, and Isaac, and Zachariah, and Benjamin, had been the simple prenomina of his ancestors. But his mother had been reading the Three Spaniards, one of those blood and thunder, chain-clanking, subterranean galleried mysterious novels, brought into vogue by Horace Walpole's Castle of Otranto, and Mrs. Anne Radcliffe's ditto of Udolpho. Now one Fernando was the hero of this famous book, a notable fellow, no doubt, at any rate much admired by Mrs. Wood, who, for such admiration's sake bestowed his name upon her son.

He learned to walk and read nearly without instruction; indeed, had very little care ever taken of his education except what he took himself. In 1820, the boy being eight years old, was sent to a class taught by Mr. James Shea, well and respectfully remembered as the competent mathematical master in the grammar school of Columbia College, as well as at the head of his own academy. At the age of thirteen, however, his father being absent in the South because of ill health, the boy fancied his education finished, and formed a strong desire to go out into the world and thus early to begin the battle of life.

He disclosed his desires for independence to his mother. and she, for jest's sake, agreed, supposing it to be a youngster's notion of which he would soon be tired. Such was, however, not the case, for he started off at once, and, borrowing a newspaper at the nearest grocer's, began to study the column of "wants," wherein he discovered that Mr. Brewster, keeper of an exchange office, wanted a boy. From the grocer's he went to the broker's, and was then and there by him engaged at the salary of *two dollars* per week. Here he was, then, a clerk; but not yet, as he thought, independent. There was a large family at home, the father was an invalid from rheumatism, and he desired to be absolutely his own bread-giver and master, to buy his own clothing, provide for his own lodging.

After much natural maternal opposition, Fernando's will prevailed; the mother of a young friend of his, Ketcham by name, and dwelling at that time in Oliver street, undertook to give him what he sought for one dollar and fifty cents per week. It was little less than his present salary; but he had faith in himself and in indomitable, persevering industry, and, taking what wardrobe he possessed, bade adieu to the mother and sisters, and went to Mrs. Ketcham as a boarder.

At eight o'clock next morning he was punctually at his post, and ever since has supported himself, and of later years aided also that good, intelligent mother of his. Mr. Brewster is now a wealthy citizen, as well as his former little clerk, his present Chief Magistrate. After some months' service the stipend was advanced to three dollars and a half; and then an exchange broker, Mr. Betts, offering five dollars for the youngster, Mr. Brewster lost him; but his chances for paying tailor's bills and such like evils were considerably better now than when the board and lodging cost seventy-five dollars and the salary was a hundred and two.

When about seventeen years old, he was sent to Harrisburgh, Virginia, on some business, and he remained there during the session of the Legislature of 1829. On returning one evening to his hotel, he found in the reading-room a number of law-makers, among whom was an important and distinguished senator, and all of whom were in a high state of excitement. It was before the passage of the Prohibitory Liquor Law. The distinguished senator, in the course of his excitement, found it necessary to his comfort to make an insulting remark to young Wood, who replied with what degree of fierce tartness was given to him at the moment. The distinguished senator, finding no crushing witticism at his tongue's end, drew his bowie-knife and advanced to immolate the boy; but he, nothing daunted, and being a stout fellow of his years, picked up a chair, and when the proper time came knocked the distinguished senator down. For this he was arrested and slept that night in prison; but early in the morning he was, without investigation, released by the distinguished senator's friends.

On his way, about this time, from Harrisburgh to Lancaster, he found in the stage-coach an old gentleman and three young girls, to all of whom he shortly had an opportunity of displaying his coolness and energy. For the horses became frightened and ran away; the coachman was toppled from his box, and matters might have gone badly for the old gentleman and the young girls if Wood had not gotten out of the window, made his way to the seat, secured the reins, and gradually stopped the horses.

So, his business in Pennsylvania being brought to an end, he started for his home in New-York. He had begun to smoke at thirteen years of age, and as is the custom among youthful New-York, the habit had attained to a precocious inveteracy. Now, leaning over the rail of the Philadelphia steamboat, enjoying his cigar, about the twentieth for that day, he was accosted by a benevolent-looking old Quaker.

"Friend, thee smokes a good deal," quoth Broadbrim.

"Yes," Fernando confessed he did.

"Well, don't thee smoke any more."

"I wont," was the reply; the half-smoked cigar was committed to the deep, and a resolution formed which has never since been broken.

Before this year of his life was out he went one evening, as was the wont of youth at the period, to the Chatham Theatre, and on coming out and going homewards, he perceived or fancied that he was followed. He increased his pace and the pursuer did the same, till

Wood turned down Lumber street, a gloomy place, flanked with huge piles of boards and other timber, and not abounding in houses. The pace of the individual behind was quickened and he had nearly reached Fernando, when the latter turned, and presenting suddenly the puffed-out finger of a dark buckskin glove, said, with whatever stern emphasis he could command:

"Follow me one step further, and I will blow your brains out."

The person addressed denied any hostile intentions, but at the same time took another way.

Soon after he was sent to Richmond to take charge of a large tobacco factory in that city, and was there smitten with a violent sock and buskin mania, which endured some months. Not many, however, for after the lapse of nine, he returned to New-York, and in June, 1832, started for himself as a tobacco dealer in Pearl street.

It was the year when for the first time the awful cholera made its appearance among us, and the city was struck aghast at its merciless ravages. From the thickly populated down town districts the merchants fled in terror. Wood's store was the only one in the neighborhood kept open, and he was enabled to do; and did good and kind service to the sick and the dying of the vicinity.

He began to think and talk of politics now-a-days, being a warm admirer of General Jackson. He wrote, too, for the press, among other things one which attracted much notice at the time, a review of South-Carolinian Governor Haynes' message in favor of Nullification.

He formed the friendship of the late William Leggett, retained it throughout the life of the latter, and proved it to his memory by projecting and liberally contributing towards the monument over his remains at New-Rochelle.

But politics is not precisely the most lucrative interest which a young merchant has; he lost time and therefore money, so that in 1835, he was obliged to leave off business for himself and become a clerk again. This time he went to Francis Secor, in West street, and served him. Industry got money, and prudence saved it, so that next year, with some help of friends, he was able to begin again as grocer, on the corner of Rector and Washington streets. Here he was very successful, coming by 1838 to be owner of two or three vessels, and then he reached his twenty-eighth year and was elected in 1840 to the Congress of the United States, in one of the most heated political contests this city has ever witnessed—the season of log-cabins, hard cider, and politics put into rhyme and sung to ancient tunes. Never, perhaps, were the Democrats so hard pushed, and the fact of his election testifies alike to the esteem in which he was held, and to that merit of his which had gained it.

CHAPTER VI.

CIGAR-MAKING — CONGRESS, AND SPEECHES THERE DELIVERED — HENRY CLAY AND THE EX-CIGAR-MAKER — POOR BLUMBERG.

MR. WOOD has ever shown an inveterate dislike to any thing like despondency, self-distrust, or doubt of his own future. During the period of his first reverses in business, instead of waiting, like Mr. Micawber, for something to turn up, he himself turned up something; no matter what, he thought, so it were work, were industry, were resolute self-maintenance. He retired for a while into Division street, and became a journeyman cigar-maker—for small enough wages, we may be sure. No matter; small as they were, he lived on them in sturdy independence, and learned another bit of knowledge—how to make cigars for other men to smoke; for himself, he smoked none. Friend Broadbrim had cured him of that.

So the cigar-maker helped himself out of that position, and in his twenty-eighth year went off to Congress to see what there was for him to do there. It was a memorable Congress that of 1840, both because of the importance of the questions debated and settled there, as because of the mighty men engaged in such debatings. There were giants on the earth in those days, and in that

Congress, an extra session called by President Harrison, there were Henry Clay, and Rufus Choate, and that human pine-knot John C. Calhoun; there were Benton and Buchanan, Woodbury and Silas Wright, Robert J. Walker and Wm. C. Rives. These men adorned the Senate chamber; while in the House of Representatives, sat, or stood to speak, old John Quincy Adams, Caleb Cushing, Millard Fillmore, H. A. Wise, J. P. Kennedy, Dixon H. Lewis, R. M. T. Hunter, and others, all men of renown.

They had the United States Bank to talk about, and the vexed and vexatious tariff question. They must decide upon the distribution of public lands, and make a law about bankruptcy.

Wood, young as he was, must have his share in all this; for he was sent thither to that intent. So when he had something to say, he rose and said it in a manly and modest manner, and then was quiet again. He spoke upon the Fiscal Bank of the United States; the operation of the Tariff Laws; the Navy Appropriation Bill; and drew up the report upon the Naval Dry and Floating Docks.

When the Americans who had taken part in the Canadian insurrection of 1837–8 were caught, and sent to expiate their acts off to Van Diemen's Land, Mr. Wood was their earnest advocate in Congress; pressing urgently upon that body the necessity of procuring their release. On this occasion, he had the honor of crossing swords with that veteran forensic warrior, ex-President John Quincy Adams. He also tried to get the U. S. Consuls classified according to the importance and the difficulties of their stations; and wisely purposed to make them salaried officers, since some get fees enough to live in splendor, and others, like our late Consul to Venice, not quite enough to pay for the painting of coat armor suitable to the dignity of this Republic.

Another thing he did of great importance. He was the advocate of the greatest step that progressive science has taken in our day—the Electric Telegraph. He introduced the claims of Mr. Morse to Congress, and strongly urged that body to make an appropriation for the experiment. The Professor wanted to run his wires along the railway track from Baltimore to Washington; but Congress was unbelieving and could not be persuaded. Still, Wood fought on. If he could not get this grant, he would content himself with a lesser one. He was, we know, a member of the Committee on Naval Affairs; and at last, for his importunity, permission was given to lay the telegraphic wires from the committee-room of the House of Representatives to that of the Senate, some four hundred feet. So the practicability of conversing by the aid of lightning was triumphantly proven; and Fernando Wood won and wears the honor of having materially aided the passage of the act which gave to the world Morse's Electric Telegraph.

The veteran legislators in some sort made a pet of the young Representative. When he had made his fiscal speech, John Quincy Adams grasped him by the hand, and said: "Young man, when I am gone, you will be one of the foremost men in this country."

Well, the old man is gone, and Clay, and Calhoun,

and other great men of that time; and the prophesy stands fulfilled to-day.

And here for a while, with his forensic honors thick upon him, the cigar-maker reäppears for a moment and then passes away out of sight up to this date.

Henry Clay was particularly fond of him; took a fancy to him when first introduced, and never lost an opportunity of paying him personal attentions. Perhaps he saw some spark of that genius in the young man, which so abounded in himself. Friends used to say, indeed still say, that the lower portions of the faces of both were strongly similar. Be that as it may, Clay loved to be with him, to walk and talk with him, and to be kind to him.

One day, the two, with an old Philadelphian friend of Mr. Clay, were going down broad Pennsylvania avenue, when the old gentleman desired them to stop in at a tobacconist's, that he might get his snuff-box filled. The three went in, and while there, Wood saw through a half-opened door, leading into a back-shop, four men seated at tables, at a work which he too understood, but for the present did not confess his knowledge of.

"What," asked he of the shopkeeper, "are those men doing?"

"Making cigars, sir," was the answer, "will you go in, Mr. Clay, and see them at their work?"

"Certainly," said the Kentuckian, and the trio entered.

There sat four artisans, dampening the leaves of the fragrant weed, or spreading them out, and cutting them up into wrappers with minute exactness and the swift certainty obtained by practice; or breaking off the dry fillers to the proper length; or rolling up the neat cigar and terminating its fabrication with a twist not unsimilar to an involute pig-tail. Use brings rapidity. From twelve to fifteen hundred in a day have been rolled up by men learned in that art; yet five or eight hundred is thought a good day's work.

The number daily accomplished by the Washingtonian fabricants has not reached posterity; but they were deft enough to make the Mill-Boy of the Slashes say:

"How very skillfully this is done! Who would have supposed that so much ingenuity was required for the making of a cigar!"

"I don't see any art in it," said Mr. Wood; "it seems to me a very simple matter; and I suspect that any one can do quite as well."

Clay looked at him and said: "Young man, you deceive yourself. Long years of patient labor are required to accomplish what these men here are doing with such apparent ease. It requires great experience to be able to do this."

"With deference, Mr. Clay," said Wood, "I differ from you. There can be no art nor skill required to do what these men are doing. See! They merely cut off a piece of the tobacco, roll some of the dry part in their hands, then wrap it up, and the whole thing is done. If this is the process, any person can make a cigar."

Clay laughed. But the shopkeeper and his men looked at the speaker with much contempt for his presumption and some wonder at his apparent self-esteem.

"If you think any one can make a cigar," said Clay,

"perhaps *you* had better try;" and he swept his arm towards the table, with a glance at the proprietor.

One of the men arose with a premature smile for the boaster's coming defeat, who sat down, saying:

"Well, I may be mistaken; but as I really do think it possible, I *will* try."

So, sitting down, he took the knife and a tobacco leaf, and with a dextrous cut prepared his wrapper; then broke the filling to the proper size, rolled all up together, twisted the small, symmetrical pig-tail at the end, cut off the top, and handed the well-made cigar to his distinguished fellow-legislator.

Clay was amazed, and vented his surprise in numerous ejaculations. The shopkeeper and his people stared with wonder at this new accomplishment in a law-maker of theirs. As for Fernando Wood, he kept the secret, and the joke ran the rounds of Congress, and was told at the expense of Henry Clay.

Apropos of cigar-making cleverness, our Mayor's father, who had a manufactory of those narcotic delights, once employed a little Frenchman, hight Blumberg, who could roll up a brace of thousands in a day. Now our Mayor loves a good joke or story as well as other, lesser folk, and the present writer thinks fit to re-produce in this place a tale which his honor tells about the same poor Blumberg.

He was a good cigar-maker, and this was the limit of his goodness. As a general rule, even his virtues leaned to vice's side; and he proceeded through life, leaping from one scrape to another, as one leaps from hussock to hussock in crossing a bog. In his last jump, he took another man's horse along with him—an action, we are informed, technically known as horse-stealing. From this hussock he leaped into the presence of the majesty of Justice.

Even here, however, the poor devil had friends. Awful Justice herself was not indisposed, in this case, to be tempered by mercy. The magistrate asked Blumberg's counsel if he could prove a hitherto good character for his client, and before the lawyer could reply, the prisoner cried out:

"Yes, sare, very best charactere: there is a gentleman who know me very well," and he pointed to a distinguished citizen, who happened to be present, and who was instantly placed upon the stand and sworn.

"Sir, do you know Charles Blumberg?"

"Yes, sir."

"How long have you known him?"

"More than twenty years."

"Yes, sare," burst forth the impetuous small Frenchman, "he know well that I am honest man: I have not steal these horse; he knows all of me; regard that which he says of me."

"Well, sir," said Justice, "be good enough to state to the jury what you do know about the prisoner."

"I have known him," said this witness for the prisoner, "I have known him for many years, and must say, that he has always borne the character of a thoroughly graceless, lazy, dissipated scamp, who has never yet hesitated to steal any thing he could lay his hands on."

The small Gaul roared with rage, leaped up in the

dock, shook his fist at his witness, and screamed, "You are one damn liar: you know me not at all: you have never at all seen me, nevare!" Then, relapsing in despair to his seat, he continued in a low voice, confidentially to himself:

"It is as so; when one commence to go down the hill, every body give to him a kick, by damn!"

In the sequel of this trial, Mr. Blumberg appears to have been supported at the expense of his adopted country, during a period of five years.

CHAPTER VII.

MRS. WOOD'S FAMILY—AN ADVENTURE ON THE ISTHMUS, AND A TRIP TO SAN FRANCISCO.

THERE were other worthy Quakers than those who bore the name of Wood. That particular one with whom we have now to deal, was known among the faithful, as among the profane, as Samuel Richardson. He had left his English home probably because of the intolerance there existing, and had sought a fuller conscientious liberty at Port Royal, in the island of Jamaica.

But Jamaica is in the West-Indies, and that, like other tropical regions, is at times subject to that peculiarly unpleasant phenomenon the earthquake. About the year 1692, friend Samuel, being with his co-religionists in meeting, was startled by the heaving and swaying of the earth. The sea roared more tumultuously than usual; the houses were shaken from their firm foundations, and toppled ruinously down. The hills seemed riven asunder, and when the people, rushing from the building, arrived in the graveyard, which surrounded the meeting-house, they may well have thought that the day of the Lord had come; for even the bands of the grave were broken, and out from the dust wherein their bodies had been laid down in hopes of resting there and commingling with it, they were thrown, as by an unkind mother; and so, those who had fled from religious persecution in what was called their mother country, found even sterner unkindness from the stepmother whom they had chosen.

But Samuel Richardson, and as many of his brethren as could manage it, embarked, as best they might, in the brig Swan there lying, and, steering a northerly course, came, with the help of God, and what knowledge the sailing-master possessed, to the colony of stout William Penn, settling not far from that Peashore of which we have had so much to say in the beginning of this biography, arriving there some thirty-six or seven years after the adventurous flight of Henry Wood from "Newport, Rhode Island." Let us add, that scarcely were they embarked, when the wild sea ingulfed the town.

Samuel, like others, purchased several thousand acres, and definitely, at last, established himself upon the pleasant river Schuylkill, some twenty miles or so above the city of Philadelphia, he and his wife, and his now grown-up son and daughter. Here he resided, a prominent man; looked up to by other colonists in that country; standing with inveterate firmness to those peaceful broadbrim principles of his, and holding fast by William Penn, "Proprietary" of that region.

Even on his arrival, he found that the worthy Proprietary, not exempt from the troubles which visit other, and non-Quaker governors, had got into serious difficulties with his colonists. Samuel Richardson, like a loyal man, stood stoutly by the Proprietary, aided him in his difficulties, with what help his quiet good common sense and some earlier experience of trouble, earthquakes included, he could bring to bear upon the question. So William and Samuel became fast and affectionate friends, a bond tightened by their official relations and more closely by the fact that their children married into the same family—that of Aubrey.

When Penn had somewhat stilled the turbulent waters, he went to England, in 1701, leaving his friend and secretary, James Logan, to rule the colony. In one of Logan's letters to his principal, under date of eighth month 27th, 1704, he gives that excellent man to know that the Assembly had voted him an address, and that such address was signed by several members of the colony, namely, by David Lloyd, J. Wilcox, Is. Norris, Jos. Wood, G. Jones, Anthony Morris, William Biles, and SAMUEL RICHARDSON. This address was reported to be "scurrilous and scandalous;" and it was afterwards repudiated by Richardson, who it seemed had unwisely signed it upon a merely cursory and insufficient view of it.

About this time, Letitia Penn, the great Proprietary's daughter, married a Philadelphian merchant, William Aubrey by name, and in process of time presented her husband with a daughter. According to the usual course of nature this infant grew, attained maturity, and married Joseph, only son of Samuel Richardson, the immigrant from Port Royal. From him descended lineally the late Hon. Joseph L. Richardson, of Auburn, and a daughter of this gentleman is the wife of the present Mayor. Fernando Wood comes by two lines from the first Quaker fugitives from persecution to this country; and his children, through their mother, trace by a third line to the same source.

It was during his honey-moon that Mr. Wood made his first speech in Congress, a period not usually considered favorable to forensic study, nor calculated to further interest in dry fiscal or other political details. Fuller remarks with reference to the Congressional career of Fernando Wood will more appropriately be found in another part of this memoir.

When his term had expired, he gave up politics, and returned to commercial pursuits, as shipping and commission merchant, in South street. This was in 1843, and from that time he met with rapid and brilliant success; and in 1847, he found himself possessor of no less than eight vessels. In September of the next year, 1848, he received from Thomas Larkin, merchant, news of the first Californian gold, brought to this country by Lieutenant Beale, of the U. S. Army. This was before the close of the war and the cession of California to this Government. However, Mr. Wood immediately fitted out one of his own vessels, the bark John W. Cator, for San Francisco, where she arrived the first, and where her cargo was sold at a profit so immense, that her owner felt enabled to retire from business finally. He purchased a good deal of real estate at a time when property was low, and now finds it quintupled in value.

After quitting business, Mr. Wood lived in retirement, applying himself to study with that resolute energy which is characteristic of him, so to supply the defects of his imperfect early education. But, in 1850, he was called out again by the Democratic party, who gave him a nomination for the Mayoralty of this city. He was not elected however to the chief magistracy.

So he stuck to his books, only once—in 1852—quitting them for a trip to the gold land. While going whither, he met with this adventure.

Prefatially, however, Mr. Wood had exchanged certain property of his in New-York for a tract of land in the city of San Francisco, the largest plot of ground belonging to any one man there, and then producing a clear annual income of $30,000. To see this, lease it, make arrangements for its management, etc., was his errand in that place.

In those days, not so fabulously long ago, there were no weekly arrivals and departures of steamers, as at this time; nor a fine railway, in the commodious carriages of which the Panamanian Isthmus might be crossed. Then one had to pole up the muddy, feverish Chagres river in flat-boats, manned by slightly-clad half-breeds. And this from Gorgona was succeeded by a long ride upon mules, down gullies and torrent beds, over improvised, insecure bridges; through thorny bamboo thickets, under tall oil-nut palms. One or more rolls in the yellow mud were usually allotted to each traveller. So our Mayor went on, until within some thirteen miles of Panama.

He wanted to get a view of that city, of its magnificent bay, of the ruins of old Panama, destroyed in 1670, by Henry Morgan and his brutal buccaneers. So he rode on before the others, and suddenly his mule, diverging from the beaten track, plunged into the dense thicket, and followed a scarcely visible path. Her rider had been told by more experienced men than he, never to contradict his mule: that she would never leave the beaten track except for some sound reason suggested by her experience and cultivated instinct. Therefore he followed such advice as he had received, and the animal carried him about a mile through the wood to a clearing, wherein stood a native mud and bamboo built and palm-thatched house.

At the door of this establishment stood a murderous-looking, ugly Jamaica negro. He looked loweringly at the traveller, and said:

"*Caramba, señor. ¿ Qué quieres aqui?*"

"Do you not speak English?" asked Mr. Wood.

"Yes, sir, very well; come, get down, and take some dinner." So speaking, he took the bridle of the mule, and fastened it to a post.

Mr. Wood knew the character of the Jamaica negro; avaricious, distrustful, utterly indifferent to human life, believing all Americans to be slave-holders, fearing and therefore hating them. He was far from his fellow-travellers; a cry for help would have awakened an echo in the tropic forest or called out a sneer from the villainous nigger, but that would have been all. Quick escape upon the back of an obstinate mule was impossible, so after an instant's thought, he said:

"I thank you for your invitation, but I have a very large party of friends a few yards from here, and must rejoin them. One man there is banker for the whole of us, and we must, if possible, keep near him. Besides, my friend, you would not have me accept your hospitality without a sixpence in my pocket to remunerate you for it."

This upset the scoundrel's hope of plunder, and there remained now only his animosity against Americans to be subdued.

"I am sorry to decline your invitation," said Mr. Wood; "because I observe the generous, noble Englishman in your face. You can not be a native of the Isthmus. Are you not from Jamaica, whose people live under the Christian and liberal rule of England?"

The scoundrel's face brightened. This skilful *ruse* had the intended effect. He returned the reins to the traveller, and said, with a wave of the hand: "*Adios, señor.* Go as fast as you can. No good for any body to stay here long."

Mr. Wood then set his will against that of the mule, and aided by a plentiful use of whip and spur, he induced that intelligent animal to obey him, and thus regained the main road. Then he rode on and entered Panama, the first of the twelve hundred persons who formed the emigration on that occasion.

He remained ten days in San Francisco, arranged his affairs, and found himself safe again in New-York, after an absence of two months and one day.

Then back to his studies and his quiet life, until called forth in 1854, by his fellow-citizens, to assume the chief magistracy of the greatest city on this continent.

CHAPTER VIII.

CONGRESS—THE FISCAL SPEECH.

We have already mentioned Mr. Wood in Congress, the names of some of the illustrious men of whom that body was composed, and the important questions there considered.

Mr. Wood was a very young man, only twenty-eight years of age, and unprepared by education to take part in debates which then exercised the genius of Clay, Calhoun, and Adams. Besides, only on the 23d of April previous he had married, as we have seen, a daughter of the Hon. Joseph L. Richardson, of Auburn, N. Y.; and, so far as the present writer's knowledge—not gathered from experience—extends, the first moons of wedlock, the matrimonial spring, is more desirably given to gentler thoughts than the science of politics can suggest.

Be this, however, as it may, the bridegroom now in question could not sit quietly and listen to the energetic and exciting debates which were going on around him; the war-horse heard the sounds of the battle, and pricked up his ears. The fiery eloquence poured from one mouth, swift answer shouted from another, charges of hot denunciation upon serried columns of stout, quiet reasons; all this roused him, and he said: "I too must have my part in this. I too feel courage and energy, and strong conviction of right within me, and I will speak it out with what power shall be given to me."

There was the great financial question now before the House. President Van Buren's Sub-Treasury system had succeeded to the United States Bank. The friends of this latter institution had opposed Van Buren's plan with vehemence. The question came to be a party issue; the Whigs advocating, the Democrats denouncing the National Bank system. The hottest opponents of the measure were the constituents of Mr. Wood, and he, both as faithful representative, as well as from strong private conviction, was determined to denounce the establishment of any national bank, with whatsoever force he had.

Several propositions had been made for the creation of a national bank, as the fiscal agent of the Government. The influence of Senator Henry Clay in both Houses, was exerted in favor of the measure. But up to the help of the Democracy against the mighty Kentuckian, came, from the Senate, Calhoun, Benton, Wright, Woodbury, Walker, Buchanan, Rives, and others; and the House flanked these troops with Ingersoll. Rhett, Hunter, Pickens, Dixon H. Lewis, Henry A. Wise, and others.

To get up and talk among these men, and against such opponents as they were to cope with, was not a very inviting first field for a young man and a younger statesman. Never mind. He had something in him to say, and he would say it, and he did; not without laurels either, for the press passed great encomiums upon him; his opponents came to compliment him on his maiden speech, and old John Quincy Adams left his seat, took the flushed orator by the hand, and said: "Young man, when I am gone, you will become one of the foremost men in this country."

The young wife was sitting in the gallery; perhaps her pleasure rewarded him more even than the praises of the great men. It is said that when he rose, he was very pale, and that his voice was tremulous; but the will was there, and by and by the voice grew firm, the color came back to his face, and the first effort at forensic oratory was for him a brilliant triumph.

What he said, we give below from the Congressional Reports:

SPEECH

ON THE

FISCAL BANK OF THE UNITED STATES.

DELIVERED AUG. 3, 1841.

MR. WOOD rose and said: Although not a talking man, either by profession or inclination, yet the importance of the question, and the recent signal expression of opinion from his constituents, demanded that he should be heard. He congratulated himself that he had obtained the floor at this early stage of the debate, and would not detain the Committee by an exordium, but proceed directly in the discussion.

But, before entering upon the main question, he felt called upon to allude to one point in the argument of the gentleman (Mr. Sergeant) from Pennsylvania, who opened the debate yesterday in an ingenious speech upon the constitutionality of a bank. He would not discuss the legal points with that gentleman; but he would say that that gentleman's remarks appeared to him as better fitted for the bar and a jury than for the House; and he would also add, that it appeared rather as a speech made to remove from the Executive certain constitutional scruples he was supposed to entertain as to the powers of the Government to create a bank, than to convince Congress or the people. But with this he had nothing to do; it was the allusion made to the sentiments of a gentleman now minister to Russia (Mr. Cambreleng) to which he particularly referred. The gentleman in the course of his remarks, alluded to a resolution reported to this House by Mr. Cambreleng from the Committee of Ways and Means in 1837—"that it was inexpedient to charter a national bank;" and drew from it the inference that that gentleman, the Committee of Ways and Means, and the House which passed the resolution, had no doubt as to the constitutionality of a national bank.

I protest (said Mr. W.) against this induction. It is not justified by the fact. It is not a logical inference. The speeches of my distinguished friend stand recorded against a bank, upon the ground of want of power under the Constitution, as well as inexpediency. The gentleman from Pennsylvania was a member when these speeches were made; and it was unfortunate their character had escaped his recollection. Besides, was this not so, he (Mr. C.) may have been acting under instruction from his Committee, against his own vote. But even if that was not the fact, he (Mr. W.) contended that the proposition of the inexpediency of a measure was not an admission of its legality. But, sir, (said Mr. W.,) I will not dwell here. My object is answered in thus briefly placing the opinion of an absent gentleman in its true light, and preventing what I conceive to be an unwarranted, and, I must add, unintentional stigma, falling upon the political character of one of the favorite sons of the Empire State.

The bill before the Committee is, in common parlance, a bill to create a national bank as a fiscal agent of the Government — a proposition which pre-supposes the repeal of the law of July, 1840, for the safe-keeping and disbursement of the public money, known as the Independent Treasury. Though the question of this repeal was not now directly before the Committee, yet, understanding it to be the determination of the administration majority to move the "previous question" immediately upon that repeal, without allowing the minority an hour for discussion, he would take this opportunity of protesting against such tyranny and against the repeal.

A proposition to strike from the statute-book a law so important in its bearings, and created for purposes of such deep interest, should be accompanied by reasons more cogent than any we have yet heard. Proof should be adduced that it had failed to perform what its friends promised for it; that it had been mischievous in its effects, or impracticable in its operations. They are not produced; nor can it be said any argument based upon its action, worthy of serious notice, has been brought against it. It is safe, then, to hazard the opinion, that no fault can be found with it in practice, although it had such strenuous opponents in theory. It has worked well, answering thus far (save, probably, in a few minor details) the objects of its creation. If we revert to the oft-repeated phophecies of the Whig party, of the devastation which the Independent Treasury was to spread with magic speed throughout the land, and now compare them with what has been our condition since its adoption, and with what is at this time our true condition, the falsity of the prophecies will be apparent. If the state of the times is used as an argument against it, it is its triumphant vindication, when compared with those which preceded it. We were told it was pregnant with lamentable consequences; that it would destroy commerce and confidence; reduce wages to ten cents per diem, the profits of agriculture to almost nothing; in short, that all interests were to be annihilated. Has this been so? Have any of these evils overtaken the people? I opine not. Without producing statistics, as I here could, to show, by irrefutable data, that prosperity—true, not false prosperity—has existed with all classes; modified, it is true, but yet has existed since July, 1840, the period at which this bill became a law; I will content myself by referring alone to the mercantile portion of my constituency, boldly making the assertion that they have less cause of complaint this year than for either of the three previous. It is true, unfortunate bankrupts, borne to the earth by indebtedness, have not been relieved, nor can any law, having for its object the custody of the public money, relieve them; nor has it re-produced the days of adventurous hazard, bringing back to the speculator dreams of glory. These its tendency has been to check, not facilitate. But mercantile New-York, in her true business character—divested of, and divided from political prejudices, thus freed from former embarrassments, and content with the profits of a safe, legitimate trade—comes not to your halls for legislative relief, or the repeal of this law; short credits and small profits seldom trouble you with lamentations; they have no cause for lamentations—they do not understand what is meant by "a war upon the currency." You can not make the merchants, who follow these simple rules, believe they are ruined and prostrate bankrupts, although they may be deluded into a support of your administration. In discussing this point, it is necessary, Mr. Chairman, to discriminate between business merchants and political merchants; for there is much necessity of such discrimination, when the advocates of the repeal and the establishment of a bank so strenuously urge their views upon the ground that they are demanded by the commercial interests of the country. Sir, I am proud of the intelligence, probity, and standing of this class of my constituency; but, at the same time, it is my duty to say, (and it is said with regret,) that a large portion of it have allowed themselves to become the tools and instruments of designing politicians; been drawn into the arena as partisan gladiators, lending the potential influence of their business titles to further schemes of adventurers: allowing their interests, and consequently the vast interests depending upon them, to be almost prostrated by a mistaken enthusiasm, engendered by imaginary wrongs. They have been put into requisition upon this occasion; but I must be allowed to say, they arrogate powers not belonging to themselves; they can not, in justice, speak for the commercial class of New-York, but more properly for the political part of that class.

I repeat, that our trading community—the safe, sound, and rational portion of it—freed from these prejudices, make no complaint. The existing troubles they attribute to past errors. In short, no argument can be adduced in favor of the repeal of the independent treasury, based upon the action or effect of the bill. The state of the times since its adoption, as compared with the three preceding years, is upon its side—evidence of some weight, and should, in this discussion, be properly placed to its credit.

But I apprehend gentlemen do not urge the repeal for the reason that it has yet betrayed any mischievous tendencies. We are told time sufficient has not yet elapsed, but the evil *will be* developed notwithstanding. Is it not wise, then, to await that time, and thus be furnished with reasons for the people? Hasty legislation, either in the enactment of laws or their repeal, is objectionable, and often pregnant with lamentable consequences. To guard against it, the framers of the Constitution devised many ways. It was a point upon which they debated long and solemnly. To repeal this law at a time when it is indisputable no argument can be produced against its operation—that it furnishes in practice none of the objections urged against it in theory—but merely because its enemies have obtained a momentary ascendency in our councils, is one of the very acts of hasty legislation so much dreaded by the founders of the Government; as, also, is it one of those self-destroying evils depicted by the opponents of republican institutions, as always connected with popular representative governments.

Much good was promised for it by its friends; much bad prognosticated by the opposition. The time necessary to prove who were in the right, and give it a fair trial upon its merits, has not elapsed. But if you force a decision, demanding a verdict now, the issue must be made up, upon its action, effect, and influence; upon which ground we are ready to meet you, sanguine of a certain triumph.

But we are told the people have decided against it. Have they, forsooth? I respectfully ask in what way? at what time? I am referred to the late Presidential election, but deny that that election had any reference to the independent treasury bill. The issue then, if there was any, (and if there was, for my life I could not discover it,) was of another kind—made up of different material than any thing having a bearing upon any question of national interest, much less the question of in what way the public revenue should be collected and disbursed. When was the subject discussed before the people? Where was a denunciation of the odious sub-treasury made the war-cry for the onslaught, as in 1838? Nowhere! Or, if so, in isolated instances, by itinerant Whig orators, who, having learned their lessons in 1838, like other *starlings* having the faculty of repetition instead of invention, doled forth their lamentations in the old repeated strains of "sub-treasury! sub-treasury!! odious sub-treasury!!!"

Was it made the issue by that illustrious convention of office-seekers who nominated the successful candidate at Harrisburg? It was not. That august body of patriots, after contemplating their act, sneaked to their homes, not daring to make an avowal of sentiments. Or was it made the topic of discussion by the candidate himself (supposed, of course, to embody the principles of his party) in his various addresses to the people? It was not. That respectable old gentleman, as far as I know, never descanted upon the subject; or, if so, by the most indirect allusion. Suffice it to say, there was no issue made at that election, involving the repeal of this law; and gentlemen know it. That battle had been fought in 1838. The election for the 26th Congress turned almost entirely upon it. Mr. Van Buren proposed it in his first message in September, 1837, and it at once became the watchword of the Democratic party, as it did the exclusive point of attack of the Federal party. The bank patriots left our ranks, in which there was no more prospect of plunder, suddenly dropping the reins which they had held with an iron grasp; thus causing dissension and confusion, producing the overwhelming though transient defeats of the fall of that year. The following spring State elections, contested upon the same ground, showed a slight reäction; but the canvass for the 26th Congress, in the fall and following summer, fought upon the broad platform of Jeffersonian democracy—the divorce of bank and State against a national bank—sub-treasury, or no sub-treasury—between the unpurified and unterrified democracy upon one side, and an unholy alliance of old federalists and bank-rag aristocracy upon the other;—an election, it may be said, held with express reference to this point of Mr. Van Buren's policy—resulted in a glorious triumph, by returning a majority in its favor, although the city of New-York was defrauded by pipe-laying, out of her representatives. Here was the issue—the only one ever made involving this question; and it is a vain subterfuge to transfer it to the late election, because you were fortunate enough to secure—no matter how—a majority of numbers against it.

As one knowing something of commerce and the influences affecting it, and being somewhat conversant with the views of that interest, and representing, in part, the most important commercial district in the Union, I regret this motion, apart from all political considerations; I regret the subject is even agitated. The debate upon it is deleterious. If it is true (as so often contended by the opponents of the late and previous administrations) that this ever tinkering with the currency—this eternal legislation upon the public finances—has a fatal influence upon trade and commerce, why do the same gentlemen now follow the course they so eloquently denounced then?—violate a principle so soon after establishing it? The first session of the late Congress, as was thought, disposed of this matter. We had a seven years' war between two powerful parties, contending with unexampled energy which should settle it according to its policy; until at last, by the passage of this bill, the question was set at rest—the public money was placed in a situation where politicians and speculators could not reach it—where it could no longer be used as investments for political defense or attack. The people, not party hacks, rejoiced at its final disposition; they felt that they were to remain for a season freed from the surges of this ocean; to have rest, peace, and security; the question was considered settled. Those who were sufferers through this conflict (and I know none who were not) would leave it where it is. Reasonable men, of all classes, rejoiced privately, if not publicly, at its conclusion. They felt relieved from the glorious uncertainty of a deranged currency. They now know upon what to depend; it was finished—disposed of; and although not according to the preference of some, yet it was disposed of; and prayed it might so remain. I tell you, sir, a majority of your party do not go with you in this repeal, when in its stead you seek to rear an institution like this proposed. The larger and more intelligent part of our merchants—a class who have contributed in various ways to place you in power, and who, according to panic-makers, were to become its immediate victims—do not ask you for its repeal, if they are to have a bank in its place. The merchants throughout the country wish you to let them alone—to let the currency alone. Instead of calling extra sessions of Congress to cater for their especial benefit, they would rather Congress take a recess for five years, and give them relief by *non-interference*. You taught them that legislation upon the currency was prejudicial; they will ask you to practise upon, in majority, the doctrines so ably expounded in minority. They do not require the political theorists who aspire to the honor of constructing a system of finance, based upon some visionary abstraction of their own, to practise castle-building at their expense; nor do they ask the adherents of Whig candidates for the Presidency to prove their fealty by the constitution of a party engine—good for Presidential aspirants, but destructive to trade and commerce.

If the sub-treasury contains errors of detail, amend and alter, regulate, but not destroy. An error of detail is not an error of principle. Give our system the same chance of developing itself that we have given a bank, and if it prove to possess any of its fatal influence, I pledge myself the Democratic party will go with you for its repeal. We never sought to wrest from the United States Bank its charter, even after its corruption had become manifest. In fact, at a time when it was notoriously subsidizing the press and squandering its money in a war upon General Jackson's administration, we never attempted the annulling of its charter. It had for years previous to its expiration proved unsafe as a public depository, unsound as a bank of emission, and a deranger instead of a regulator of the exchanges; yet we never dreamed, in the plenitude of our power, of laying hands upon it. I contend that the charter of that bank was violated, and yet General Jackson never proposed its demolition. It was at one time spoken of, in the political circles opposed to it; but the friends of the institution cried for quarter, and quarter was given. And so with our nine hundred State banks, which have been for years preying upon the vitals of the people, putting at defiance all law, human and divine. We have not sought their destruction, nor do we now; their friends admit there are errors in their system, but ask us to regulate, not destroy them. We make no admissions of errors in our system; but if there are errors of detail, regulate, but not destroy. For forty years this Government has tried a national bank as its fiscal agent; what has been our financial condition for these forty years? We have been periodically visited by panics, revulsions, and distresses, inflations and reäctions, astounding exposes of defalcations and forgeries, agricultural killing low prices, and mechanical and operative killing high prices—a see-saw between inflation and depression,. aptly represented by Daddy Lambert times and Calvin Edson times. But, sir, have any of these delectable bank followers visited us since the adoption of our plan? They have not. I shall be answered, it has not been in existence long enough. Very well: it is admitted. Give it a trial of ten years—one quarter the period you have had for yours; and if it harass and beggar the people in the same manner, we will give it up, and strike our colors.

The truth is, no argument based upon common sense can be adduced against the independent treasury. There are two motives actuating its opponents—the one, malice; the other, to rear in its place a political institution, which will enable them to comply with certain promises made previous to the late election. There is a class of the Whig party not provided for by the distribution of the spoils; the wheel does not revolve fast enough for them; and another, who look for payment in a less laborious manner, by moneyed facilities.

There is an interest also across the water, too powerful to be denied, and to whom, if report speaks true, the dominant party is somewhat indebted. But if these exist only in the imagination, I repeat, malice—deep, unrelenting malice—has much to do with this repeal; a motive the more unmanly and contemptible, as it is veiled under pretexts of what the public good requires. By deception was the power obtained to do this deed, and by deception is the deed perpetrated. As the pirate decoys the merchantman under a friendly flag until the sides of the victim are scaled and the deck is in his possession—so did the Whig leaders decoy the people, until, having them fast bound and powerless, as far as their action here is concerned, they unfurl the red banner, bring forth the bloody instruments of torture, exhibit the portentous engine yclept a bank, and prepare the manacles and chains. But, thank God, here the simile fails; for, unlike the victims of the corsair, they shall be freed from this subjugation, and deal a just retribution upon the actors in this treachery—ay, sir, reaching the pirate captain himself, whether enveloped in robes of senatorial dignity, (Mr. Clay,) or doffed in the *brown* habit of a puritan secretary, (Mr. Webster.) These dazzlingly-bedecked chieftains wear but the people's livery. Is it not enough that you should have purchased popular support by allying yourself to popular passions; but must you now exercise your ill-gotten power, without dignity and without respect, by indulging this spirit of pitiful vindictiveness? But what can be expected of an administration coming into existence as it did, and controlled by the men it is—men whose object was to obtain office, and, until they are stripped of this power, standing forth as naked of government patronage as they are naked of principle? There is no rest for an abused and deluded people.

Sir, I have not the ability or disposition to go into an elaborate defense of the sub-treasury, if any were required. It was the principal topic of discussion in every legislative body in the country, from the moment of its proposition to its passage. The ablest talent battled for it and against it; the public press teemed with it; scarcely a child but is conversant with the arguments upon either side. I will not spend the people's money, or weary the patience of the Committee, by repeating them. The mandate has gone forth—"*it must be repealed.*" It may be said with propriety, that any discussion in the premises, or any opposition, here or elsewhere, is folly—madness. *It must be repealed.* A distinguished Senator has said it; and, like Mandarins under a special edict of the Celestial Emperor, it is the duty of the majority of this House to "*tremble and obey.*" But as it is not pretended we are to be left at sea without a rudder, a substitute is proposed; or, rather, would it not be more correct to say several substitutes? all, however, in the language of the official gazette, "central or fiscal agents." The time has arrived when the lead-horses of this motley group, now in the possession of the Government, can, as they think with safety, take their course without fear of the consequences. It is not now with the Kentucky Senator as it was when pressed upon by the Democratic Senator of New-York, previous to the closing of the last Congress. Then he replied to a question as to the substitute, "that sufficient for the day was the evil thereof." "He had then nothing but the sub-treasury to handle, and that was sufficient for him." It was too soon to play trumps. He (Mr. Clay) was not ready. A premature disclosure may have effected certain congressional elections, not at that time holden. Of course, at *that time* he had nothing but the sub-treasury to handle; it was entirely too soon to make further "disclosures for the public eye." But now, secrecy was no longer necessary; the elections have been held; a federal majority is secured; the administration is thrust into the breach; the hand is shown; the card is played; and the Whig trump is to "incorporate the subscribers to the fiscal bank of the United States."

Sir, if the people of this country decided in the late election against the sub-treasury, (which I deny,) did they decide in favor of a national bank? They did not. That issue was never made; the question was never raised; nor are they now in favor of such an institution. I am aware efforts are being made to foist upon Congress the interested action of a handful of brokers, bankers, and speculators, as the popular voice. But the mantle of deception is too flimsy. Gentlemen refer me to what they are pleased to term the mammoth petition from New-York, presented to the Senate a few weeks since. Sir, they may term it the mammoth petition, but I christen it the bastard petition; ay, sir, the illegitimate offspring of illegitimate parents. Sir, it purports to have been signed by some fifteen or twenty thousand petitioners; whereas, if my information be correct, it did not contain eleven thousand; and four thousand of them were purchased by hired loafers at the corners of the streets, at four dollars per hundred. Thus will the mammoth, which took three persons to bring it to the Capitol, lose more than half of its rotundity, and all of any thing formidable in its appearance. I have alluded to the three persons who assumed the responsibility of acting as its guards and escorts; I should have said *Committee*, for they were dignified by such official cognomen by their wire-pullers in Wall street. And who were the members of this Committee? The same gentlemen who went "cap in hand" to Mr. Biddle, in March, 1837, begging him to save New-York from annihilation; and who, in October, 1839, advocated a suspension of specie payments by our banks—fit instruments to be the tenders of such a petition. There has also been presented a memorial from the Chamber of Commerce of New-York, praying for a similar favor. I have a word to say as to this memorial. Unsophisticated gentlemen, unacquainted with the way in which *cliques* contrive to manufacture public sentiment, would not think it possible that a memorial coming from such a source could be any other than a representation of the opinion of commercial men; but, sir, in this instance it is not so. Our Chamber of Commerce is an association of about two hundred gentlemen; there were but fifty-six present, when a resolution was passed to memorialize Congress for a bank: thirty-six voted in favor, and twenty against it. Under this resolution, a Committee of five was appointed to draw a memorial—and were they merchants? No, sir, there was but one merchant upon that Committee. This is not an empty assertion, without authority, but is the fact, as I will convince the House, by producing their names and occupation. The first-named gentleman was James G. King, senior partner of the house of Prime, Ward, & King,' an old-established Wall street *banking-house*, largely connected with British capitalists and British interests—a banker, (or, in common parlance, a *broker*,) and not a merchant. I intend no disrespect when I characterize him as a broker. This word, in its original and true definition, has nothing disreputable in it; its present taint has arisen from the fleecing propensities of the modern order of that profession. Among them are many honorable exceptions, and I believe him (Mr. K.) to be one; but he is not a merchant, and, consequently, is not the proper person to speak through the Chamber of Commerce what the mercantile interests of New-York require. The next is Mr. James Brown, of the house of Brown, Brothers, & Co., another *banking* establishment, largely connected with capitalists across the Atlantic, and, as I believe, a partner in a similar firm in Liverpool or London. As a representative of the commercial classes, he is in the same category with the former gentleman. I intend no disrespect. Well, sir, the third is Mr. James Depeyster Ogden—not a banker, it is true, but a cotton operator—or, in other words, a cotton speculator. This gentleman (whom I understand to be a very worthy man) is the author of several labored treatises in favor of a bank, and is the reputed author of the memorial. He is not a merchant, and can not speak for the merchants of New-York. The fourth is

Mr. John R. Hurd, president of an insurance company, who is also a gentleman of respectability, but not a merchant; nor can he with propriety speak for the merchants of New-York. The fifth, and last, is Mr. William H. Aspinwall, a *bonâ fide* merchant, practically and theoretically, and one of the most enlightened and prosperous of the class. He was the only merchant upon the Committee. In connection with this point, I will add, that at the time this cheat was in preparation—this merchants' petition being drawn up by brokers and speculators for the Congressional market—there were conspicuous British bankers in Wall street, anxious observers, if not co-laborers in the movement. Among them might be named Mr. Bates, partner of the celebrated house of Baring, Brothers & Co.; Mr. Cryder, of the equally celebrated house of Morrison, Cryder & Co.; Mr. Palmer, Jr., son of Horsley Palmer, now (or late) *Governor of the Bank of England.* Nor, Mr. Chairman, were these "allies" seen alone in Wall street; their visits were extended to the Capitol; and since the commencement of the debate upon this bill in the other House, they have been in the lobbies, attentive and apparently interested listeners. I make no comment; comment is unnecessary. I state facts —undeniable facts; and it is with feelings akin to humiliation and shame that I stand up here and state them.

Sir, the voice from the city of New-York in favor of the national bank is from Wall street and its purlieus; from the brokers, bankers, speculators, and their dependants, and not from the solvent and prudent merchants, or the small traders and mechanics. The merchants of New-York, in the aggregate, without reference to party, are opposed to any bank you can create, under any name, with any checks of any character. But, sir, I repeat: suppose the people have decided against the sub-treasury, (which I deny,) and suppose they decide in favor of a national bank, (which I deny,) and suppose the people are now in favor of it, (which I deny,) will it perform what its friends in Congress promise for it? It will not. We are told, among other benefits to be conferred by its creation, a uniform currency will be established, and exchanges will be regulated. Gentlemen often revert to the late bank as proof of this assertion. I will take them on that issue, and leave out of the question, as they unfairly do, the Pennsylvania Bank of the United States.

It is an error, an unpardonable error, in either practical men or statesmen, to say that the late United States Bank produced steadiness of currency, or regular exchanges. In the first commencement, it so inflated the money market that a revulsion soon followed, which swept off the merchants of the day by thousands. The father of the humble individual who addresses you (said Mr. W.) was one of the unfortunate victims. This revulsion nearly prostrated the bank; but, by breaking every thing else, it saved itself. Its safety was secured by its management falling into the hands of Mr. Cheves, who took the reins, and saved it from bankruptcy and ruin. An able and impartial writer, who avows himself in favor of a bank, says, in speaking of the close of Mr. Cheves's administration:

"The bank then passed into other hands, and from that time to 1836 there were no causes developed which threatened a general suspension of the State institutions; but there were various important minor *crises* which were *all* more or less *aggravated* by the action of the bank of the United States; and with the causes in operation from 1830 to 1836, (independent of those arising from the war between the Government and the bank,) *had its charter been renewed, it would inevitably have failed.* These causes are well known: they were chiefly in a series of years of high prices for cotton, of introduction of foreign credit and capital into the foreign trade of the country, the gradual increase of loans to the States, and the stopping of payments on account of the national debt. The operation of these causes brought in a gradual and continual accession of capital, and enlarged the bases of credit and confidence in that degree that engagements were infinitely multiplied and business expanded, and together with the immense increase of Government deposits in the bank, make it all but certain that, under its then management and great and increasing circulation and extension, it would have been the first to fail and carry the country with it; and we believe the time is not far distant when this will be considered beyond question. It behoves us, therefore, if we *are* to have another bank, to have it so restricted and constructed as to place it out of the power of enterprise or cupidity to endanger its safety, and to lessen the mischief which *always* accompanies the action of such large bodies in times of difficulty."

Again: another able writer on finance gives a statement which can not be controverted. I challenge contradiction here or elsewhere.

The fact that, for a few years during the existence of the United States Bank, the exchanges were uniform, proves nothing but that a combination of extraordinary events tended to produce a greater supply of credit than could for some years be absorbed in the regular course of business. These were created partly by the yearly payments of $10,000,000 on account of the national debt, which went through the United States Bank as the fiscal agent, and the creation of a large amount of State debts that formed the bases of bills. From the creation of the United States Bank in 1817, up to 1823, the exchanges were in as bad a condition as they are at this moment. The banks of the South and South-West did not pay specie, and the United States Bank had no power over them. In 1820, large issues of State stocks commenced as follows:

STATE STOCKS ISSUED FROM 1821 TO 1830.

Issue commenced—	1820	South-Carolina,	$1,560,000
	1823	Pennsylvania,	7,980,000
	1823	Virginia,	1,499,000
	1823	Alabama,	100,000
	1824	New-York,	8,496,781
	1824	Louisiana,	1,800,000
	1825	Ohio,	4,400,000
		Total,	$25,835,781

In this we find that nearly every section of the Union had large credits to draw against, created by stock sales. In these stocks were invested a large amount of the money paid out through the United States Bank to the public creditors. This was an important element in regulating the exchanges; and as during that period the movements of the bank were confined to regular business only, there was but little speculation abroad; and these credits were all to be absorbed in regular business. A sufficiency of bills was thus created that effectually prevented any extraordinary rise in rates. Let us now see the movements of the bank during the whole existence, as follows:

BANK OF THE UNITED STATES, FROM ITS ORGANIZATION UP TO JAN., 1841.

Year.	*Loans.*	*Stocks held.*	*Specie.*	*Circulation.*	*Deposits.*
Jan., 1817	$3,485,195	$4,829,234	$1,724,109	$1,911,200	$11,233,021
1818	41,181,750	9,475,932	2,515,949	8,339,448	12,279,207
1819	35,786,263	7,391,823	2,666,696	6,563,750	5,792,809
1820	31,401,158	7,192,980	3,392,755	3,589,481	6,568,794
1821	30,905,199	9,155,855	7,643,140	4,567,053	7,984,985
1822	28,061,169	13,318,951	4,761,299	5,578,782	8,075,152
1823	30,736,432	11,018,552	4,424,874	4,361,058	7,622,340
1824	33,432,084	10,874,914	5,813,694	4,647,071	13,701,936
1825	31,812,617	18,422,027	6,746,952	6,068,394	12,033,364
1826	33,424,621	18,303,501	3,960,158	9,474,987	11,214,640
1827	30,938,836	17,764,359	6,457,161	8,549,409	14,320,186
1828	33,682,905	17,624,859	6,170,045	9,855,677	14,497,330
1829	39,219,602	16,099,099	6,098,138	11,901,656	17,461,918
1830	40,663,805	11,610,290	7,608,076	12,924,145	16,045,782
1831	44,022,057	8,674,681	10,808,040	16,251,267	17,297,041
1832	66,293,707	2,200	7,038,023	21,3[illegible]5,724	22,761,434
1833	61,695,913	....	8,951,847	17,518,217	20,347,749
1834	54,911,461	....	10,031,257	19,208,379	10,828,550
1835	51,808,739	....	15,708,369	17,339,797	11,756,905
1836	59,232,445	....	3,417,988	23,075,422	5,061,456
1837	57 393,709	....	2,638,449	11,477,968	2,332,409
1838	45,258,571	14,862,108	3,770,842	6,768,067	2,616,713
1839	41,618,637	17,957,497	4,153,607	5,982,621	6,779,394
1840	36,839,593	16,316,419	1,469,674	6,695,861	3,328,521
1841	20,942,508	10,822,717	2,569,705	7,157,517	2,970,069
April, 1841	19,349,079	10,913,240	756,454	3,249,576	1,462,239

We find here that, from 1819 to the election of General Jackson in 1828, the discounts of the bank varied but little, and never ran so high as its capital. In 1828 it increased its loans $6,000,000, and in each successive year up to 1832, there was a large increase of loans and a decrease in stocks. For a period of five years there is no return made of stock, but in that time large loans were made on stocks. In March, 1835, these loans were $4,797,936 ; and in March, 1836, they were $20,000,000. In March, 1835, the loans by the Exchange Committee commenced, and ran from $6,000,000 to $8,000,000 in two years. In all this period speculation ran very high. The State loans created from 1830 to 1835 were as follows :

STATE STOCK CREATED FROM 1830 TO 1835.

Louisiana,	$7,335,000	Mississippi,	$2,000,000
Alabama,	2,200,000	Tennessee,	500,000
Indiana,	1,890,000	Illinois,	600,000
Ohio,	1,701,000	Virginia,	686,000
Maryland,	4,210,311	Maine,	554,976
Pennsylvania,	16,130,003	New-York,	2,204,979
		Total,	$40,012,769

United States Bank bills were paid out on those stocks to a great extent, and they thereby got an immense circulation, which ranged near $23,000,000 in 1836. The credits created thereby went far to support the exchanges. In 1832 the immense fund that had yearly been thrown off by the payments on the public debt ceased by an extinguishment. In 1833 the deposits were removed, and the bank proceeded to curtail the loans on mercantile paper ; and as it did so, employed its funds on stock loans. Hence the discounts in 1835 had decreased $15,000,000, and the stock loans, according to the late Committe report, were $20,000,000, while the specie had accumulated to $15,000,000. In 1838, according to the table, there was a further reduction of $14,000,000 in discounts, and an increase of $15,000,000 in the stock account. In the following year the same feature was apparent. The whole contraction of loans from 1833 to the present time is $49,000,000, which of course was good. The remaining $19,000,000 is the refuse ; and when we take into consideration the circumstances of its creation, it may be put down as worthless. The late report states that " very little of it is mercantile paper." The details of these bills would be very interesting.

From 1835 to 1838, the creation of State stock amounted to $108,423,808, almost all the States participating. Under the inflation of the bank, the fictitious business had become so great as to absorb all the bills based upon these credits. The banks stopped, their paper became depreciated, and the exchanges fell into confusion.

Although the bank called in its loans on regular paper after 1833, it re-loaned the money on stocks. The officers speculated with it in all kinds of ways, and when, in 1836, the charter was to be paid for, the bank was obliged to borrow $5,000,000 in London, and 12,500,000 francs in France. The creation of stock gave to each section an excess of credit on the financial centre of the Union, *that of itself regulated exchanges, and would have done so in the hands of private dealers, without a national bank;* and exchanges would have worked as regularly as they do throughout Europe without any bank.

Now, sir, let us hear no more of the beneficent operation of the old bank. It is dead, but its disastrous consequences still live.

We need not a Government bank to regulate exchanges; they are regulated by the immutable laws of nature—by supply and demand. Artificial remedies for currency disorders are like artificial stimulants to the prostrate animal—the resuscitation, to be permanent and healthful, must be produced by the inherent vigor of the system, which depends upon the inherent vitality of itself. What is exchange? It is simply the transfer of property or its representative. If banks confine their business to the legitimate objects of their creation—making loans upon short *bonâ fide* business paper, and no other—exchanges can not be deranged, because then the notes discounted represent commodity; capital is loaned, and not credit—which, as all writers on commercial banking agree, is the only thing a bank should loan. We require nothing to regulate exchanges, if our nine hundred banks do their duty; but if they will only in part perform it—one portion of the country suspending, and the other paying specie—the exchanges will become disturbed, and human ingenuity can not devise a national bank to remedy the difficulty.

But, sir, granting that every merit you claim for a national bank was well founded, and that it would perform all the beneficent action promised, it can not be put into successful operation, nor can it ever obtain public confidence. The people of our country have had a surfeit of their banking system. Of all the evils of corrupt legislation, the creation of banks, whether State or national, has been the worst. I think the assertion can be established, that nearly all, if not all the periodical derangement in our monetary affairs has had its origin in it. Banks appear to be the instruments selected by man to subvert God's blessings. Look abroad upon the face of our beautiful country; see its expanse of empire, stretching almost from the rising to the setting of the sun; its climate of every variety—the soft zephyrs of the South, and stern frigidity of the North; its soil sending forth spontaneously, almost without the force of man's labor, the richest products of earth's bosom; its bounteous supply of rivers for navigation, and watering-streams for tillage; its mighty oak, for the construction of the world's commerce, and the skill and energy for its speedy monopoly. And were these not given—had God not lavished upon us these gifts — look at the governmental fabric bequeathed to us by "the sires of whom we are the degenerate posterity!" See its adaptation to our physical and mental being; its invisible operation upon our cohesion and fraternity. Again: see the resources of our strong arms, native intellects, and indomitable enterprise, raising us aloft in all the attributes of gifted man; but, alas! turned upon ourselves, the weapons of our own destruction—the engines by which we perpetrate a suicide upon our own prosperity. It is ourselves, then, and not God, who produce, by the creation of credit, and not capital, the evils of which we complain. The munificent Bestower of all blessings has allotted to our portion of his domain, fair verdure, congenial climate, and individual adaptation of character; but by our own hands have we fallen victims to the abuse of what was intended as blessings, sacrificed by legislation, destroyed by turning our back upon the benevolence of God, looking to banks and not industry.

Sir, do you know what banks have cost the people? I will show you.

In a report made to this House by the Committee of Ways and Means in 1830, it was estimated that, previous to 1817, the Government lost by loans made to it in depreciated currency, and paid in specie, $33,000,000

The late Secretary of the Treasury, in a report to the Senate, tells us that, since then, the Government has lost	15,492,000
That the people have lost directly by bank failures, ...	108,885,721
Losses by suspensions of specie payments by banks, and consequent depreciation on their notes, ...	95,000,000
Losses by destruction of bank-notes by accidents, ...	7,121,332
Losses by counterfeit bank-notes, beyond losses by coin, ...	4,444,444
Losses by fluctuations in bank currency affecting prices, extravagance in living, sacrifices of property, and by only a part of the other incidents to the banking system, not computed above, at least	150,000,000
	$413,943,497

But, sir, we do not stop here. This is an enormous aggregate, but this is not all. The losses by fictitious banks and their notes—operations of mere swindling—are very considerable; and they are justly chargeable to our system of paper currency. Besides, there are frauds, robberies, and defalcations, connected with the banks, which might be properly set down under this head: but these are not easy to compute.

The amount paid by the country to the banks, during the last ten years, for the use of their agency and their notes, after deducting six per cent. interest for the use of bank capital and the reasonable expenses of managing the banks, is computed at $94,000,000; being an annual sum of $9,400,000.

Of the aggregate losses sustained by the community since 1789, Mr. Woodbury computes that there must have happened within the last ten years an amount of $200,000,000; which is at the annual rate of $20,000,000.

Is not this a frightful exhibit of what banks have cost the people? But it is not all. Where is the gatherer of statistics who will attempt to compute the losses sustained by men who, seduced from the small earnings of an honest avocation, have been insnared into the temptation of a bank discount? What master hand shall delineate the wreck of morals and loss of character, to say nothing of domestic happiness, produced thereby? Who will furnish us a record of the defalcations, forgeries, dishonest self-appropriations, with which our press is almost daily teeming? Sir, these are evils of the system. The wisdom of this, or any other country, never created banks, as such, without these concomitants. These evils appear to be a necessary consequence—a certain result. Is it not strange, then, we find in this House advocates for a bank as an agent of the Government—as a keeper of the public finances—men willing to strike from existence a law with which they have not, and can not justly find fault; and place in its stead one, the result of which all experience proves is pregnant with the worst of evils—the very impersonation of national disaster?

But, sir, in conclusion, let me say, Go on—pass this bill—charter your bank—fasten this iniquity upon the country; the mighty shout of *repeal* has gone forth from my lion-hearted constituency. Ay! repeal! repeal!! repeal!!! From that ground from whence first floated to the winds the bright banner of "*Divorce* of *Bank* and *State*"—borne aloft by the stout arms and honest hearts of the down-trodden, but indignant masses—now is heard, trumpet-tongued, the voice of REPEAL. New-York has spoken: she never speaks in vain. I echo her voice in these halls. It is the proudest moment of my life that I have been the first in this debate to ring into the ears of great men's satellites: "Bind the chains of this bank upon us, and the Democracy will rend them asunder by a speedy repeal of its charter."

CHAPTER IX.

CONGRESS — THE TARIFF SPEECH.

Among other questions which were greatly discussed in this Congress was the question of the tariff; a point which has produced more excitement and agitation, and has excited more bitter feeling between North and South than any other matter, except slavery. Mr. Clay had already promulgated the doctrine of protection for American labor, and by his extraordinary ability and commanding eloquence, succeeded in creating and sustaining a powerful party around him.

Although himself a slaveholder, and an uncompromising enemy of Abolitionism, his great talents brought to his side the manufacturing interests of the North and East, regions so hostile to slavery. According to the prevailing fashion with questions started by great statesmen, this too became a matter of party, and fealty to party dictated the position to be taken by the popular representatives.

The Democratic party opposed Clay's doctrine on the ground that American labor, being able to compete with the industry of the whole world, it needed no protection from discriminating imposts or duties in its favor—that every dollar of duty levied by Government upon imports, beyond the money absolutely needed for governmental expenses, was taken from the pockets of the whole people to benefit a single class, to wit, the manufacturers. Clay and his followers said that American labor should be protected against the *pauper* labor of Europe, with many another strong argument. And the excitement throughout the country was great in this matter.

The Democratic party had sustained an immense defeat. Not only was Mr. Van Buren ousted from the Presidential chair, but the Whigs had elected both Houses of Congress by a decided majority. The Democratic majority in the lower House was only twenty-five. Mr. Wood's district, a commercial one, was from its interests anti-tariff, and opposed to obstructions of foreign commerce, such as discriminating duties on foreign manufactures. Mr. Clay found against him the commercial, importing, and shipping interests of New-York. Mr. Wood went with his constituents.

Mr. Clay's party, among other things, instructed the Committee on Manufactures to send for witnesses who might bear testimony on the subject of the tariff laws, etc., which Committee being known to be in favor of a tariff, was not thought likely to be influenced by any adverse testimony. Mr. White, of Kentucky, a warm partisan of Clay, had formed the Committee in furtherance of the project, and the mover for the testimony, Mr. Saltonstall, of Massachusetts, who represented a manufacturing district, knew that the Committee would report in favor of the tariff.

These instructions, Mr. Wood opposed in the speech

which follows, and with so great success, that immediately on resuming his seat, it was moved by Mr. Williams, of North-Carolina, that the resolution be laid upon the table. This was carried by a majority of twenty-nine, in a House almost entirely Whig and Protectionist.

SPEECH

ON THE

OPERATION OF THE TARIFF LAWS.

DELIVERED FEB. 9, 1842.

MR. SALTONSTALL, from the Committee on Manufactures, reported the following resolution:

Resolved, That the Committee on Manufactures be authorized to send for witnesses and take testimony on the subject of the present tariff laws, their operation upon the interests of the country, and the alterations which those interests require.

Which being under consideration,

Mr. Wood rose, and addressed the House, in substance as follows:

Mr. SPEAKER: I am in favor of all information which it is possible to gather upon this important question, and desire, as earnestly as any gentleman, that every legal and just means be taken to procure it. I am willing to go far, very far, to obtain light; for none more than myself believes it is required. Of all questions affecting individual and Government interests, directly or indirectly, that is paramount; therefore light should be had, that we may legislate knowingly and understandingly. This House, of all the world, requires it. The discussion of the revenue bill of last session, and motion of reference of the tariff portion of the President's message this session, have convinced me we have too little of the requisite knowledge. We are lamentably ignorant of the practical operation of our import system, or in what respect it needs modification or alteration. The country is in want of light. The manufacturing districts should have the light of reason and experience, to show them the fallacy of submitting their interests to the control and jurisdiction of demagogues. And from whence must it come? From practical men, of all classes, professions, and occupations. The dreamy theorist of the old world, or one-sided, interested advocates of this, can not, if they would, impart it to us. It must be drawn from a philosophic study and comparison of facts, and not from inventive political economists. We must go into an investigation as expansive and deep as will be the bearing of our decision upon the interests of the people and prosperity of the Government. All men must give us the result of their experience. In disposing of a question which involves every interest—the ramifications of which extend to every man, woman and child in the nation—which is inseparably connected with and controls the public treasury, a precise and positive knowledge is unquestionably indispensable.

There must be no surmises, no guessing, no speculation. Facts, indisputable and beyond impeachment, must be the basis of our action. I would examine the merchant. I would ask him how and in what manner a high tariff affects commerce; whether a tariff sufficiently high for protection is not inconsistent with a tariff for revenue; whether tariffs should be discriminating, or an unvarying *ad valorem;* how the English warehousing system, and the proposed home valuation, would be adapted to this country, and what rate of duties would best prevent smuggling and other invasions of the revenue laws, and the other numerous inquiries of detail. I would ask the agriculturist under which system, high or low duties, the native products of the soil would find the most advantageous market; whether he was willing to pay an additional tax upon implements of husbandry, not to raise revenue by which to meet necessary national disbursements, but add to the already large profits of manufacturers; and whether a restrictive duty on foreign importations would not in time cut off much of the foreign demand for his own productions? The manufacturer should be consulted. I would ask him whether, without protection, under low duties, with a business insuring a fair remuneration, his interest would be subserved by encouraging the competition and rivalry of speculating adventurers; if in those countries of Europe where the restrictive policy had been thrown off, the manufacturers had not surely flourished in proportion to advantages of material and labor; and if American manufacturers can not subsist and flourish without the aid of Government, by what right does it demand a tax upon the whole industrial as well as non-producing population for its particular benefit. I would ask whether he was ready to admit that, with our free institutions, superior industry, ingenuity, and advantages of home-raised raw material, we could not compete with European monarchies? And I would now appeal to the consumer of all classes and occupations—to the backwoodsman of the Far West, and the sturdy operatives of the Atlantic cities.

Of the hardy pioneer, whose capital is as much in the ax as the sinews which deal the blows, I would learn how he is affected—whether he is willing the instruments with which he levels the mighty oak of the forest, and the weapons with which he drives its original owners from their coverts, may be taxed to build up and cherish Eastern monopolizing, manufacturing corporations. Sir, in part, I have the honor to represent a large manufacturing district; for I contend that he who planes a board, or makes a shoe, or constructs any work of art or mechanism from prepared or raw material, is as much a manufacturer as the denizens of your New-England associations, and should be as much consulted. To the manufacturers, or, in another word, the mechanics of the city of New-York, I would apply—I would ask them whether they desire that the doctrine of protection be put into practical operation, and that the fostering care of Government be exerted for their particular benefit, to the detriment of every other class, and destruction of our present means of raising revenue? Whether they are willing to carry out the principles of the Home League, by paying thirty dollars for a coat which previously had cost but twenty-five? I know them too well to do them the injustice not to anticipate their answer. *They* require no protection but the reward of honest industry. They come not to your halls for fostering care. If there is a favor they would ask or accept at your hands, it is *non-interference*—to let them alone—

to cease your officious intermeddling, and, least of all, keep away the protection of a high tariff, which they look upon as

> "Such protection as vultures give to lambs—
> Covering and devouring them."

They will turn to you and say, "Gentlemen, last session you squandered the public treasure upon bankrupt, profligate States, giving away, in a corrupt bargain, that which cost our fathers blood and treasure, and now come to us with the conciliatory notes of kindness, with a base bribe to buy our favor. We will none of it. We *question* that the policy of high duties is beneficial to us; but we *know*, if it were so, that it is iniquitous, anti-democratic, and unequal. We have principles dearer to us than pecuniary advantage. We would not have you destroy the harmony of the glorious and beautiful Union, or do aught to impair the fabric of our political existence, to put in our pockets the wealth of the Indies. We are no dollar-and-cent patriots; they may be found in your marble palaces, but not in our obscure workshops. It is true we produce every thing and get nothing, and you produce nothing and get every thing; yet your injustice to us shall not compel us to be unjust to others." This would be their answer, as it would, if I mistake not, the answer of the same class throughout the Union.

Sir, I am in favor of getting, in this manner, the facts upon which to base our action, but object to the medium through which it is proposed by this resolution to procure them. I am not willing to trust the Committee on

Manufactures, as now organized, with the power of making those inquiries; better have no investigation, and depend upon the lights of our own experience, than be fatally misled. In searching for facts, let us beware of false facts. If we desire to enter the haven safely, let us take pilots whose interest or enmity will not drive us upon the beach. I can not give my vote to intrust this responsible and important duty to the Committee on Manufactures.

It is no small part of our legislative rights that this resolution asks shall be given them. Under an ingenious construction of the Constitution, power can be found in it to do almost any thing, in the name of the House of Representatives of the United States; it can command the attendance of witnesses, whether for real or pretended examination, and institute an inquisitorial scrutiny into accounts and papers. In many ways it can, if it will, encroach upon the rights and property of citizens. Nor is this all. Admitting no individual rights were violated, I ask if it is, as now composed, two thirds of its members having pre-judged, representing constituents loudly clamorous for protection; I ask, is it the proper Committee to undertake this inquiry? It is truly and emphatically a Committee for protection. Let us look into the districts of a majority of the members. The honorable chairman (Mr. Saltonstall) has, in the two counties which he is set down in the Congressional Directory as representing, 19,567 persons engaged in manufactures and trades.

[Here Mr. Saltonstall inquired of Mr. Wood what portion of them were engaged in mechanics, and what portion in trading. He said his district was commercial, agricultural, and navigating, and that he premised the gentleman from New-York (Mr. W.) was mistaken in his district.]

Mr. Speaker, for the counties composing the gentleman's district, I quote from the Congressional Directory, furnished to this House by its officers, and for the statistics from the sixth census, recently taken. I presume the authority is good—it has never before been questioned. The next member is the gentleman from Rhode-Island, (Mr. Tillinghast). In the county of his residence, (Providence,) I find there are 14,302 persons engaged in manufactures and trades, although its whole industrial population, including all employments and professions, is but 24,645. The gentleman and one colleague represent the whole State, in which there are but five counties. So in truth he is the representative of, it is safe to estimate, in all, at least double that number. The next on the Committee is the gentleman from New-Jersey, (Mr. Randolph.) Himself and five colleagues are elected by general ticket. He has no district. The whole State had 27,004 engaged in manufactures and trades, which, giving him one sixth, make him the representative of over 4500.

We come now, sir, to the distinguished advocate of high protection and abolition, the gentleman of Vermont, (Mr. Slade.) He is set down as representing Rutland and Addison counties, which have, together, 2232 of the same class. The fifth is my colleague from Rensselaer county, (Mr. Hunt,) who has 4787 in his district. The sixth is the gentleman from Pennsylvania, (Mr.

Henry,) who represents 2612. There are but nine members on the Committee. The branches of industry and principal business of the constituency of six of them, are here shown. They are gentlemen elected to this House by manufacturing districts, for the avowed purpose of procuring from Congress a high tariff for protection. They are fully committed to the advocacy of such a law. Had they not been, their seats would now have other occupants. They could not have been elected holding opinions adverse to the opinions of their people. Those opinions have been repeatedly expressed, accompanied by uncompromising demands of protection. I repeat, therefore, this is a Committee of protection—for an ultra high tariff.

Now, sir, is this the proper medium through which to collect the necessary information to guide us to a fair, equal and wise disposition of the tariff question? It is not! A large majority of its members would go into the investigation with interests and prejudices misleading their judgments and controlling their decisions. Local preferences would be consulted. The political power which created and can destroy, would have the preponderance. That comprehensive view of this widespread country, with its diversified and delicate interests, could not be taken. All classes and occupations would not alike be called upon for evidence; nor would the evidence collected receive dispassionate consideration. A report would be made to us and go forth to the country, with all the authority of a Congressional document, with false inductions from doubtful facts. Is the House prepared to give this power to the men who ask it?—to place in the custody of the representatives of one class the vital interest of all other classes. Will the people support us in it if we do? I think not. The gentleman from Rhode-Island (Mr. Tillinghast) tells us the power is safely intrusted, for we give it to honorable men. It may be so. I question no man's honor; but has the honorable gentleman forgotten that the most beautiful object in nature will appear hideous if seen through a jaundiced vision? How often have men's passions made the brightest truth seem to them the foulest falsehood? Who does not remember the error, misery, and bloodshed, which have been perpetrated in the world by counsels that had pre-judged? Or is the judicature of the holy inquisition forgotten, whose victims passed through the form and ceremonies of trial, before judges, who, out of their own evidences, adjudged the innocent to torture? But, that the application be more direct, who would willingly submit a cause at common law to the decision of a jury of opponents? or what member of this House would like his general veracity tested by the testimony of personal enemies?

The case is plain. The Committee on Manufactures are one-sided and partial. We must have an unbiased investigation or none. We want light, not darkness; and, sir, it is not the evil which may be inflicted now, the erroneous opinions that may spring up in an honest community at this time, or the improper turn to be given to present legislation, that excites all my fears. I look to posterity. It is our duty to the "generations which come after us," not to hang out false lights. Legislators are wedded to precedents and the quotations of authorities. Hand not down to our children the record of their fathers prostituting every thing to mammon. This report would become a portion of our parliamentary history, and go to the world and after ages as a statement of facts with warranted inference. It will gain force by time. Hereafter, when years may have obliterated the data by which to expose its fallacies, it will become, if not an absolute law, certainly a powerful weapon with which to perpetuate the evil now effected. These are important considerations.

But, Mr. Speaker, suppose the objections here urged against the present character of the Committee cease to operate by changing its members. Let us imagine it freed from the charges I bring—in all things irreproachable and unimpeachable, without prejudice, interest, or passion. Is there time at this session to perform the work? There is not. Witnesses are to be summoned from beyond the White Mountains in the East—from the Texan border in the South—the frozen regions of the North, and the forests and prairies of the West—American citizens, alike interested in our impost system of taxation, are to be drawn from their homes, separated by more than a thousand leagues. Innumerable questions of detail, as well as general principles, are to be asked practical merchants from different seaports. An almost incredible amount of commercial intelligence is necessary to commence the basis of the proposed structure, and it can only come from the enlightened of those who have learned by experience. This is a wide field of investigation, demanding careful and exact inquiry. The manufacturers have much to impart; they have honest differences upon cardinal points, which should be entertained and reconciled; their several classes are to be consulted. The agriculturist would have mighty claims upon our attention: this noble art is cultivated in our country by near four million inhabitants, whose rapidly increasing prosperity begins to look for outlets in foreign markets. Of all the avocations of man, tilling the soil is most legitimate, and in accordance with his nature. It should be guaranteed the full earnings of his labor, and the imposition of indirect taxes be freed from unequal exactions.

Is it possible to thoroughly perform this duty in the most extended time allowable at this session? How long do the majority intend to keep us at the Capitol? Reference was made yesterday to the report of Mr. Hume to the British House of Commons. It is argued that that report had been the work of far less time than was necessary in our instance. I am glad the advocates of this resolution have alluded to that precedent. If they are so chained to the examples of British legislation, I wish them more judgment in their selections. For myself, I repudiate the policy of drawing upon English habits and English customs, whether social or political. I desire that some of these days we may become less dependent and menial. I know it is said, by the friends of Britain upon this side of the Atlantic—and she has many—that our interests are inseparable. I deny it. The true interest of America is to sever all connection with the worn-out and rotten monarchies of Europe—to be as independent in her pecuniary relations as she is gloriously independent in her political relations.

As she rests upon no nation on earth to assist her in maintaining and carrying out the undying truths of democracy, so should she rest on no nation on earth in assisting her in the simple walks of republican legislation. We have the examples set us by the able and patriotic sires of their country. Our own few Congressional archives will furnish guides enough for the full deliberation of laws adapted to freemen. When we go back again to bondage, I will not complain of gentlemen who seek to adopt the rules of bondsmen to the abeyance of freed men. But Mr. Hume's report has been referred to. I accept the issue. What are the particulars of its history? On the 6th of May, 1840, by a resolution of the House of Commons, a select Committee was appointed, on motion of Mr. Hume, "to inquire into the several duties levied on imports into the United Kingdom, and how far those duties are for protection to similar articles, the product of manufacture of this country, (Great Britain,) or of the British possessions abroad, or whether the duties are for the purposes of revenue alone; and to report the minutes of evidence taken, to the House." Upon this Committee were nine of the most prominent and able members of the Commons, at the head of which was Mr. Hume, the author of the proposition.

I have no data of the day upon which it entered upon its duties, but suppose, as the session had far advanced, it commenced immediately. Twenty-nine witnesses were examined, each of whom was a resident of London; not a man was summoned from beyond the precincts of the capital. Those who gave testimony were at the door;

but few practical men underwent examination, and in no instance was the investigation lengthy or full. Notwithstanding these favorable circumstances to a short and speedy termination, the sittings were continued until the 6th of August—precisely three months from the day of commencement. Nor were the Committee satisfied they had accomplished the objects of their creation. We have the recorded minutes to show they were not. At the last meeting, when the report was formally decided upon, Sir C. Douglass, a member, offered the following amendment: "To strike out all after the first word of the report, and insert: 'the evidence, although partial and limited, is of so various and valuable a character, that your Committee do not feel they should be justified in expressing any opinion founded on the impressions it is calculated to create. Your Committee consider that further information ought to be afforded, before they can make *any recommendation* as the result of their labors, and consequently they do not hesitate to suggest the *reäppointment of a committee*, early in the next session, to continue the investigation of this important subject.'" And in the report, as finally adopted and presented to the House, I find an admission that, "owing to the period of the session at which the inquiry was begun, the Committee have not been able to embrace all the several branches which come within the scope of their instructions." If gentlemen can find encouragement here to vote a similar proposition under auspices as far adverse to the procuration of reliable results as can well be, then their confidence in miracles is much greater than my own. Mr. Hume's Committee sat three months, in which it examined twenty-nine witnesses, every man of whom was within an hour's call, and finally made an admitted *ex parte* report, without having touched "several branches which come within the scope of their instructions." Now, sir, how long would it take our Committee on Manufactures, whose witnesses must be called from far-distant sections of our empire, and whose inquiries must embrace the feelings, views and predilections of people as opposite in sentiment as they are distant in geographical position? If the London investigation took three months, how long ought ours, *pro rata!* Further argument upon this point would be an insult to your understandings. It is obvious there is not time to carry out this scheme properly, were it possible to do so with such a committee, and make a report for action at this session of Congress. Dog days would be upon us before these gentlemen's gathered light would throw its rays upon this benighted body, and it would be really August when their *august* dignities were prepared to render an account of their stewardship.

Mr. Speaker, my friend from Tennessee, (Mr. Brown,) who addressed us yesterday, informed the House that the Committee (of which he is a worthy member, and to his credit let me add, is opposed to this imprudent request,) have been already receiving volunteer information. They have been anticipating our action by opening the doors of their committee-room to the swarms of hungry applicants for favor who invest this city. I know not by what authority this is done. But with authority or not, it can not influence my opinions. If it is volunteer testimony they require, I doubt not it will be supplied. Every mail from the East is loaded with circulars and letters from parties having dollars and cents at stake. Where direct advantage follows the enactment of laws, there is no lack of *disinterested patriotism* to volunteer assistance. The doctrine of free trade is called an abstraction; if so, it gives no prospects of practical personal gain, and, therefore, has few energetic, spirited advocates, who will travel hundreds of miles to the Capitol, to enforce upon law-makers its truths. The volunteer assistance procured by the Committee will come from the *disinterested patriotism* of those who desire the prohibition, by high duties, of the commodity which they themselves manufacture.

One other objection. This investigation, if instituted, should be by joint commission of both Houses. We are joint in action—dependent upon each other in the final passage of laws. The information is as necessary for the Senate as ourselves. It is not my purpose to detain the House longer with arguments against this resolution. I have already said more than was my intention at rising, but less than I believe the subject demands. I have attempted to show (with what success the House will decide) that an impartial and an instructive report, really useful as a guide to our legislation, can not follow the deliberations and searchings of this Committee—that it is one-sided, and has pre-judged the case upon which it desires to act the umpire—that there is not time, were it without these objections.

Mr. Speaker, if I were to follow the example of some learned gentlemen, members of this House, I would now proceed and discuss the merits of the tariff question.

But believing such deviation from "order" is "better in the breach than the observance," I shall withhold. At the proper time, when the great question is legitimately before us, I hope to be allowed to give my views. Then I shall attempt its discussion in every one of its multiplicity of phases. In advance, I beg leave to give notice that when a bill is reported, I shall, to the extent of my ability, impress upon the House the following points:

1. Special laws, granting exclusive privileges, or encouragement to particular classes or professions, are unequal and consequently unjust, and in violation of the genius of our institutions, and of the Constitution. A protective tariff is of this class.

2. Protective duties are high duties laid upon foreign products, whether manufactured or raw, to prevent their importation at prices less than the same products of our own country, and must, to be effectual, be mostly prohibitory. Now as the impost system of taxation was originally adopted to raise revenue to defray national expenditures, and as a high tariff is an abolition of revenue, some other mode of taxation must be devised. What shall that mode be?

3. But if a tariff for protection was consistent with a tariff for reveuue, and both would follow the same regulation of imposts, yet would it be suicidal to commerce. For if it is true that decreased importations, by the operation of an increased duty, will pay the same revenue, yet commerce suffers; additionally from the fact, that the excluded nations would seek out other buyers, and of course other markets for purchase.

4. A high duty is a tax upon the consumer to the amount of duty paid upon the foreign article, and whilst it increases the price of the home-made article to that of the foreign, yet in the former instance (the home-made) the increased price goes into the pockets of manufacturers, and not into the treasury; therefore, if the object of protection was fully attained, of excluding the competition of foreign commodity, and supplying its place solely with home-made, the seventeen millions of consumers would be extra taxed, over and above the necessary expenses of government, for the benefit of the less than eight hundred thousand engaged in manufactures and trades.

5. Protection is injurious to manufactures. It restricts its market to home consumption, for other nations will retaliate the policy of exclusion, and if they do not, the enhanced price of our manufactures would prevent their competing with other countries; and would raise a vigorous, speculating competition at home, which would destroy the present progressive prosperity by inducing to enter the business, men without principle or fortune.

6. Commerce is the greatest protection to manufactures, and high duties are destructive of commerce. For high duties discourage importations, induce other nations to turn to manufacturing, which before were content to purchase by exchange of raw materials; encourage smuggling and other evasions of the revenue laws; cause similar restrictions upon our productions of the soil, and onerous port charges and vexatious maritime regulations.

7. The protective policy is hostile to the prosperity

and good condition of the laboring manufacturer. It is in extended commerce, which coëqually extends the field of labor, a free, untrammelled interchange of commodity with the whole universe, and the entire absence of all legislative interference or bounties, that labor will find its best reward, and industry its best protection.

8. The spirit of the age is tending towards free trade. The nations of Europe have recently become anxious inquirers into its political and social advantages. The general assimilation of customs regulation, the mutual dependence of an unfettered intercourse, the beautiful and harmonious working of a system beyond the control of ambition or avarice, would in time bind mankind in bonds of "amity, good will, and peace," driving war and famine for ever from the world.

CHAPTER X.

CONGRESS — SPEECH ON THE NAVY APPROPRIATION BILL.

THE next effort of Mr. Wood was his speech on the Navy Appropriation Bill, which was delivered in the House of Representatives in May, 1842.

The subject was of no vital importance as a national question, but the speech must be essentially interesting to the citizens of New-York, inasmuch as it exhibits that keen outlook for public economy, that resolute opposition to unnecessary public expense, since exhibited in the mayoralty messages, and entitling His Honor to so much gratitude from the people whose interests he knows how to, and will protect. His knowledge of federal finances and disbursements is shown in the proposition (page 124) to reduce the expenses of Government, and by his pointing out in what departments such reduction would be useful.

SPEECH

ON THE NAVY APPROPRIATION BILL.

DELIVERED MAY 20, 1842.

MR. CHAIRMAN: The Committee will remember that, on yesterday, the House resolved, on motion of the honorable chairman of the Committee of Ways and

Means, to take this bill out of Committee, and close debate thereon, on Monday next at 1 o'clock. The Committee will also remember that, though it has been before us longer than a week, and though it contains twenty-nine sections, and proposes an appropriation of nearly eight millions of dollars, we have not as yet closed the debate upon the first section. In pursuance of the resolution adopted by the House, but two days remain to discuss the twenty-eight sections not approached. I submit it to gentlemen, whether it is possible to do justice to the examination which these numerous details, not yet reached, require, within so short a period. For myself, I can not vote understandingly upon them, with the little information now before me. Without reasons more cogent than any thus far offered, my vote shall be found recorded in the negative. I have listened attentively to the chairman of the Committee on Naval Affairs, (Mr. Wise,) and to the gentleman from Massachusetts, (Mr. Cushing,) who appears as first lord of the admiralty; and I respectfully deny that either, with all his ability and ingenuity, has adduced arguments sufficiently exculpatory of the largeness and extravagance of this appropriation.

Declamation and oratorical flourishes about the glories of the American navy can not induce me to give support to a profligate expenditure of the public money. I desire reliable facts, figures, and official statements,—something tangible, addressed to reason, and not the fancy. Since the establishment of this Government, there never existed a greater necessity for close investigation and care in voting away revenue, than the present; yet we see honorable members ready to vote, without discussion or examination, every dollar asked of them. The haste with which it is sought to close this debate, and in a moment part with an amount which, under preceding administrations, constituted one third of the whole annual expenditure, is evidence in behalf of this remark.

Have gentlemen reflected upon the responsibility they assume in yielding assent to a demand so unwarranted? Have they looked into the enormous executive requisitions upon our table, and made comparisons with those from the same source under the late much-vilified regime? I opine not. What do facts tell us? The Secretary of the Navy has, in his annual report, estimated that the necessary outlays of his department for the year 1842 will be—

For the naval service	$8,213,287 23
" marine service	502,292 60
	$8,715,579 83
To this add the unexpended balance remaining to the credit of the department	2,965,594 96
	$11,681,174 79
Congress have already voted for an iron steamer	500,000 00
Various bills reported from the Committee on Naval Affairs, estimated	500,000 00
	$12,681,174 79
To which may be added the Home Squadron Appropriation of last session	789,000 00
	$13,470,174 79

Now, how does this amount bear comparison with the sums estimated for, and appropriated by, the Democratic party when in power? I will take the four years of Mr. Van Buren's administration. The official reports made to Congress show the following sums as estimates and appropriations:

	Estimates.	*Appropriations.*
1837	$5,513,721 00	$5,679,021 00
1838	5,185,124 91	4,135,270 00
1839	4,776,125 64	4,776,125 64
1840	4,647,820 00	5,762,120 00
Total,	$20,122,791 55	$20,352,536 64

Here it will be seen that the highest estimate for either of the four years was in 1837—the year in which the exploring expedition was fitted out, at an expense of about $500,000; and, notwithstanding that charge, it amounted to but $5,513,721—being $3,201,858.83 less than the estimate for the present year. But, if this large difference exists in the estimates, how much larger will be the difference in the actual appropriations, if the Committee and the House pass the bill now presented. The largest appropriation made for any one year of the last administration was in 1840, and amounted to but $5,762,120; whereas I have shown that, with the bills already passed, the bill before us, the estimate of the Secretary, and the unexpended balance, there will have been appropriated this year, $13,470,174.79—an excess of $7,708,054.79, and thirteen twentieths of the Van Buren *four* years.

The amount demanded is equal to the whole sum expended for both army and navy in any one of the last five years. I can not vote for it. I can not give my support, humble and inefficient as it may be, to this rapid progress towards the accumulation of a public debt, from which it will be impossible to recover. I can not give my support to the rearing, in this home of simple republicanism, a powerful and splendid navy, with all its paraphernalia of pomp and tyranny. I could not return to an honest and truly Democratic constituency, after having aided in a system of profligate squandering; especially when the deficit is to be drawn principally from the earnings of their industry. Hereafter, should it become my province to denounce (as it will be the duty of every good citizen) the enormous expenditures of the *patriots* now in power, I can not give them the privilege of pointing to my vote as having aided in the act.

Sir, if the condition of our foreign relations bore a threatening aspect, and danger of collision was anticipated from any quarter, no man sooner than myself would prepare and do battle for defense. The unanimous voice of my people would be heard first in behalf of invigorating the maritime army. The only sentiment which could rise in my breast, if the position of pending negotiations were such as to leave "a hinge to hang a doubt upon," as to the speedy and amicable arrangement of all questions at issue, would be to arm, and "to arms"—"millions for defense, but not one cent for tribute."

But it is not contended that war is probable. No gentleman has advocated this bill upon that ground. The honorable Secretary has not proposed the increase predicated upon the slightest fears of difficulty with England. Nothing has been said in this debate, giving color to the idea that an increase of the navy is necessary in anticipation of any such event. It appears to be generally conceded that this is to be exclusively a permanent peace establishment. Nor are there causes for apprehension of war. Great Britain will not attempt the subjugation of the American prowess. It has never been her policy to declare hostilities against the brave, the powerful, and the just, when diplomacy or corruption of honor by gold could reach the negotiating officer and obtain her object. So long as Daniel Webster wields the Department of State, and holds within his grasp the thoughts and will of the pliant Executive, so long will the peace of this country be maintained, if with England is the only contention. Her policy will seek other means of preserving peace and obtaining her desires than by the cannon and the sword. Experience has taught her that here are to be found, not imbecile Chinamen—not enervated Indiamen—not tyrant-ridden Europeans—but men in the full growth of intellectual and physical manhood; who, when in embryo and comparatively powerless, stood up in two contests, unshrinkingly and successfully against her overgrown might. She knows we were refractory in childhood, and have never repented the contumacy: on the contrary, when what she conceived to be wholesome chastisement has been attempted, we have turned upon the parental assailant with other than filial mercy. For this we have not been forgiven; nor do we ask forgiveness. It is true we are a sprout from her trunk; but we have grown a rival tree. We claim with her a common origin; but, thank God! we are not linked to a common fate. We will perpetuate her language, and all that is ennobling in her virtues and glorious in her institutions; but trample under our feet her threats, defy her prowess, repudiate her vices, and, if bloody strife ensues, sink into oblivion the last foothold of her trans-Atlantic power.

Mr. Chairman, is now the time to enlarge the navy? The wheels of Government but yesterday stood still, and the machinery of the Executive was stopped, for the want of a small pittance wherewithal to proceed. A permanent debt, heretofore unknown to the present generation, has been, within a twelvemonth, fastened upon us by the party in office. But yesterday, the public faith was hawked up and down Wall and Chestnut streets, an humble suppliant to *British capitalists* for favor. Pecuniary dishonor—the first since the establishment of an American mint—has been permitted to visit and rest upon our escutcheon. Out of money, out of credit, embarrassed and financially disgraced—is this the chosen opportunity to appropriate the millions asked? The vicious banking system having spread its evils through the land, our industry is borne down by oppressions which paralyze every sinew of production. The great bubble of extended credit-system, created and upheld as it was by the credit party, has exploded over our heads with terrible devastation, making a wreck of fortune, character, and life, and sinking the iron deep into the bosom of the wife and mother. With the yeomanry and trading population, "chaos is come again"—man looks upon his fellow as a foe. Self-preservation and interest are now the predominant springs of action. The biting want of maintenance has driven the mind to expedients for a sustenance, as it has taught a lesson in economy which *force*, that unyielding tutor, has driven him to practise. Men have realized want. It is no longer an unpleasant day-dream reverie, arising upon the vision in crossing the path of the tattered mendicant; but has become a painful reality, from which there is no escape by passing on. Retrenchment and reform is now the domestic economy of the American people; and be assured, sir, the time is not far off when it will be their political economy. The time is not far off—for it is now! The people of this country *now* demand, through their representatives, a reduction of the public expenses. They call upon that party, and those men, some of whom have the full control of the executive branch, and others of the legislative branch, to carry out in practice a general system of contraction. They ask it at your hands. They say, "We will not revert to the oft-repeated promises and solemn pledges with which you made the air of 1840 vocal; nor will we tell you of the professions for our own prosperity, which, without stint and without bounds, were lavished upon our credulous ears. Let them pass. It is true, the odious *sub-treasury times* were the heydays of thrift, compared with the present gloom which our 'generous confidence' has given us. But of this, no matter. Our own folly has produced much of our own distress; but to the Government we look, not to put money in our pockets—not to enact laws by which idleness may get rich and labor be defrauded—not to lend its aid in the reëstablishment of a cormorant monopoly, which, like the locusts of Egypt, will overshadow the land with its pestilential progeny;

we look to it to contract its power, to reduce its expenses, and to cleanse its abuses. These are of the thousand reforms so loudly promised us; and having given you the power—the full and absolute control of the law-making power—we call upon you for action, speedy and efficient action. It is no answer to say you have fallen out among yourselves; that in the struggle for the mastery of the spoils, the Executive has been separated from the Legislature; that, without harmonious action of both, nothing can be accomplished; and that your President is a traitor, or that your ex-legislative leader is a dictator. Of your criminations and recriminations we know nothing. By your joint and combined advice and proffers, we drove the late incumbents from power, placing you joint and combined in their stead; and, in your joint, combined, as well as individual character, we hold you responsible." This, sir, already is the language of the people. How is it met? In what have their expectations been realized, and your pledges redeemed? Where has been furnished the evidence of the so-violently-denounced Florida war corruptions? Where are the proofs of the Executive malpractices? Where the slightest testimony of a single profligate expenditure? And who are the thieves and peculators in high places, whom, so soon after getting the reins, you intended to identify? Give us the record; produce the data. It can not be done. These vile charges, like the viler inventors, have sunk into silent insignificance. The brains which conceived them, and the tongue which gave them utterance—though still following their wonted avocation of abuse by calumniating each other—have not the hardihood to reïterate, or the slightest proof to adduce in substantiation of a single slander. That part of Whig promises can not be performed. Not so as to the retrenchment of expenses. There is no impediment to a full compliance in this particular. Coming into office with at least forty majority in this House, and nine in the other—with the President and heads of the departments—no obstacle presented itself. Why has it not been done? Why has it not been proposed? You have the power, and there exists the necessity. The expenditures are too great; they are far beyond the simplicity compatible with the Republic, and very far beyond what is compatible with the present means of defraying.

Retrenchment is the order of the day in private life; why should it not be the practice of those who are honored with stations in public life? You have held power over a twelvemonth, during which Congress has been in session nine months; and no retrenchments worthy the name proposed or adopted. It is true the honorable gentleman from Virginia, (Mr. Gilmer,) to whom much praise is due, early in last session moved a committee for some such purpose; but no measures have yet been offered, save what relates to our own franking privilege and mileage, which, although commendable reforms, are minor, indeed, compared with the overshadowing costs of this Government. I desire good faith upon this part of Whig promises. Why are not efforts made for a compliance? The treasury is empty—the credit of the country prostrate; and yet nothing is said of a reduction of outlays. The last Democratic

Congress voted you five millions to commence with; at the extra session you voted an additional twelve millions, as a permanent loan; and at this session another five millions—making, in all, twenty-two millions in less than a year; and yet pennyless and bankrupt, and a daily crying give! give! give! Why, instead of the lamentations of the chairman of the Committee of Ways and Means over the lack of funds to replenish our exhausted treasury, have we not substantial bills of retrenchment and reform, which will lop off the causes of our distress? The people do so. It is not their practice, when involved in embarrassments, with burdens greater than their income, to borrow, borrow, borrow. They retrench—that is the first principle of their domestic economy; and I mistake them if they will not exact similar economy of their public servants. What would be thought of that man, in private life, who, a creditless debtor, kept up a splendid establishment, without apparently knowing he could not afford it? But who would pronounce him honest, if sane, if such a one made voluntary bequests of one tenth of his whole income? You have done this; while an avowed bankrupt—with expenditures greater than receipts—you gave away the proceeds of the public lands, averaging three millions annually. This is only the suicidal policy of knaves. Surely "he whom the gods wish to destroy, they first make mad." Sir, the expenses of this Government are as far beyond what, under a proper system, would be necessary, as they are beyond our ability to support. This fact was fully established by the twenty-sixth Congress. That Congress, though repudiated by the people, who thought best to substitute a *hard cider* Congress, was satisfied of this fact. Its acts prove this remark. It made great progress in the work of reform, commencing in the right way and in the right quarter. It reduced the emoluments of the collectors of our large seaport cities to an amount within the bounds of reason; but yet leaving them far beyond, in my opinion, a sufficient recompense. The collector of New-York, who, under the old law, considered himself poorly paid if his salary and perquisites netted less than twenty thousand dollars, was limited to six. The postmaster at New-York, whose yearly income had grown from five to over twenty thousand, was reduced and limited to five thousand dollars. The district-attorney and marshal also came within the pruning-hook. Here was serious retrenchment. Hundreds of thousands of dollars annually were thus brought into the coffers of the nation, which had previously been the pay of public officers.

Thus has the example been given you by the Democratic Congress which you have so much animadverted upon. Why not follow in its footsteps? Why not go and continue this work? None can question the policy —nay, justice to the tax-payers. It must de done, sooner or later, or national degradation will surround us. A Democratic Congress commenced it in good faith, which its successors promised should be continued and perfected. And it was but commenced!

Sir, I have taken some trouble to look into the yearly cost of carrying on this Government for the last twenty years; and am convinced that, estimating it at present at twenty-five millions, there is room for striking off at least one fifth, leaving it at twenty millions. Indeed, Senators, whose long experience in public life and whose ability to judge of these matters qualify them thereto, have asserted that sixteen or seventeen millions would be sufficient. I would take the estimate of twenty millions, which my examination assures me will leave every department in full vigor.

To do so, I would propose reductions in the following branches of the public service, which a close examination of the whole subject has convinced me can be done without detriment:

From the mileage of members of Congress:

Length of the sessions, one quarter.

Contingent expenses of Congress.

Expenses of the Judiciary department.

Salaries of the President and heads of the departments.

Expense of intercourse with foreign nations.

Home expense of State department.

Expense of Treasury department.

Expense of collecting revenue, and light-house department.

Expense of General Land-Office.

Expense of Coining department.

Expense of the War and connecting offices.

Expense of the Department of War, including a reduction of the military establishment, etc.

Expense of the Navy, including a general supervision of yards, purchases, abolition of Navy Board, etc.

Expense of Post-Office department, including restriction of the franking privilege.

I would thus relieve the treasury of millions, and not cripple a sinew of defense, or impair the full efficiency of a single office. Nor is this all. I would bring in several hundreds of thousands of dollars annually, which would find their way into the pockets of the office-holders. I would bring into the treasury all fees and emoluments received by the following officers, over and above a fair recompense for their services:

Consuls abroad,
Deputy postmasters,
Marshals and attorneys,
Revenue-collectors,
Pursers,
Navy-agents,
Commissary General Purchases,
Military store-keepers.

Now, Mr. Chairman, holding these views, can my vote be expected for this bill? I have shown by figures, which do not lie, that it is extravagant, unnecessary, and far beyond any appropriation for corresponding purposes made for the late administration, when there was as much necessity. I have shown that not only is the sum proposed exorbitantly large, but that the treasury is bankrupt, the tax-payers poverty-stricken, and the spirit of the people in favor of "retrenchment and reform." I have shown the already enormous useless expenditures, by pointing directly to them.

But, sir, let us look a little further. Suppose the objections thus far urged were without existence. Let us imagine that the treasury is full, and without indebtedness; that the people are prosperous, and willing to bear additional burdens; that extension, expansion, and prodigality characterized the age, and there were no existing evils of this character; would it be consonant with propriety and correct legislation to pass this bill? I think not. It was not intended by the fathers of the Republic that upon their plain and unostentatious foundation should be built a gorgeous and powerful nation. They did not establish this political community for conquest or plunder. It was no part of their design that posterity should rear, upon the corner-stone laid by their hands, a splendid edifice of naval or military glory. Their policy was essentially peaceful. Meek and humble in spirit, they banded themselves for protection, and for protection alone. The Union was a confederacy for mutual defense and preservation, and not to form a league, the consolidated strength of which could reduce nations, impart glory, or make too strong the arm of the Executive. Simple and republican themselves, they sought to establish a Government thoroughly imbued with their own faith—one assuming no power not necessary, exerting no authority not required, antagonist to no principle of popular rights. Would a naval armament numbering its hundreds of ships and millions of tonnage, employing its thousand commanders, disbursing its millions on millions annually, and extending to an almost unlimited degree the already overgrown privileges of the President, who, by virtue of the Constitution, is "commander-in-chief of the army and navy of the United States," be consistent with simple republicanism? It would not. But pass this bill as now before us, and the first step is taken; the first stride towards consolidation, Executive mastery, and an incubus of debt, is taken—irrevocably taken.

Another objection: Ships, after construction, must be supported; officers, men, supplies, and stores, must be furnished. The end is not with the cost of building. The keel is but laid for a continuous and never-ending expenditure. They must be kept afloat. If unemployed, they rot at the depots, and the whole is lost. The error once committed of saddling the country, in a time of peace and embarrassment, with a large floating naval world, you must go on appropriating annually a proportionably large amount to keep it sea-worthy and from falling to decay. It is a permanent expenditure now presented to us. The aggregate of this bill, enormous as it is, will be less onerous than what will be necessary to preserve it from ruin. And when once made, there can be no receding. As with State appropriations for internal improvement, you must go on *ad infinitum*, or all will be lost.

Again: I find no provision in it, or in the several bills for the reörganization of the Navy Department reported by the Committee on Naval Affairs, to remedy the evils of the present manner of procuring supplies. The door for corruption, which long practice, from the foundation of the navy to the present moment, has opened, has not been closed. I would remedy this objection before voting so large an amount. Under long-established usage, the navy agents are authorized to make open purchases without contract, without agreement or supervision. A large portion of the material, and many heavy articles of stores used at the yards, as well as nearly the whole outfits of ships preparatory to sailing, are procured in this manner. These officers have permission to disburse hundreds of thousands annually, without check as to prices or quality. They buy of whom they please, and at such prices as they please. I am not prepared to say that, of my own knowledge, there are mal-practices; but I do say, that if none have been, it was not for want of opportunity; we may thank the integrity of the officer, and not the strictness of the laws.

Before placing at the disposal of the Secretary the millions comprehended in this bill, I would supervise the laws regulating purchases. I would not, in these days of want and peculation, place in the power of any agent the opportunity of profiting ten and twenty per cent. by his disbursements. Every article should be supplied by contract. It should be the duty of the Secretary, or of the Board of Navy Commissioners, or the agent, to advertise for estimates in the public prints; thus giving to every citizen an equal opportunity to benefit by this immense patronage; and incurring no loss to the Government from bad quality, high prices, and collusion between the officer and the factor or merchant. But, Mr. Chairman, there is another consideration which, though not relating directly to either of the points thus far urged, is a subject for serious reflection, and is equally applicable to every money-bill presented to the House. Is this the proper stage of the session to discuss and act upon bills to appropriate money? Is it wise policy to make these large bequests at this time, within a few weeks of the expiration of the sliding scale of the compromise act, without any adequate provision to insure revenue; and, in fact, without a law to carry into effect the only existing law which can give us a dollar? The leaders of the Whig party in this House (the very men who are urging on these cormorant bestowments from an empty treasury) tell us that a high tariff is necessary for revenue; and that, without a new law to take the place of the compromise law, and without a general supervision of the whole subject, there will not be revenue enough to meet one half the public expenditures.

We are told that, to keep the wheels of Government in motion, it will be necessary to lay additional duties upon imports, and to settle upon a permanent basis this greatest of all questions. I ask whether, under the avowed condition of our collecting laws, it is wisdom to pass this, or any bill for similar purposes, before some action is taken on the revenue bill? Can it be the correct policy of Congress to go on appropriating, appropriating, appropriating, with empty coffers, an admitted want of laws to bring in and secure the usual fiscal income, and with a probability of a heavy falling off of imports, under any rate of duties? Certainly not. Were there no other objections, this alone ought to prevent action at this stage of the session, or until the other and more important business is disposed of. And is it not strange we find here men advocating measures so contradictory; telling us, in one moment, that we must pass a high tariff, to preserve the nation from bankruptcy; and in the next proposing the most extravagant outlays? Is it not singular consistency, to use the mildest phrase? If it is true, as alleged by the high-tariff party, that it will be impossible to carry on the Government, under the lowest reduction of expenditure, without a material advance on the present rate of duties, why is it that, before action is had on the tariff question, so much anxiety is evinced to enlarge our appropriations? Why are the gentlemen in such hot haste to make these heavy requisitions upon the public coffers?

Sir, I think the astute eye of prophecy is not necessary to divine the reason. I do not believe that any but a Talleyrand or a Metternich can unravel this seeming secret. In my humble conception of the ruling motives of men, the "why and the wherefore" is to be found in the same reason which made them bequeath to the States the public domain, without consideration and without cause. It was, to drive us by necessity to a high tariff, to fill up the vacuum thus made in our finances; to force us, by appeals to national honor to preserve the national credit, to go with them in their unhallowed designs upon the rights and liberties of the people; to give away our anticipated receipts, that means may be taken, through the operation of an increased tariff, to favor particular interests at the cost of the tax-payer. It is for this we have systematic expansion, instead of the systematic contraction the times demand. Besides the tendency of Whig principles to inflation, as evidenced in every instance where they have obtained the power—besides their love for debt and detestation of liquidation

—besides their contempt for every thing *locofocoish*, as is the pay-up system, there are now at work other motives and other inducements. The expenses must be increased, because there must be a deficit between revenue and disbursements. Having embarrassed and exhausted the finances, it is supposed the people will rise *en masse* in favor of devising a remedy, which they are prepared with in a high tariff, and thus accomplish, by a trick, that which they dare not ask for as a principle.

I mistake very much if this is not the object hidden under the bill before us. In fact, the veil of public necessity, with which it is sought to hide the scheme, is too flimsy to deceive the most unsuspecting. No party could drive so recklessly on, after the many protestations of reform, without some such intention.

Mr. Chairman, we are told that an increase of the navy is advantageous to commerce, and that every member representing a commercial district is expected to support this bill. It has been said, by gentlemen who have advocated it, that the principal employment of our naval marine is to protect the commercial marine. The interests of the Representatives from the Atlantic cities have been appealed to, to come forward in behalf of what they are told is the vitality of commerce. Sir, I am not old, but yet too old to be caught by pretexts so weak. Could arguments like these (which, at best, are addressed to our interest, the most selfish of all legislative influences) affect my vote, I should be incapable of performing the trust confided in me. I am yet to learn that in any quarter of the globe the American shipping has suffered for the want of Government protection. No cases have come to my knowledge where our flag has been insulted, or our property destroyed or taken from us, because of a restricted navy. There have been isolated instances of encroachments, but none that could have been obviated had every ship of war been a fleet. England and France, with the most extended navies in the world, have occasionally met obstacles to their trade. But the stars and stripes are a passport upon every sea to the hull and spar which bear them. Our bright bunting floats unmolested over the wide expanse of the ocean, for there are none so daring as to do it injury. Under its broad folds legitimate trade is secure and respected.

And were we liable to frequent losses for the want of the proposed increase, I am far from being satisfied that, of the two evils—the passage of this bill, and the chances of occasional injury without it—the latter is not the least. Can it be advantageous to the city of New-York to adopt a policy which drives us into a restrictive tariff? If by large drafts upon the treasury, the necessity of additional duties is forced upon us, commerce will undergo a diminution, because your increased duties will decrease importations. The foreign trade can not thrive if legislative impediments are thrown in the way of its free action. It is not reasonable that, where an exorbitant toll is demanded for ingress, that ingress will not diminish. It is a well-established axiom, that the imposition of higher duties upon imports immediately and seriously affects the commercial trade; hence the rallying-cry of a party not many years since in this country, of "free trade and sailors' rights." Therefore, admitting that an accession of a ship-of-war is required to protect our flag, it would be suicidal to protect it at a cost so great: better arm our merchantmen at private expense, for self-protection, than lay them up in ordinary, without employment. Gentlemen had better use other arguments militating less against them. It is not wisdom in Congress to attempt to give protection to any branch of trade, when such protection is only to be obtained by the inflicting of harm. In this instance the injury would be twofold; first, to the interests intended to be the recipients of favor; second, to all other interests which are taxed for its support.

There are other arguments which press themselves upon my notice; but I fear the patience of the Committee is already exhausted. I could go on elaborating the objections which are continually arising before me, but the allotted time for cutting off the debate, and the many other gentlemen who are anxious to be heard, warn me not to trespass much further. It is a grave topic, and admits of a wide range of discussion. At any time, in any condition of the treasury, a bill to appropriate money involves important considerations. To vote money, is to expend the proceeds of taxation; which is to part with that portion of the capital or results of industry which is bestowed upon the Government for its necessary disbursements. If the people are interested in the amount of taxation levied upon them, to a corresponding extent are they interested in its disposition.

If the amount expended is drawn from the tax-payer,

we are but his agents to appropriate his money for the maintenance of law and order. It is equally criminal to make lavish or impolitic use of it. I conceive that we would be as guilty of dereliction of good faith by complying with exorbitant behests from the executive departments, as if we put our own hands into the treasury to fill our own pockets. By the Constitution, we are more the guardians of popular contributions than of the popular liberties. We are made the peculiar conservators of the money-power. It behoves us, therefore, to scan closely all requisitions. Endowed as are the members of this House with the high privilege of representing the great body of American freemen, it behoves us, in the plenitude of power, not to forget the poor tax-payer at home.

In conclusion, Mr. Chairman, I beg leave to say that it is with regret that an imperative sense of duty has compelled me to address the Committee on this subject. It is with no little fear my position has been assumed. The almost overshadowing popularity of the navy, and its adaptation for American defense, connected with the recollection of the glorious victories which crowned its success in the last war, make me feel I have been treading on dangerous ground. Had my inclinations alone been consulted, my voice would not have been heard; but convictions, matured from deliberate reflection, have prompted my tongue, and it has spoken. I regret to be thus seemingly placed in opposition to it; but, at the same time, beg to be understood that it is to the unprecedented increase at this time I object—not to the service. I object to this extravagant proposition, believing it to be impolitic, unnecessary, anti-republican, and premature. I am willing to vote the usual annual sum, and will go to the highest of either of Mr. Van Buren's years; but can not give support to the bill as now before us, without material reduction.

CHAPTER XI.

CONGRESS—NAVAL REPORT.

UNTIL the year 1843, the subject of Floating Docks for the raising and repairing of Government vessels, had not been proposed. The old-fashioned stone docks at Gosport and Norfolk navy-yards, were still in fashion. So were old fogies, and they did all they could to prevent improvements—innovations, we believe they called them. But Mr. Wood prepared the Report; Mr. Wise, the chairman of the Committee on Naval Affairs, presented it; it was approved, and now is presented to the intelligent reader.

REPORT
ON
NAVAL AFFAIRS.

JANUARY 10, 1843.

THE Committee on Naval Affairs, to which was referred a Report of the Secretary of the Navy, with accompanying documents, relating to dry and floating docks, and the Brooklyn Navy-Yard, called for by a resolution of the House of the 19th December, beg leave to report:

That they have given the subject the consideration which its importance demands. Dry-docks attracted the attention of the Government at an early period. The Navy Department was established in April, 1798, and the following December the Secretary officially expressed his strong conviction of their necessity. February 25th, 1799, a law passed both Houses of Congress, and received the sanction of the President, authorizing the construction of two docks, and appropriating $50,000 for that purpose. December 15, 1802, the President, (Jefferson,) in his message at the opening of Congress, strenuously urged the construction of docks, and in March, 1813, $100,000 was appropriated for a dock-yard for repairing ships of war. These appropriations were not expended, owing, as is supposed, to the inadequacy of the sums voted. In 1814, the Secretary, in a communication to the chairman of the Naval Committee of the Senate, again urges the building of dry-docks. In 1824, the Navy Commissioners made similar recommendations. In 1825, the Secretary, in a report to the Senate, enters fully into the advantages of dry-docks, showing conclusively that no navy-yard should be without one, or its substitute: and in 1826, in a communication to the House of Representatives, he says, "that docks have become absolutely necessary for the prompt and speedy use of the vessels belonging to the navy."

Every administration, since the creation of the navy, has given its sanction, either by the approval of laws or official recommendation, to the erection of docks and other necessary facilities for repairs. As yet but two dry-docks have been built: the one at Charlestown, the other at Norfolk. Either of these points is eminently entitled to it. The sites are excellent, and other advantages great. Previous to the commencement of these docks, New-York was considered as the first position to be selected. The first survey made of the several points upon the Atlantic coast, which offered inducements for the establishing of navy and dock-yards, placed that harbor among the most favorable. The report of the survey, made to the Department in 1818, states that, "next to Boston, it is the most suitable place for such an establishment, and one worthy of the attention of the Government as a naval depot."

But opinions have varied as to the advantages of different sites within the waters of the harbor. Since the location of the yard, repeated attempts have been made to effect a change. The Secretary has, more than once within the last ten years, contemplated its removal to supposed more advantageous positions. To procure a better site for a dry-dock, has been among the motives given for desiring another situation. In May, 1835, Loammi Baldwin, Esq., was appointed by the Secretary "to make the necessary soundings and examination, and to ascertain whether any more advantageous site for a navy-yard and dock presented itself within the harbor of New-York." June 3, 1836, the House adopted a resolution calling for information, etc.; in reply to which the report of Colonel Baldwin was presented. February 23, 1837, the subject was again brought before the House by a resolution requiring "examinations to be made of the various positions not heretofore examined within the waters of New-York and vicinity, which are adapted to the establishment and construction of dry-docks," etc. In pursuance of this resolution, Professor Renwick, of New-York, was appointed to make the examination. His report, made in December, 1837, was against the Brooklyn Navy-Yard, and in favor of Constable's Point, opposite New-York, on the New-Jersey shore. March, 1838, the result of an unofficial survey, by Messrs. Swift and McNeill, civil engineers, in favor of Barn Island, was presented to the House. It gave great preference to that over any other site. In the same month, a communication was laid before Congress from the Navy Commissioners, in which the relative merits of Brooklyn, Constable's Point, and Barn Island are fully discussed. A decided preference is given to Brooklyn. The next and latest, and, it may be added, the most satisfactory examination, has been recently made at the instance of the present Secretary, who appointed Captains Conner and Shubrick, and Moncure Robinson, Esq., as a commission for that purpose. Much care and labor were bestowed by these gentlemen in the discharge of the duty. Their report confirmed what had previously been declared by Colonel Baldwin, that a more advantageous site than the present one was not to be found within the waters of New-York harbor. Nearly ten years' agitation and investigation leave the matter precisely where it was found. The original selection was a proper one. It does appear that an attentive perusal of the reports which have so often been made, would have long since precluded the supposition that a change was necessary. It is now, however, permanently settled. No further doubt need exist as to the permanency of the present position.

It would be little less than folly or madness to adopt another. That the uncertain disposition of this question has operated against the erection of a dock in Brooklyn, can not be disputed.

The citizens of New-York and Brooklyn have frequently manifested their wishes in favor of some provision by the Government for the repair and coppering of ships of war. They have held public meetings and memorialized Congress, believing there was cause for complaint. It has been thought by them as little less than miraculous, that a naval station of its importance should remain neglected; that a Government almost exclusively mercantile, whose defenses and warfare were principally maritime, should have left its commercial emporium, for nearly a half-century after the establishment of its navy, without a work so indispensable. Her tradesmen and mechanics have conceived themselves deprived of a portion of the public patronage and labor, which is due alike to all. The concentration of national employment at one or two favored points was looked upon as hostile to their interests, and not in keeping with the true interests of the country.

It was deemed a grievance. It may be said these are not points for the consideration of the Committee; that the opinion and wishes of the immediate citizens of New-York and Brooklyn are entitled to no greater weight than a corresponding number at any other part of the Union; that the construction of public works is paid for out of the national treasury, and for which the whole people appropriate, and of the propriety of which the whole people are judges. But the people of New-York and Brooklyn, without doubting the soundness of these positions in their general application, conceive their case an exception. Their reply is, that when any portion of the people, conscious of great advantages, believe that, in the distribution of patronage, a discrimination is made against them, they have a right to be heard, and it is a fit subject for the deliberation of Congress; that there is cause of complaint not only of an individual wrong, but a national evil; for a division of public employment "improves and augments our mechanics and artificers; gives bread to a portion of the laboring classes; induces the improvement of our cities and navigable waters; contributes to a more efficient and general defense of the places; renders our citizens more patriotic and contented with their Government, and, by the additional interest which it gives them, more willing to defend it." Nor must it be forgotten that the navigating and ship-owning interests of New-York have a deep stake in the adequacy of the naval marine to protect the commercial marine. The harbor, filled with shattered and disabled ships of war, without means of repair, would offer but slight resistance to hostile fleets upon our coast. Innumerable cases will suggest themselves, in which serious consequences may ensue, and the loss of public and private property be beyond the expense of many dry-docks.

As a naval station, New-York has peculiar fitness, besides the extent of her commerce. Her harbor is spacious and well fortified; her channels sufficiently deep and unobstructed; her position central and commanding; and her advantages for the supply of materials and skillful workmen unsurpassed, if equalled, in any other port. No local obstacle prevents; and a longer continuance of the absence of some provision for the repair of ships of war would be as hazardous and detrimental to the property of the Government as it is unjust to her commercial interest.

The largeness of a sum sufficient to build a dry-dock there has attracted attention. To vote it at this time has elicited opposition. It can not be denied that the exhausted condition of the treasury presents a serious impediment. But there are occasions when the outlay of money will conduce to the advantage of the Government, even in a pecuniary sense. In any state of the treasury, it is wise to erect works necessary to preserve existing works. It will not be asserted that it is impolitic, even under our present embarrassments, to vote such an expenditure. The present would seem an instance of this kind. It has been represented that two ships of the line, the Washington and Franklin, now lying at the Brooklyn station, not movable without heavy repairs and expense, will require docking very soon, to save them from abandonment. The latter is a noble ship, which, by razeeing, could be made one of the finest frigates in the service. It would certainly be unwise to leave them in their present situation, fast falling to decay, without an effort to save them from a total loss. It can be done only by docking. The frigate Hudson, also lying there, has already been sacrificed. A survey was held upon her in November, 1841, and she was condemned as unworthy of repairs. The Washington and Franklin, if much longer neglected, will most assuredly be placed on the same list.

Much interest has recently been shown by the public in floating dry-docks. It is contended that, in many respects, they possess advantages over the excavated docks, besides the difference in cost and comparatively very short time required in building; the latter of these considerations is essential, with reference to saving the ships in Brooklyn. Fears are entertained that they would be lost before the expiration of the six or eight years required in building an excavated dock. Many gentlemen of intelligence, whose opinions are entitled to confident reliance, give the strongest assurance of their belief in the utility, safety, and superior advantages of floating dry-docks, and have recommended the speedy construction of one at Brooklyn to raise and repair the Washington and Franklin.

It can be readily conceived that a proposition to construct a dock of this kind will be received with alarm by those who have not given them careful investigation. It will be looked upon by many as an experiment, and fraught with danger. The idea will present itself, that an attempt is to be made to raise from their element our ships of war, each weighing thousands of tons, by the frail and uncertain aid of a wooden machine, slightly and insecurely constructed. Unsteadiness, instability, and want of durability, will at once appear insuperable objections. Upon attainment of knowledge of the principles and practical operation of the approved dock, it is confidently asserted, all such fears must vanish. As in all inventions, when first presented, prejudice is to be combated and beaten down before acquiescence in their utility or practicability can be obtained—there are men who, though intelligent and honest, appear to be opposed to every thing which did not come upon the stage before themselves, to whom innovations are as revolting as an attempt to change the Government or revolutionize the social system. As applicable to improvements in the navy, this hostility has been paramount. Inventions of the first merit, promising economy of time and money, and the addition to existing usages of warfare of great facilities, have frequently been rejected. No branch of the public service more requires the application of the production of intellect, and in none is such obstinate resistance manifest. The world is following progress in its onward march to the amelioration of the condition and advancement of mankind; the arts and sciences are being exerted for the simplification of mysteries which for centuries have slept in night, and the discoveries of philosophy are spreading their beneficent influences over every movement of man. The governmental policy of the powerful of European nations has been forced into an opposite current to that in which it ran for ages; international law is no longer expounded by the cannon and the sword; the military tactics of Charles XII. and of Napoleon, each in their day so formidable and perfect, have been bettered by improvement; and even the every-day utensils of husbandry and mechanical tools for the present time would not be recognized by the original inventors. Mind, in this myriad of diversified applications, has, with superhuman effort, given birth to a new world, comparatively regenerated and disinthralled from the bigotry and prejudices of the old world. The navy alone has apparently resisted change. She has nearly stood still amidst the surrounding advancement. The vast improvements which commercial enterprise has bestowed upon the merchant marine have been avoided and decried by those who have had charge of the naval marine. It should not be. The efficiency of the nation's right arm deserves the benefits of the genius and skill of the world; not only is it entitled to all meritorious improvements of our own country, but to those of any other people.

The present head of the Department has evinced a desire to adopt an opposite course. Credit is due to him for a disposition to pursue another policy than those who doubt the merit of every thing new, and adhere tenaciously to every thing old. He evidently desires to keep pace with the spirit of the age. Several experiments have already been made, to the adaptation of science to useful ends. The recent discoveries of Professor Johnson in detecting the impurities of copper, thus enabling the Government, as well as individuals, to detect impositions which, it is reasonable to suppose, have cost many millions, are beyond estimate in importance. Other experiments have been made, which will prove highly beneficial to the service.

Floating dry-docks have been heretofore but imperfectly understood. The generally-received opinion, that nothing but an old-fashioned excavated or walled dry-dock could safely perform the duty of docking and undocking ships of the larger class, has prevented that attention to them to which they are so justly entitled. Practical gentlemen have too often taken it for granted "that they would not answer," refusing a fair, dispassionate, practical test. To this spirit, so prevalent in our naval service, is chargeable the tenacity with which old ideas and old customs are rigidly followed.

It is not contended that the principle of docking ships by means of a floating vessel is entirely new. The general leading feature has been in use many years; but it is believed that there have been recently added to it such guards, checks, securities, facilities, and advantages, as to render it, in every necessary particular, capable of docking and undocking the largest vessel of war. In some respects, advantages over the excavated dock are claimed for it by those who understand the principles of each. These advantages will be enumerated and explained, and it is thought satisfactorily, to every casual observer.

Among the papers from the Secretary, referred to the Committee, is the report of a commission appointed in October last, to repair to New-York, to examine and witness the performance of the floating dry-docks there, and investigate such plans as should be submitted. The gentlemen composing it were Capt. Beverly Kennon, United States Navy, Col. Samuel Humphreys, United States chief naval constructor, and Walter R. Johnson, Esq., professor of mechanics and natural philosophy. It can not be disputed that it would have been difficult, if possible, to have formed a court of investigation with more capacity and sounder judgment. The scientific and practical information necessary to insure safe conclusions was here happily blended. Nothing can be hazarded in yielding to the opinions of this report. The required knowledge, and the patient investigation which is indispensable in procuring a proper understanding of a subject so intricate and intimately connected with, and depending upon, scientific principles, were laboriously bestowed. The report is full and conclusive. Seven different plans of floating docks were presented, though only two were exhibited in practice, which received minute examination, being subjected to the nicest calculation. Their comparative advantages and disadvantages went through the ordeal of severe scrutiny; and though it was thought but one would answer for the naval service, the other was pronounced meritorious. They were the balance floating dry-dock of Mr. John S. Gilbert, and the sectional floating dry-dock of Mr. S. D. Dakin.

The operation of docking and undocking the largest class of merchant ships was performed in the presence of the commission—a full and detailed account of which is given in the report. The comparative advantages are fully shown. A preference is given to the balance-dock, in the most decided language. Insuperable objections against the other are enumerated, one of which (namely, that much greater depth of water than can be found at the Brooklyn yard will be required for its action) is enough to put it out of the question, as far as that station is concerned. The balance-dock is free from this difficulty, owing to its construction upon an entirely different principle. In it, the ship intended to be docked is admitted, as in an excavated dock, between the sides; whereas with the former, the whole dock must rest under the ship, and consequently, drawing not only the draught of the vessel, but also of the dock. As, for instance, if a ship draws twenty-five feet water, and the dock twenty feet, it will require forty-five feet water to dock her in. The assertion that floating dry-docks have advantages over the excavated dry-dock is fully made out by the balance-dock.

The objections to excavated docks are:

1. Want of light and room. They are constructed extremely narrow, having but space enough for the vessel. The narrow construction arises from the necessity of lessening the pressure of water on the gates and under side of the bottom, which being computed by the area of the bottom, will be found immense. This pressure of water is frequently the cause of accident, and always of unpleasant consequences. Commodore Stewart, in a communication made to Mr. Paynter, member of the Naval Committee in 1838, writes that, "owing to this constant pressure of water upon the gates, they are always leaking, and the water springing into the dock, and the bottom is kept overflowed and wet, which requires almost constant pumping for the purpose of draining it off." It is to obviate this difficulty, by lessening the pressure, that they are built as narrow as the admission of the vessel will allow. Hence it is that not sufficient light is thrown upon the hull. In clouded days, artificial light must be introduced, to enable the workmen to perform their work. It follows, that the quantity as well as the quality of the work is not as it would be if done under the bright rays of the sun, or if not restricted from the usual light by high walls. A diminution in quantity and deterioration in quality must ensue. It may well be a question whether the enor-

mous expense attending the repairing of vessels of war has not, in part, been contributed to by this want of light in dry-docks. It is well ascertained that, with artificial light, the caulking of seams and coppering can not be as well performed as with the natural light of day.

Another evil, arising from the same cause, is the difficulty in getting long pieces of timber into the dock, and preparing them for being placed upon the keel or bottom.

The balance floating-dock is without these objections. There is no necessity for narrow construction or high sides. The pressure of water is upon all its parts. To give room to workmen, it is made double the width and much longer than the largest ship to be inclosed in it—thus at once securing light, room, air, and effective power.

2. The health of the workmen. The extreme dampness of an excavated dock is detrimental and sometimes fatal to those engaged in them. The mechanics are crowded together eleven hours daily, in wet and cold, and a humid atmosphere. Diseases of a peculiar and serious character are frequently the result. Floating dry-docks are without this evil. In them the labor is performed on a dry floor, with good light, and sufficient ventilation.

3. The labor in docking a vessel upon the excavated dock is *increased* as the size and weight of the vessel docked is *decreased*. Greater power is necessary to dock the smallest sloop of war than the largest ship of the line; which is not the case with the balance-dock.

With the latter, the reverse is the fact. The smaller the vessel, the less the required labor and power, and *vice versa.*

4. There is less safety in the excavated docks. The gates, being of wood, are liable to decay, and to be forced open by the pressure against them, which is increased by the necessity of constructing them high, to keep out extraordinary tides. The alternate exposure to wet and dry increases the chances of accident, by decreasing the strength of the wood of which they are made. In 1838, the gates of a dock in France gave way, thereby drowning and killing fifteen persons. Similar accidents, destroying, in one instance, eighty persons, are said to have occurred in England.

The balance-dock is without this objection. As has been seen, there is no extraordinary pressure upon any part, and what there may be is equal upon all its parts. The strain which, in the excavated dock, is brought to bear upon the gates, is borne by it upon the sides and ends, thus operating as a preventive to accidents, and not inviting them.

5. The time required to build. It is estimated that from six to eight years will be required to build an excavated dock, and but as many months for a balance-dock. Upon this point, the report of the commission properly remarks: "If the Government were at war, and had, in the harbor of New-York, several disabled vessels which could not make their way to Norfolk or Charlestown, and the question was the most speedy method of getting docked, it would doubtless render this consideration important, independent of the loss of

interest or cost between the commencement or completion of a walled (excavated) dock."

6. It is stationary. The balance-dock could be removed from one position to another, whenever convenience or safety required. The advantage of this quality is too obvious to need comment.

7. Difference in original cost. The estimates for an excavated dock (at Brooklyn) are from $900,000 to $1,300,000.

Mr. Gilbert, the inventor and constructor of the balance-dock, offers to contract with the Government to build a dock on the plan, 240 feet long, 85 feet wide, and 33 feet high, (large enough and with power enough to raise the ship-of-the-line Pennsylvania,) for $250,000; if built inside of an iron tank, as high as the load line, $260,000; and if all of iron, or such parts as would be necessary, but little variation from that sum. Of course the price would vary according to the size and material of which it was built. Take $1,100,000 (a medium sum between the estimates for an excavated dock) as about the cost, and it will be seen that there will be $850,000 difference in cost of building. The interest on the cost of the excavated dock would be $66,000 per annum, when calculated at 6 per cent., and would, in four years, amount to $264,000—a greater sum than is required to construct a balance-dock. Thus it is seen one of them could be built every four years for the interest of the cost of the excavated dock. It would not take many years to place a dock at every southern port, where they are so much wanted, by the appropriation of merely the interest of constructing one dry-dock on the old plan. Another consideration, too important to be overlooked, is, that there would be much greater distribution and quantity of labor given to mechanics.

These are the prominent advantages of the balance-dock over the excavated dock. In several material points, they are worthy of further discussion and amplification than can be given in this report.

We will now proceed to notice the common supposed objections to floating dry-docks.

1. They are constructed of perishable materials, and are subject to decay and accident.

If built in a galvanized wrought-iron tank, as proposed by the commission, this objection and its consequences are at once dissipated. Its durability would be secured; nor would it require repair—having, in that particular, an advantage over the excavated dock. The gates of the latter being of necessity built of wood, and, as has been stated, alternately exposed to wet and dry, their liability to decay is increased. Frequent examinations are required; and, when repaired, it is in some cases necessary to build a coffer-dam, at a heavy expense. No accident to the hull of the balance-dock can affect its stability, or its retention of upright position—the space between the outer and inner walls being divided into small cells. If it were possible to perforate it, the water would flow over the whole platform, thereby preserving a perfect level.

2. A vessel of the first class would be unsafe if for any length of time in a floating dock.

The fact that the floating dry-docks of New-York have sustained the largest merchant ships as long as it could be probable would ever be required in the navy, is a sufficient reply to this objection. No accident from this cause, nor, indeed, any other, has happened. It is no reply to say that the danger is increased with the size of the vessel docked. A floating dock which will lift and sustain one thousand tons will lift and sustain four thousand tons, provided it is constructed large enough to admit the vessel, and all its parts are increased in strength in proportion to its increase of size. Its width is always nearly double that of the largest ship intended to be docked; consequently, the effective power and strength is superior to that which is required to safely sustain any ship which it is spacious enough to hold. If made of iron, all doubts upon this point must certainly vanish.

In reply to a letter addressed to Professor Johnson, since the report of the commissioners, asking whether, in his opinion, the naked hull of a ship-of-the-line (having reference to those now at New-York) could be safely lifted and sustained in a floating dock, he says: "In reply to the specific question which you propound, I would say that, if built in a substantial and workman-like manner, I see no reason to doubt that a dock on that (Gilbert's) plan could safely lift and sustain the naked hull of a ship-of-the-line." He evidently alludes to a wooden dock. If built of iron, there could be but little, if any, difference between it and the excavated dock, as to accident and strength.

3. The unsteady position and chances of straining or hogging the ship whilst in dock.

This objection, however true of floating dry-docks

generally, can not lie against the balance dry-dock. It is guarded against fully. There is a perfect adaptation of the line of keel-blocks to the line of the keel of the vessel, which gives it an unyielding and firm support. It has a counterpoise to the weight of the ship, which is distributed over the whole platform.

The large area of water covered by the length, width, and weight of the dock keep the whole in an immovable position. The one now in the Hudson river, at New-York, lying in the most exposed part of the harbor, where severe north-western winds prevail three months in the year, has never met with hindrance or accident to either dock or vessel.

If the advantages claimed for the balance dry-dock rested upon no other basis than theory, or its operation by a model, it would be temerity to recommend one for the Government. The value of a vessel of war, or, indeed, the cost of the dock, would be too great to intrust to the hazard of an experiment. However urgent may be the necessity, New-York had better remain without a dock than to adopt one which, if failing, loss of property so great would ensue. It could not aid the cause of progress and improvement to adopt any plan of dock as a substitute, or even auxiliary to a dry-dock, which would not entirely answer the purpose. An experiment is not made in constructing a balance-dock. It is already in successful operation at New-York for 1500 tons, and at Amsterdam for 4000 tons.

The Dutch East-India Company paid 12,000 guilders for simply the model and drawings from which (so simple are its principles) it was constructed. At the latest intelligence, this dock was efficiently performing its duty, and no accident had occurred. Its lifting power, being 4000 tons, is nearly 1000 greater than the ship-of-the-line Pennsylvania, and more than the Secretary tells us will be required, owing to the intention of the Department to dismantle before docking.

The Austrian Government has also made application to Mr. Gilbert. Baron Ghega, chief engineer of Austria, in behalf of his Government, after examining all the means in use in raising vessels in Europe and America, gave the preference to this plan, and made official report to that effect.

After mature deliberation, and a review of the many considerations to be weighed in arriving at correct conclusions, the Committee recommend that the existing appropriation of one hundred thousand dollars, voted at last session towards the building at Brooklyn of a dry-dock or floating dock, according to the discretion of the Secretary, be applied to the construction of a balance floating dry-dock, and report a joint resolution to that effect.

CHAPTER XII.

ELECTION OF MAYOR WOOD—DIFFICULTIES IN THE WAY OF GOVERNMENT—DISPOSITIONS OF THE NEW MAYOR—COMPLAINT-BOOK.

OF New-York, and of the difficulties it presents in the way of government, we have said nearly all we have to say, in our initial chapter. It was an odd, wild metropolis, wherein if we had not two or three murders or a spicy riot or two with our matutinal tea or coffee, we were disappointed. We lunched upon improprieties; we dissipated upon frightful bills of mortality; rollicked in muddy streets; and looked upon our rulers chiefly as divinely-appointed guides to Schuylerism and other modern accomplishments.

The citizens were disheartened, or had grown callous, and so careless. There was a sort of blind confidence in a protecting fate, on the part of some; while the more energetic talked in a revolutionary manner about re-obtaining a good government. The press was filled with complaints of official corruption, useless expenditure of public money, over-taxation, and improper contracting. The streets were filthy to an abominable degree, and the health of the city exceedingly endangered; paupers in myriads were emptied from polluted ships upon our shores, to become the prey of the emigrant-runners, or a burden upon the charities of the city.

Such was our condition in the month of November, 1854, when the election for the Municipal Government of New-York was held. The Democratic party was at variance with itself; the secret Know-Nothing organization was fresh and powerful; the Whigs, though not numerous, were resolved to be Whig, and a new Reform party had been established. So there were four parties in the field, the Whigs nominating Mr. J. J. Herrick as their candidate for the Mayoralty; the Reform party nominating Mr. Wilson J. Hunt; the Know-Nothings, Mr. J. W. Barker; and both sections of the Democratic party uniting on Fernando Wood.

Against three candidates, then, and with disaffection in his own party, Mr. Wood, after a violent struggle, was elected to the chief magistracy of the city of New-York. Many citizens abstained entirely from giving any vote for Mayor, for the number of gubernatorial votes cast was 60,367, while for Mayor but 59,643 were given. Of these, Herrick received 5696 votes; Hunt, 15,397; Barker, 18,547; Wood, 20,003: total, 59,643: making the majority of the victor over his chief opponent 1456, and securing his election.

On the first of January, 1855, at noonday, he was solemnly inaugurated, taking the oath of office, and entering instantly upon the execution of the duties of that office.

There were immense difficulties in his way. Parts of six different city charters had created no less than *nine* executive departments, each claiming sovereign authority and independence. What power the Mayor possessed was hidden by long neglect, or want of definiteness, or sluggishness of former incumbents, till it appeared to be non-existent altogether.

But a resolute, energetic, untiring, persistent, strong-willed man had been called to the head of affairs. He supposed himself elected to do something, and resolutely set to work to find out what that something was, and then to do it. His idea of a government was the simple one—a power which governs. He intended to discover whether he had any such power. If he had, he meant to use it to the fullest and most absolute extent which the interests of the people and the welfare of the city required.

To judge of the immense difficulties, almost inconceivable, in the way of ruling this huge town of ours, the first two messages—the inaugural, and the message of January 11—must be carefully read. The latter sets forth, in the most distinct and masterly manner, the obstacles to be overcome, the needs existing; and both exhibit the quiet, immovable determination of a strong man to crush or surmount those obstacles, to satisfy those necessities of the people.

He does not hide his knowledge of the difficulty, nor yet his will to conquer it. In his inaugural, he says to the Common Council:

THE present is not an auspicious time to commence a new administration; it is beyond the ability of any man, exercising the duties of this office under the city charter, to give this people that government which appears to be so generally expected, and which is certainly so much required.

However we may differ as to the cause, there can be no doubt of a pervading dissatisfaction with the municipal affairs of this city. That this feeling exists, and that there are sufficient grounds for it, all must admit; whether it arises from defects in the fundamental laws, or from improper local legislation, or from mal-administration upon the part of those intrusted with the executive duties, are questions upon which there is diversity of opinion; in my judgment, all of these are the causes.

The amended charter of 1830 was preferable to the present system. Admitting that it required modification, the subsequent amendments have but increased the difficulties.

The allegation that it was inadequate to the increased size and wants of the city, was, in my opinion, entirely without foundation.

The Constitution of the United States is as applicable to the present greatness of the Republic as it was to the Federal Union at the time of its adoption. Had amendments been made to it at the instance of every party or statesman who deemed it insufficient, we should have fallen to the same condition as a nation that this city has as a corporation.

The mistake in disturbing the charter of 1830 was not only in the alteration effected, but also in the introduction of an uneasy spirit in the people, who, by the continual application to State legislation, have been taught to look to foreign remedies for domestic abuses.

Thus have we transferred to Albany much that could

have been better cared for among ourselves; forgetting the old republican maxim, that no power should be delegated which can be exercised by the people themselves. This principle should never be forgotten. It was faithfully adhered to by the framers of the national Constitution. In all countries and in all ages, the utmost caution has been observed in granting to representatives the right of even ordinary legislation.

We should not present the first instance in which a people voluntarily surrenders the power to form the organic laws—yielding that highest of all prerogatives to men who owe us no responsibility, are not chosen by our suffrages, who are foreign to our interests, do not understand our wants, and who, consequently, are liable to become the tools of designing men, having selfish or corrupt objects of their own to obtain.

Amendments to the charter of 1830 have, one after another, been adopted at Albany, until now we are administering the government by portions of *six different charters, which create nine executive departments, having undefined, doubtful, and conflicting powers,* with heads elected by the people, *each assuming to be sovereign, and independent of the others, of the Mayor, or of any other authority;* and beyond the reach of any, except that of impeachment by the Common Council, which never has been, and probably never will be, exercised.

This irresponsibility has been productive of carelessness in expenditure, and negligence in the execution of the ordinances.

Thus, in the attempts to remedy defects by foreign aid, which could have been accomplished at home, we have fastened upon ourselves a complicated, many-headed, ill-shaped and uncontrollable monster, which has not, in my opinion, developed its worst characteristics.

So far as my duties are defined, I feel some embarrassment. Even coördinate powers with the several executive departments are denied to me in some quarters; and the fact that my predecessors, under the new charters, have not attempted their exercise. is relied upon as sustaining this position.

Without desiring to question the wisdom of those who have preceded me in this office, I must be permitted to construe my powers and duties as I understand them. Restricted as the prerogatives of the Mayor have been by almost every legislative act appertaining to the government of this city, for several years, still there is sufficient left to instill more energy into the administration than now exists, and to hold at least a supervisory check over the whole city government.

It is true, that though ostensibly head of the Police Department, he is not so practically, in the essential element of authority—that of controlling the retention or removal of his own subordinates. The Chief of Police holds his place independent of the Mayor, that officer having been appointed during "good behavior," by the late Mayor and Board of Commissioners, under the law of 1853, which they construed to give that authority. He can not, *solus*, appoint or remove the humblest subordinate in the service, nor make the rules and regulations for its governance. Of these requisites of power, so necessary to make an efficient police corps, he is by law deprived. Discipline can only be obtained and maintained by the firm hand of unrestricted power; besides, it is wrong in principle to make any public officer responsible for the acts of subordinates who are placed beyond his individual power to remove.

These are some of the evils arising from the frequent application to State legislation for this city. Instead of a simple form of government, easily understood, the power of its officers so well defined that there could be no conflict or misunderstanding, we have one full of the objections referred to.

It is not my purpose, at this time, to indicate a substitute, though I can not omit to add my belief, that the most perfect form of government was that adopted by the framers of the Federal Constitution. Its clear and simple provisions are equally applicable to municipal corporations, or to a nation of a hundred millions. The Mayor should be to the city what the President is to the General Government. There should be corresponding executive departments, with heads selected by the Mayor, (subject to the confirmation of the Board of Aldermen,) who should have entire control, and be, himself, responsible to the people. The Mayor and heads of departments should meet in council, and have a general uniformity of action and coöperation with each other, in carrying out the laws, and preserving the general interests of the city. Over the whole should govern the Chief Magistrate; he should have the one-man power, which history teaches is the least dangerous, and the most positive for good.

Certainly we have suffered more from legislative assumptions, or misconduct of subordinates in authority, than from the tyranny or corruption of a chief ruler.

Precedent shows there is safety in the latter, not only in the exercise of authority for the public weal, but as a barrier against the wrong doings of the former. The stronger the head the more healthy the body; but if strength is taken away by diverting it to a multitude of heads, the whole becomes enervated, and unable to discharge its functions.

Concentration, with ample power, insures efficiency, because it creates one high responsible authority. Decentralization is subversive of all good executive government.

This want of concentration has been the prime cause of the immense load of taxation which we now bear. To compare the relative taxation per individual, under the charter of 1830, and that now existing, will prove this assertion.

In 1843, the amount raised by tax for the support of the city government, was one million seven hundred and forty-seven thousand five hundred and sixteen dollars and fifty-nine cents; whereas, in 1853, it was five millions sixty-seven thousand two hundred and seventy-five dollars and sixty-nine cents; and this year it is nearly six millions; a startling increase. Need you be told that this addition of two hundred and fifty per centum, is the result of either corruption or wasteful extravagance, the natural consequence of irresponsibility?

And here let me diverge to remark that to tolerate profligate outlays of the public money, whilst nearly one tenth of our whole population are in want of the necessaries of life, is as shocking to humanity as it is injustice to a large and valuable class of our suffering fellow citizens.

Surely we are admonished that if this rate of taxation be continued, more of it should be devoted to the relief of the poor, whose industry bears most of its burdens, and who are now ringing into our ears their cries of distress. Labor was never so depressed as now. Employment is almost entirely cut off, and if procured, its remuneration is totally inadequate, owing to the high price of articles of subsistence. The prices of labor and of food bear no relative equality.

In ordinary times of general prosperity capital possesses advantages over labor.

Capital can always protect itself, and it is only at periods of inflation, when capital is directed to speculation in the products of labor, that the operative is appreciated, and his industry rewarded by competent compensation.

But now, when capital either timidly retreats, through fear, to the bank-vaults, or is diverted to the oppression, for gain, of those who employ labor, his condition is sad enough. Does it not behove us, not only individually, but in our corporate capacity, to throw ourselves boldly forward to his relief?

This is the time to remember the poor!

Do we not owe industry every thing? It is its products that has built up this great city.

Do not let us be ungrateful as well as inhuman. Do not let it be said that labor, which produces every thing, gets nothing, and dies of hunger in our midst, whilst capital, which produces nothing, gets every thing, and pampers in luxury and plenty.

It is our duty to take and administer this government under the charters and laws as we find them, until a change is effected for the better. Valuable improvements can now be made, notwithstanding these objections to the system. All the evils of which the people complain are not chargeable to wrong legislation. If the Common Council will be more cautious in the passage of ordinances, especially those involving disbursements of money, holding fast to the purse-strings as against the harpies, who for many years have hovered around its chambers, and if the executive bureaux will coöperate with me in the rigid enforcement of the laws, and particularly in restraining expense, and exacting a faithful performance of every contract, we may do much towards removing the present discontent.

Most assuredly the people pay enough for the better administration of their public affairs; and it has never appeared to me that they were unreasonable in their requirements.

They ask public order; the suppression of crime and vice; clean streets; the removal of nuisances and abolition of abuses; a restriction of taxation to the absolute wants of an economically administered government, and a prompt execution of the laws and ordinances. Let us endeavor to meet their expectations.

For myself, I desire to announce here, upon the threshold, that, as I understand and comprehend my duties and prerogatives, they leave me no alternative, without dishonor, but to assume a general control over the whole City Government, so far as protecting its municipal interests may demand it. I shall not hesitate to exercise even doubtful powers, when the honor or the interests of the public is abused.

The public good will be sufficient warrant to insure my action. Under this law I shall proceed, not doubting your concurrence and the support of the people, for whom the responsibility is assumed.

[And in the next remarkably clear document he exhibits the real condition of that Augean stable which he has been expected to purify.]

THE several annual reports from the executive departments have been several days before you, and no doubt thoroughly examined. In taking a survey of the affairs of the city, the first object to present, is the condition of the finances. A statement with reference to it is herewith furnished.

Permanent city debt, redeemable from the Sinking-Fund, January 1st, 1855:

5	per cent Water stock,	redeemable,	1858	$3,000,000
5	" "	"	1860	2,500,000
5	" "	"	1870	3,000,000
5	" "	"	1875	255,600
5	" "	"	1880	2,147,000
5 & 6	" Croton Water Stock,	"	1890	1,000,000
7	" Water Loan,	"	1857	990,488
5	" Public Building St'k,	"	1856	515,000
5	" Building Loan Stock, No. 3,	"	1870	75,000
5	" Do. " 4,	"	1873	75,000
5	" Fire Indemnity St'k,	"	1868	402,768
	Amount carried forward			$13,960,856

Amount brought forward.............		$13,960,856
Corporation stock and bonds held by the Commissioners of the Sinking-Fund, on account of redemption of the city debt....................	$4,252,289	
Additional assets (bonds and mortgages) held by the Commissioners on said account...	911,886	
Balance in bank, Jan. 1, 1855...........	17,240	5,181,415
Actual amt. of permanent debt, Jan. 1, 1855, say......		$8,779,441

which is a reduction, as compared with the amount of debt, January 2, 1854, of $460,246.

Funded debt redeemable from taxation, and payable (with the exception of Public Education Stock) in annual installments of $50,000, January 1, 1855.

6	per cent	Building Loan Stock, No. 2, redeemable in 1855 and 1856......................	$100,000
5	"	Public Building Stock, No. 3, redeemable in 1857 and 1864......................	400,000
5	"	Stock for Docks and Slips, redeemable in 1867 and 1876......................	500,000
5	"	Public Education Stock, redeemable in 1873	154,000
		Total amount of funded debt, Jan. 1, 1855.........	$1,154,000

which is an increase, as compared with the amount of debt January 2, 1854, of $204,000.

The revenues of the Sinking-Fund, for the payment of interest on the city debt, are fully adequate for the payment of interest on the above stocks. The balance to this account, January 1, 1855, being $60,000, invested temporarily in revenue bonds of the city corporation, and cash in bank $317,106.11, thus rendering it unnecessary to raise *any amount* for "interest on city debts" by taxation.

In connection with this statement another is presented, of the amounts which have been raised, by taxation, from 1844 to 1854, inclusive:

1844....................	$1,988,818 56
1845....................	2,096,191 18
1846....................	2,520,146 71
1847....................	2,581,776 30
1848....................	2,715,510 25
1849....................	3,005,762 52
1850....................	3,230,085 02
1851....................	2,924,455 94
1852....................	3,380,511 05
1853....................	5,067,275 69
1854....................	4,845,386 07
And to be raised in	
1855....................	5,918,593 25

By this it will appear that the expenditures have gradually and steadily increased, though it is well known that the character of our Government has deteriorated.

The people of this city can not realize that the actual cost of conducting their municipal affairs amounts to the sum annually expended. They do not believe that all of the money appropriated is devoted to public wants. In my opinion an examination of the subject, and close scrutiny of the various items composing the accounts of the disbursing officers, will show that it is the undue, unnecessary, extraordinary outlays, without sufficient equivalent, that have swollen our taxes to their present enormous amount.

It behoves us, as guardians of the public interests, to look to the subject. If it is longer permitted, we are *particeps criminis*, whether the money is spent under our own eyes or not. Besides greater caution in appropriations, we are called upon to exercise more vigilance over, and demand severer accountability from, those who spend the money. The smallest items of expenditures should be guarded as sacredly as if amounting to hundreds of thousands. *The principle which will permit a disbursing officer to divert the value of one dollar, in money or property, to his own or his friend's purpose, will, in time, render him a defaulter or a peculator.*

The treasury can be relieved in many ways; several present sources of expenditure can be abolished entirely, and large sums be brought into the treasury, which now go to the pockets of individuals.

THE STREETS.

The street openings and subsequent heavy outlays for that purpose in regulating, grading, paving, sewering, repairing, etc., are one of the heaviest burdens we bear. It is no answer to reply that much of it is returned to the treasury by assessments upon the property benefited; it is of little importance to the party who pays, whether the money is procured from him, under pretext of adding to the value of his real estate, or whether under the plea of supporting the Government.

We have no right to make distinction It is our duty to protect the private property of the people, as well as their public treasury. As now conducted, the public business appertaining to streets, is under the direction of *six of the departments, besides several outside commissioners, inspectors, surveyors, appraisers, and other temporary selected agents.* The law officer superintends the selection of Commissioners of Estimates and Assessments to open, examines titles to property affected, and counsels the legal proceedings, necessary in opening, widening, and altering streets.

The Street Department advertises for proposals to open, makes contracts therefor, and through its bureaux makes and collects assessments; it also has charge of the opening, regulating and paving. The Croton Aqueduct Department attends to the sewerage, and laying Croton water pipes.

The Repairs and Supplies has control of repairing, re-laying pavements, curb and gutter, etc.

The Streets and Lamps places lamp-posts, and superintends the lighting and cleaning.

The City Inspector's Department attends to the removing of nuisances, carrying off dead horses, and other animals, and has general charge of every thing relating to the streets, which affect their sanitary condition. Each has numerous subordinates with light duties, but large compensation. Commissioners are appointed for each job, even to "*declare*" a street opened, but for one block, and though it may remain closed for a quarter of a century afterwards. Many of these persons, really and in fact, in person perform no actual duties, and are compensated in proportion to the delays produced, and money expended. These places are often given as the reward for other than official service, which is not of much value to the city; some of this class may be called "professional street-openers," whose time is devoted to the procuration of jobs of this kind, and by getting resolutions through the Common Council to "open" when there is no necessity for it; they are strong in partisan influence.

The law which gives to a majority of the property holders to be affected by an improvement when unnecessary, the power to prevent, is inoperative before them; several instances have been recently brought to my attention, in which their influence over the Common Council has suppressed the voice of two thirds of the parties in interest who had remonstrated against their further proceedings. If pressed, they obtain delay in the Common Council, until all they can make out of the job is procured, when they magnanimously withdraw their opposition, and the city must foot the bill, and their "estimate and assessments" amount to nothing. Some of these persons have several streets on hand at the same time, and make large sums of money. It is but proper to add, that sometimes there are commissioners who are not comprehended within this description of them as a class.

Another class more useless, though not so expensive, is the inspectors appointed to superintend the grading, regulating and cleaning of streets, building of sewers, docks, piers, etc. Some of these people seldom see the work for which they are appointed inspector, and if they do, they know nothing of it, or do not wish to know, provided the contractor *is a clever fellow*, and does "what is right."

These departments frequently come in conflict with each other; it sometimes happens that they are nearly all engaged at the same time, upon some part of the same street. It often occurs, *that soon after the paving is completed, it is taken up* to lay down a sewer, Croton water or gas pipes. Each department being independent and sometimes inimical to the other, no concert exists, but every one, upon its own notions, proceeds to do what it deems best, without thinking or caring of expense or public convenience.

It is no exaggeration to say, that sometimes *twenty* officials, belonging to different departments, are engaged in doing, at the same time, that which could be accomplished by *one* man, if acting for himself, in *one twentieth the time, and at one twentieth the cost.*

Each department is its own master, and acts upon its own volition, without consent or consultation, and not unfrequently strives to thwart the plans of each other, and produce confusion. Every person having the control of private business or interest, can see, without further comment, the reason why so large a sum is expended upon our streets.

The business care, concentration, uniformity and regularity so essential to the success of any enterprise is entirely wanting.

A general cutting up and distribution of authority, creating irresponsibility and negligence is productive of profligacy in expenditure and inefficiency in the performance of work. This abuse must be reformed. It has become too serious to be permitted longer.

The little time which has been left me for investigation, consistent with other duties, has satisfied me that the whole business should be entirely under the control of one department, and at least one of the existing departments could be abolished entirely. There should be a Street Department having sole jurisdiction over the whole subject; some part of the duty could be advantageously given to other departments, without detriment or additional expense.

There should be a permanent Board of Commissioners, instead of three for each job as now, which should have the power to appoint permanent surveyors for the whole city, instead of one for each work as now. It should be made the duty of the law officer of the Corporation to give his services without any additional compensation, directly or indirectly, and if receiving fees, the amount should be paid into the treasury.

There should be one or two permanent inspectors for the whole city, provided any is required, which I doubt, instead of one for each job as now. The duties now performed by the Bureau of Assessments should be done by the present Board of Tax Commissioners, without additional compensation, who have not only sufficient leisure, but the surveys, maps, and the assessed values of every improved and unimproved lot in the city within their own office, by which to facilitate the duty. The collection of assessments should be made by the Receiver of Taxes.

That branch of the service coming under the head of repairs should be severely scrutinized, and every dollar accounted for under the most stringent rules of accountability; and nothing should be expended except upon previous appropriation, with specific reference to the object for which the money was intended. The inconvenience and delays which would attend previous appropriations upon detailed estimates for even small sums could be of little consideration as compared with the principle of unauthorized expenditures, with the official profligacy which too often follows in its train.

TAXABLE PROPERTY.

Another matter of much importance is the feasibility of enlarging the basis upon which to levy tax. The Board of Tax Commissioners, organized a few years since, has added much to the taxable basis of real and personal estate. There is yet room for increase.

Notwithstanding the vigilance of these officers and the assessors, a very large amount of personal property escapes, and an undue proportion is consequently put upon real estate. A distinction is thus created entirely unjust to real property, calculated not only to affect its value, but to retard the growth of the city. There is no solid reason why distinction should be made in the kind of value, whether real or personal, upon which we levy tax. So long as the principle of taxation is upon *property*, *all* property should bear alike.

Besides the large amount of personal estate that escapes in consequence of the inability to discover it, there are immense amounts belonging to foreign manufacturers and traders, in the hands of agents resident here, who refuse to recognize our authority to collect. A very large sum thus gets clear.

This foreign property receives all the protection which the city government affords, in common with that of our own people, which pays the expense.

These foreign owners not only enjoy equal privileges

with native citizens, but in not paying taxes upon their property, possess an exemption which enables them to compete with American labor, and affording them undue advantages.

People who pay taxes can not sell merchandise as low as those who pay none. Means should be taken during the present session of the Legislature to procure the passage of a law, making the property of foreign manufacturers and others liable to taxation.

ABOLITION OF FEES.

As a further means of revenue, I recommend an application to the Legislature for a law which will bring into the treasury the large sums now received by the Register, County Clerk, Counsel to the Corporation, Corporation Attorney, and other county officers, who receive fees as their own perquisites.

In some instances these sums are said to amount to from twenty to thirty thousand dollars per annum to one person. Whilst it is right that every public officer should be sufficiently compensated, yet there can be no good reason for permitting a few to amass large fortunes, whilst other officials, who perform more labor and more responsible duties, are paid one fifth the sum, and the whole community is burdened with taxes. *Give liberal salaries, but let all fees go to the treasury.*

INTEREST TO BE CHARGED.

A further relief may be found in requiring interest on deposits with the City Treasurer, and collecting and disbursing officers generally. The equity, practicability, and importance of this measure is so apparent, that it surprises me it has not sooner been adopted. A very large revenue could be thus derived. There was to the credit of the city in the hands of the Treasurer on the 28th of November, 1854, over one million of dollars; the 1st December, 1854, over one and a half millions; from which was drawn on these dates about a half-million, leaving about two millions to the credit of the city. Additional large sums have since been drawn, leaving, however, on the first of January, inst., a balance remaining to the credit of the city of one million two hundred and eighty-three thousand four hundred and seventy-four dollars, for which the city receives no allowance of interest whatever.

It is proper to add that it frequently occurs that the City Chamberlain is in advance to the city, and that during the last year he advanced fifty to sixty thousand dollars on claims on the treasury, for which warrants could not be given, thus offering facilities to individuals having claims, who otherwise would be obliged to wait the slow process of legislation, to be paid their just dues. Notwithstanding, however, this accommodating disposition upon the part of this officer, I can see no reason for conducting the financial affairs of the city upon any other principle than that which governs the commercial intercourse of individuals.

I am satisfied that the nearer we approximate the laws of trade, the better will public business be conducted, and the interests of the treasury protected.

The city is obliged to pay interest when using the

funds of individuals, and it should receive interest from individuals who have the use of its money.

Last year the Comptroller borrowed upon revenue bonds, three millions six hundred and ninety-three thousand dollars, nearly the whole of which was borrowed at the rate of *seven* per centum, and for which we are still paying interest, notwithstanding the large amount now lying to the credit of the city in bank. How long could an individual or a banking institution retain its credit or its capital, that conducted its affairs upon so ruinous a principle? The State of New-York discovered the value of its own revenues when lying in bank-vaults, as early as 1826. It then adopted the policy of requiring interest upon its canal funds, which has been followed since without deviation. My last advices from the Capitol state, that two millions and a half of dollars have been already received from that source, for interest exclusively on the deposits of this fund with the banks. And it is well known that some of the heads of the city collecting and disbursing bureaux, have been in the practice of receiving interest from various city banks, on the public money in their hands, which has gone into their own pockets as private perquisites.

In recommending a revenue from this source, I beg to be understood that no step should be taken in effecting it, which would in the least jeopard the security of the money. Security is the first consideration.

A prudent business man never hazards his principal in efforts to accumulate interest; but if safety and profit can be combined—and in my judgment it can be—we should be largely the gainers, and to that extent taxation lessened.

ESTIMATES AND APPROPRIATIONS.

Another object of importance, by which large sums now extracted from the treasury could be saved, is the necessity of adopting some mode, by which all disbursing officers should be prevented from the expenditure of money, or creation of obligations to pay, for which the city is liable, without previous appropriation, and a balance unexpended to meet it.

Many abuses have grown up under the present loose manner of expending money.

It is useless to ask the departments for estimates upon which to base the appropriation, if they are disregarded afterward. *So long as the Common Council pass resolutions incurring expense, and the departments execute them, frequently by using funds appropriated for other purposes, so long will our taxes continue to increase, and the enormous annual deficiencies, now so common, continue to startle us at the end of the year.*

Means should be taken to stop this altogether; the head of a department should not be allowed to exceed his own estimates, or the appropriation made; he and his bonds should be made responsible to the city for any liability thus incurred.

Disbursing officers must be confined within the spirit as well as the letter of the charter, which provides that *no money* shall be drawn from the city treasury except the same shall have been previously appropriated to the purpose for which it is drawn.

An honest version of this provision makes it as applicable to the creation of an obligation to be liquidated out of subsequent appropriation, as it is to that directly referred to.

SUSPENDED SALES FOR TAXES AND ASSESSMENTS.

You should also take measures to collect about seven hundred and fifty thousand dollars from the suspended sales for taxes and assessments, which can be obtained upon the necessary legislative action, empowering the Comptroller to proceed. The sum is sufficiently large to demand your immediate attention.

CONTRACTS.

The present mode of making contracts is defective. Notwithstanding the improvement of late years, in exacting more publicity in opening bids, and in guarding against favoritism in granting contracts, yet it is supposed much wrong still exists. There is no doubt that frauds are still perpetrated in this branch of the public service. Bids are frequently put in in the name of fictitious persons, ranging from a high to a low estimate—speculators standing ready to take advantage of any embarrassment to the department, owing to the non-appearance of the false bidder, and to get the contract at the highest possible limits. Again, it is the practice to put in estimates, not with the expectation of making and performing a contract, but to be bought off by some more responsible party, who has been under-bid. Various other ways, the details of which are known only to the initiated, are in vogue, by which to defraud the treasury. If the head of a department acts in collusion with these outsiders, it is next to impossible to prevent frauds under the present system.

One of the best safeguards may be found in more general publicity in offering to receive proposals. The expense of advertising is of no importance, as compared with the benefit to be derived from it.

The object of offering public proposals to make contracts, is to invite competition, and prevent the high prices which monopoly produces; it is defeated if the advertisements are published in obscure papers, unknown to and unread by the mass of the people.

Too much publicity can not be given to the offering of contracts; the expense of general advertising will be more than made up by the increased bidding, and consequent reduced prices.

CITY RAILROADS AND OMNIBUSES.

I also recommend the taxation of city railroad cars. It appears to me that these companies should pay at least one hundred dollars license upon each car, besides keeping the streets and avenues through which their tracks are laid in complete repair, and always clean.

The City Government receives no equivalent for the privileges these roads possess, which are now very valuable. So far as rail-travel in this city can affect them, the present roads may be said to have a monopoly. A recent State law secures their grants, and in effect precludes opposition or annoyance; they occupy, to the exclusion of all other citizens, the centre of our best business avenues.

Exclusive privileges are always to be deprecated, but when granted, the city should in return receive an ample pecuniary equivalent. A revenue of forty thousand dollars could be procured from this source, besides the saving of the very heavy cost of repairing and cleaning the thoroughfares.

The omnibuses should also keep in repair and clean the streets through which they pass, or pay into the treasury a sufficient sum for that purpose.

These vehicles do more injury to the pavements than all the rest of the travel together, and the city in return receives no pecuniary aid from them for that purpose whatever. The existing lines of omnibuses are well secured in their privilege, having, by the law of 1854, made it so difficult to procure licenses for competing lines, that they now enjoy almost a monopoly. How far the out-town railroad lines, entering the city, are subject to municipal regulations, I am not at this time enabled to advise; my opinion, however, is, that there is nothing in their charters entitling them to exception from any tax which you may deem a fair equivalent for the right of way they now possess.

If, upon consultation with the Counsel of the Corporation, there be no legal obstacle, I make the same recommendation as to a car-tax, and the cleaning and repairs of the avenues and streets through which they pass, as made with reference to the city railroads.

EMIGRANTS.

It is well known that for many years extortions and oppressions of the most inhuman character have been practised upon the emigrants coming to this port.

There appears to be a series of organized classes of persons, all connected, and acting from a common impulse of plunder, who take, and keep possession of their victims as long as a sixpence is left to rob them of. These vampires form a cordon, stretching from Sandy Hook to the lakes—and to the far West.

They act in concert, with a well-formed understanding, and spend large sums to protect themselves from detection and punishment. Common humanity, as well as the honor and prosperity of this City and State, call for more stringent laws and regulations governing our whole emigrant system. I regret that this already too lengthy communication prevents more extended comments upon this branch of the subject, consistent with others demanding attention.

Much inconvenience to the shipping interest is caused by the present mode of landing emigrant passengers.

As now conducted it is a serious evil, not only to the passengers, but also to the vessels from which they land, and to other vessels, with which they materially interfere. This is also an evil calling for some action at your hands; as now conducted it is productive of great hardship to the emigrant and injury to others.

Now a ship arrives from sea with her decks crowded with hundreds of men, women and children, and hauls outside and alongside another vessel at her berth, discharging or taking in cargo, which may be composed of fine goods in valuable packages.

As soon as the emigrant ship nears the wharf, she is boarded by an army of runners, cartmen and others, having business with, and too often design upon, her passengers, and the passengers are dragged over the vessel discharging, to the shore; her cargo, which may be on deck, or upon the dock, is not only materially injured, the packages soiled, broken or stolen, but an embargo is laid upon all work for the time being. Thus a serious injury is inflicted. This evil has grown to be intolerable. The remedy is very simple. One or two piers should be set aside, away from the pressure of shipping, and exclusively devoted to the landing of emigrant passengers. They should be inclosed, and only persons properly clothed with authority, and of good character, be permitted within the inclosure. The police could be stationed there to protect and direct the emigrants, and, as the boarding-houses and forwarding officers would, of course, locate in the vicinity, the emigrants would be benefited, as well as the present injury to other shipping entirely removed. These suggestions are worth attention, and, I hope, will be acted upon.

It has long been the practice of many Governments on the continent of Europe, to get rid of convicts and paupers by sending them to this country, and most generally to this port. The increase of crime here can be traced to this cause, rather than to a defect in the criminal laws or their administration. An examination of the criminal and pauper records shows conclusively, that it is but a small proportion of these uufortunates who are natives of this country. One of the very heaviest burdens we bear is the support of these people, even when considering the direct cost; but when estimating the evil influences upon society, and the contaminating effect upon all who come within the range of their depraved minds, it becomes a matter exceedingly serious, and demanding immediate and complete eradication. I know no subject of more importance; certainly we have the power to protect this city against the landing of so vile an addition to our population; the health, as well as the life and property of the people for whom you legislate, requires some action at your hands. I am confident the General Government will listen to any representations from you, relating to it, and interpose its national authority in our behalf. On the 2d instant, I made this grievance the subject of an official communication to the President of the United States, a copy of which is annexed, marked A.

The constantly increasing expenses of the Alms-house Department, and the want of control of the Corporation over them, should not escape your notice. I am satisfied that, whatever may be thought as to the exercise of proper economy upon the part of the Governors of the Alms-house, there can be no doubt that one cause for the present large outlay required, is the maintenance of persons who should be a charge upon the fund under the exclusive control of the Emigrant Commissioners. It is evident that the object in creating this Board was to have full control over the whole subject, and to bear the entire costs of the support of these unfortunate people, at least until they have been five years in this country. In practice, this appears not to be its operation. At least a portion of the inmates of the institutions under the control of the Alms-house Governors, who are supported by the city, are properly chargeable to the Emigrant Commission. In my opinion, the whole subject requires revision. An entire alteration of the present system is absolutely demanded. As it is now, the tax-payers of this city have not only to support the poor of the city, and a portion of that belonging to the surrounding country, which find their way here, but also a very large portion of the paupers of every nation in Europe.

The absolute cost of supporting *our own* poor would be a trifle too small to be worthy of comment; but when required to perform the duty for so many other communities, its burden has become of too great a magnitude to be submitted to longer. The Board of Emigrant Commissioners was created in 1847, to protect and provide for the emigrants arriving at this port; a fund is provided for this purpose. It is a State institution, mostly under the control of officers appointed by the Governor and Senate, and, in all respects, independent of our municipal action. Its existence is a recognition of the position that the persons called emigrants should in no respect be a tax upon this county. As now conducted, it is a grievous tax. We support the emigrant criminal sentenced to Blackwell's Island, and other city penal institutions. A large number of policemen are detailed especially for their protection, for which our treasury pays. The Mayor's office and no inconsiderable portion of his time are occupied in hearing and determining cases involving the rights and property of emigrants, to say nothing of that branch of his duties relating to the proper licensing and regulating of emigrant boarding-houses and runners. In my opinion the city should be relieved altogether from these duties and expenses. So far as the State assumes to take charge of these people, she should carry out the work entire; we should be relieved from it.

[Then follow some instructions on the Police, which will more fitly be considered in the chapter which shall treat of that department.]

SPRING CHARTER ELECTIONS.

I can not omit expressing my conviction that much benefit could be derived to the city, by separating the election for charter officers from that for State or national officers.

As now conducted, our local interests are almost entirely lost sight of in the conflict on State or national issues. As the lesser is always absorbed by the greater, so is the apparently smaller affairs of our City Government lost sight of in the contest on candidates for higher offices.

The magnitude of our municipal interests calls for the closest scrutiny into the qualifications of persons to take charge of them; no other considerations than those connected directly with local questions should be included in the canvass for city rulers. The evils of frequent elections are of little importance as compared with the danger of the selection of improper men. In the struggle for a Governor or a President, persons entirely disqualified will sometimes slide unobserved into a local place of trust and power.

The election law, which places the candidates for county offices on the same ballot with candidates for State officers, increases the evil. At the late election there were twelve names on the same ballot. In the haste and excitement of election day, it is very difficult for even the most intelligent voter to select the names for whom he desires to vote when found upon the same ticket; but where the duty is imposed upon the illiterate or ignorant, it is seldom exercised, especially if there be a cunningly devised ballot, not permitting erasure or substitution.

CENTRAL PARK.

The commissioners appointed to open the Central Park are progressing with the work. Since the organization of the Board, it has collected and examined evidence of title to the lands to be taken for the park; in causing the necessary surveys, maps of blocks and profiles of grades to be made, in personal view of the lands to be taken, and in procuring such information in regard thereto, as may serve to guide to a just valuation of the same; also in determining the area of assessment for special benefit, and procuring maps of the same, and in procuring evidence of the value of the improvements on the land to be taken; and are now engaged in the valuation of the lands themselves. It will be remembered that this park is to be bounded south by Fifty-ninth street, north by One hundred and sixth street, east by the Fifth avenue, and west by the Eighth avenue; and will comprehend an area of seven hundred and seventy-six acres, say........................... 776

From which, deduct

State Arsenal,............ 14
Croton Reservoir,......... 38
Proposed " 112
Streets and Avenues,......190
Belonging to the city,...... 34–388

Leaving to be paid for—acres........ 388

Which, by estimating at sixteen lots per acre, makes six thousand two hundred and eight lots to be paid for by the city, and by assessments upon contiguous property. The important question of the valuation of these lots has not as yet been positively fixed by the commissioners. The subject is now before them, and I advise all who are interested to appear at their office. Another question of much public interest, in connection with this matter, is the territorial limit to which the commissioners shall extend their assessments upon property of individuals, and what proportion of the whole cost shall be made a tax upon the city.

These questions are entirely under the control of the commissioners. I am informed, unofficially, that the disposition of the Board is to extend the area of assessment three blocks east and west, and a greater distance north and south; and to make two thirds of the whole cost payable by the city. If this be the determination, it can be easily ascertained about what sum the park will cost. Estimating the average value of the land at five hundred dollars per lot—a liberal estimate—the whole cost would be three millions one hundred and four thousand dollars; deduct one third to be paid by individuals whose property is supposed to be benefited, it will leave two millions sixty-nine thousand dollars to be paid for by the city—a smaller sum than was anticipated at the time of passing the act. The commissioners expect to close their duties early in the ensuing summer. There can be no doubt as to the necessity of some such park conveniently located on this island. In my opinion, future generations, who are to pay this expense, would have good reasons for reflecting upon the present generation, if we permitted the entire island to be taken possession of by the population, without some spot like this, devoted to rural beauty, healthful recreation, and pure atmosphere.

NEW PUBLIC BUILDINGS.

It is to be regretted that we are still without some definite action in this matter. It is a year since the old Alms-house buildings, which for several years were used for the purposes of a court-house, were destroyed by fire, and no conclusion has yet been arrived at with reference to the erection of a substitute. This should be one of the first measures to receive attention.

The present City Hall and its appendages are insufficient. The accumulation of public business of all kinds has rendered it imperative upon this city, regardless of expense, to make provision for it without delay. Many plans for a new City Hall have been proposed, none of which have been examined by me, and of which I am not competent to judge, had they been. I will suggest, however, that, inasmuch as the day can not be far distant when that portion of the city lying south of Grand street will be entirely occupied by wholesale business, to the exclusion of resident population, and that, as a City Hall, to contain the courts and offices for the transaction of municipal business should be in the vicinity of the numerical centre of population, whether it is politic to expend large sums of money in permanent improvements in the Park, as now located. We have no guarantee that the next generation may not demand their removal to a more convenient position. There can be no doubt that public offices, to which all classes, without distinction, are drawn, should be equally accessible to the whole population.

Nor can I recommend the adoption of a proposition recently made in the Common Council, by which the Legislature is to appoint commissioners to superintend the erection of a new City Hall. The folly of transferring further legislation for this city to Albany, except to get a charter that will return to it a form of government commensurate to its wants, is so apparent, that I hope it will not be indulged in again. One legislative act after another has been adopted at Albany, until we are almost without any government whatever. There is now in preparation a proposition for the Legislature to appoint six commissioners, with power to name every officer under the city government, which, if it becomes a law, will give the extinguishing blow to what little power is left to the people of this city over their own municipal affairs.

PUBLIC SCHOOL EXPENSES.

Complaints are made of the largely increasing expenses for public school education, and the want of power of the City Government over the disbursements of the Board of Education.

My attention has been called to this subject, and though there is no doubt room for improvement as it regards the economy evinced in the erection and fitting up of school-houses, yet the benefits derived from the system are of too great a magnitude to be jeoparded by illiberality in defraying its cost.

I have no doubt that it is the general approval of our public schools, as now conducted, that induces the people to submit to the present onerous taxation. The great improvements in the mode of culture adopted, and the evident advantage of the public schools over the private schools of this city, have made them the general academies of tuition for the children of nearly the whole population. The cost to us in taxation is not one fifth the usual expense for an ordinary pay-school education. Indeed, there are few real estate owners, with families, who cannot get their whole tax returned by sending their children to the public schools, with the advantage of a better and more thorough education, and a discipline and moral training far more perfect than our fashionable "academies for young gentlemen" can pretend to.

Therefore, while discountenancing extravagance in

any public department, yet having full confidence in the gentlemen who have charge of the public education of this city, and deeply appreciating the system, I can not recommend any step towards interfering with the management of it, so long as it continues to improve in efficiency and public benefit, and holds, as it does now, the position of our brightest ornament, with the prospect of being the fruitful source from whence we are to derive yet higher honor and more brilliant results.

REVISION OF THE ORDINANCES.

I can not too earnestly impress upon you the necessity of a revision and a collecting of the ordinances into one or more volumes, and a codification of the laws applicable to this city. It would be almost incredible to a stranger to be told that there is no collection of the laws by which this city is governed.

A collection of ordinances has not been published since 1845, and of that but few copies remain; since 1845 material amendments have been made to the charter, and numerous resolutions and ordinances have been adopted, which are now to be found only by a voyage of discovery in the office of the Clerk of the Board of Aldermen, with the chance being very much against success, even with the guide of the accommodating officers who have charge of that office. The memory of persons who have for many years been connected with the Common Council is the only index in existence.

The mere statement of the fact will, I am confident, procure action.

THE DOCKS.

The dock accommodations for the shipping of the city, is another subject which should receive notice. You need not be informed that at present they are totally inadequate, both in extent and quality. There is no commercial city in the world, of the magnitude of New-York, so deficient; substantial stone or iron docks and piers should be constructed, which would not only be durable, but in the result far more economical than those now in use.

A funded debt could be created for the payment of the cost, leaving to posterity, who are to be the recipients of the advantages derived from the construction, the liquidation of the obligation. The present, as well as the future accommodations for the shipping, which constitute so great an element in our prosperity, demand some action at your hands on this subject.

NON-PAYMENT OF CONTRACTORS AND OTHERS.

Much distress has recently been caused to persons having demands against the city, owing to the non-payment of salaries, and for supplies furnished, and contracts performed. Great injury has resulted to many individuals of small means, from this cause. At any time, disappointments of this kind bear oppressively, but at a period of great monetary stringency, like the present, it is a hardship exceedingly onerous, and should not again occur. Besides the wrong done to the party having a just claim, in omitting to meet the demand, the injury to the treasury is not insignificant. We need not be told that a poor paymaster has to pay higher prices than he who meets his engagements promptly.

It is not unreasonable to expect that the city creditors will provide themselves against the loss arising from the difficulty in getting their dues, by charging sufficiently to cover the loss arising from these delays. Without recommending any relaxation in adherence to the laws and ordinances governing the disbursement of money, I can not omit to express the hope that you will take immediate means to prevent a recurrence of so great an evil to the creditors of the city, and preserve its faith and credit from dishonor.

RELIEF TO BROADWAY.

Another relief to the citizens could be found in the adoption of some mode to prevent the large collection of omnibuses in Broadway below the Park. In my opinion this evil should not be longer permitted.

If the stages now permitted to go to the South ferry were limited to one half the present number, the whole difficulty would be remedied. The many lines entering Broadway below the Park, not only obstruct the passage of each other, but frequently cut off entirely the passage of smaller vehicles. Foot-passengers are excluded almost entirely from the cross-walks.

This evil is increasing, though the police, at an expense to the city, is kept on duty to prevent disorder, and to aid passengers in crossing.

The present laws deprive the Mayor of power over the omnibuses, so far as controlling their routes or their number, but I recommend that an ordinance be passed preventing any one line sending more than one stage in ten minutes, below the Park, in Broadway. The little inconvenience which this restriction would cause to persons having business below the Park would be of no consideration compared to the present difficulties.

I also recommend that the Russ pavement in Broadway be grooved. Though this beautiful and durable pavement is an ornament as well as advantage to the city, yet its smoothness renders it dangerous to horses. Its solidity retains moisture, which, when freezing, presents a surface of ice, rendering its use extremely dangerous.

CATTLE-DRIVING.

The practice of driving cattle through the streets of the city is another evil calling for prompt action. It is an abuse which our citizens have submitted to too long. In my opinion, this Common Council will deserve the severest censure, if, like its predecessors, it timidly skulks from its duty in ridding us of this dangerous nuisance. Not only is the health of the whole population jeoparded by the unwholesome odors arising from the collection of these animals, but it not unfrequently occurs that life, limb and property are destroyed by it.

DIRTY STREETS.

In April, 1854, contracts were entered into for the cleaning of streets and avenues of the city. The specifications of these contracts are stringent, and there would be no cause of complaint if the contractors performed them. They provide that every thoroughfare shall be thoroughly and properly cleaned and swept, and all the dirt, manure, ashes, garbage, rubbish, and sweepings, of every kind, removed twice a week; and in Broadway and the leading avenues, three times a week. If these conditions were complied with, there could be no grounds of complaint. I regret to say they have not been complied with, and though it is stated that in consequence of the low rates at which the contracts are taken, compliance is impossible, without heavy loss; yet, in my opinion, there is no other resource than to demand a rigid fulfillment. If contracts are to be thrown up, or only half performed, at the will of contractors, because not profitable, the bargain is all on one side. Under this ruling, the city is to suffer in any event. So far as the law gives me power, I shall require a strict compliance with the existing contracts to clean the streets; and that I may know which of the contractors are derelict, the police have been ordered to make the condition of the streets, in their several beats, the subject of observation, and to report, every day, the result.

[Since 1830, the charter had been tinkered and re-tinkered, patched, clouted, and otherwise quasi-mended, until it resulted in the extraordinary composition now extant. Read, O my friends! this extract from the proposed amended charter referred to by His Honor the Mayor—read it, and let your heads swim:

"Sec. 35, Chapter 122, of Laws of 1830, and an act to amend the charter of the city of New-York, passed April 2, 1849, and an act to amend an act, entitled an act to amend the charter of the city of New-York, passed April 2, 1849, passed July 11, 1851; and an act further to amend the charter of the city of New-York, passed April 12, 1853; and an act supplementary to an act, entitled an act further to amend the charter of the city of New-York, passed April 12, 1853, passed June 14, 1853, are hereby repealed."

Not being yet repealed, what have we? Nine independent chiefs of city governments; five bureaux to take care of the streets—("too many cooks," say the vulgar, "spoil the broth;") executive officers with independent powers, and legislative bodies who interfere with the executive; doubtful or restricted power in the hands of the executive, and strong inclination to take even that away from him.

What, then, is to be done? Homœopathy alone can cure this: the principle, *similia similibus curantur*, must be applied here. If legislation have reduced us to chaos, let us legislate ourselves back again out of that chaos, into some sufferable shape. So a new plan of charter is formed; first to repeal that dreadful sentence quoted as "Sec. 35," above, and then to make New-York government a simple legislative and executive one, the Mayor being the head of this latter division. Most of this proposed amended charter met Mr. Wood's views; of important points, he zealously opposed one—that which set down general and local elections for the same day.

He speaks of this in his letter to Mr. Blatchford, which follows here :]

MAYOR'S OFFICE, NEW-YORK, *February* 13, 1855.

HON. R. M. BLATCHFORD, IN ASSEMBLY, ALBANY :

Dear Sir: In relation to the proposed City Charter, I can express a favorable opinion of its leading features. With the exception of the continuance of *the great error of leaving our local issues to be decided at the general election,* I find much to approve. Its leading features correspond with my ideas of a good form of government as expressed in my Inaugural Address to the Common Council. In the main it is very like that adopted by the framers of the Federal Government in the present Constitution. With slight modifications it will be a most excellent substitute for that now in force. It is an error, however, to suppose that good government depends upon the organic law. It does not, because, without honest, fearful and capable executive officers the most perfect form of government ever devised by human intellect will prove entirely inadequate to the wants of the people. Therefore, we require not only a good Charter, but also good functionaries to execute the laws under it. These must be chosen with exclusive reference to their fitness and capacity for the places filled by them. To secure officers of this kind no other than local issues should be permitted to enter the canvass, which can only be accomplished by an entire separation of the elections for national and State officers from those for municipal officers, and this is the objection to the Charter now proposed. It leaves us as we are, with our own local interests entirely at the mercy of the exciting and at times overwhelming issues of national and State politics. As favorably as I think of this new Charter, it will, in my opinion, entirely fail in removing the difficulties under which we suffer, if it does not also provide for the election of Charter officers at some other time than that at which are chosen State and national officers. In the Message sent by me to the Common Council, January 11, 1855, I refer to this subject in the following language :

"I can not omit expressing my conviction that much benefit could be derived to the city, by separating the election for charter officers from that for State or national officers.

"As now conducted, our local interests are almost entirely lost sight of in the conflict on State or national issues. As the lesser is always absorbed by the greater, so are the apparently smaller affairs of our City Government lost sight of in the contest on candidates for higher offices.

"The magnitude of our municipal interests calls for the closest scrutiny into the qualifications of persons to take charge of them; no other considerations than those connected directly with local questions should be included in the canvass for city rulers. The evils of frequent elections are of little importance as compared with the danger of the selection of improper men. In the struggle for a Governor or a President, persons entirely disqualified will sometimes slide unobserved into a local place of trust and power.

"The election law, which places the candidates for county offices on the same ballot with candidates for State offices, increases the evil. At the late election there were twelve names on the same ballot; in the haste and excitement of election day, it is very difficult for even the most intelligent voter to select the names for whom he desires to vote when found upon the same ticket; but where the duty is imposed upon the illiterate or ignorant, it is seldom exercised, especially if there be a cunningly-devised ballot, not permitting erasure or substitution."

Though in office but one month since the above was written, yet the experience of that month has confirmed these views. The connection between local politics and that of the State and nation is detrimental to the interests of this city. New-York has a government and a municipality of its own, of too great a magnitude to be jeoparded by being made secondary to the overshadowing influences centered at the capital. The power derived from the patronage of the General Government in this city, overwhelms all other political considerations, and it is almost invariably the fact, when the central power at Washington has a direct interest in the result of an election here, that our local interests are submerged entirely. When a President is to be chosen, or a congressional majority is to be secured, or any measure to be sustained or opposed, this power is unhesitatingly exercised, and carries in all the candidates as well for municipal officers, as for those directly required. The General Government has never been beaten in this city, when it had a direct stake in the result. At every Presidential election for twenty years, the then existing national administrations have been sustained in this city, and all the candidates of the party with which it was identified have been successful. There is no arguing against these facts. The conclusion is inevitable, that other interests than our own influence if not control the selection of our own rulers when elected at the general election. If, under these circumstances, honest and capable men happen to be designated for us, we are indebted for it more to accident or the interposition of Divine Providence in our favor than to the forethought and discriminating action of the voters themselves. No, let there be a separation, irrevocable and entire. Let there be but one issue when local officers are to be chosen, and that referring to the welfare and prosperity of New-York. If, differing upon national and State questions, we can unite without embarrassment or obstruction upon men fitted for charter officers without reference to their party affinities or associations, the consideration will then be not whether they are in favor or against any outside issue involving matters of national import, but whether in favor of an economical government for this city, and opposed to vices, immorality, corruption and bad government. I shall not have time to present several other points equally worthy of attention. If this change is made in the charter now proposed, I could give it my support though not approving all its details.

I look upon spring charter elections as essential to the well-being of this city. It is in my opinion paramount to all other questions appertaining to the City Government. With this alteration, the paper now submitted by the Board of Aldermen will be applicable to our wants, and will give us the best government we have had in thirty years.

Very respectfully, yours,

[Signed] FERNANDO WOOD, *Mayor.*

With these principles to guide him, with his energetic, strong nature to help him, Fernando Wood set out upon his attempt at reform—his attempt to give to this great city a government somewhat worthy of it.

The first step in all reforms is to know the evil. It was Mayor Wood's first step. Previous to his administration there was not one of the departments to which the citizen could apply with certainty of having his grievance redressed. The duties and the powers were so indefinite, and the officials so little desirous of having trouble, that a complaint was sent from one department to another, and back again, or to a third. His sorrow appeared to be every body's, or, what is tantamount to that, no body's business, and when finally reduced to petition the Common Council, he discovered that such a process was somewhat like a suit in the court of chancery, a decision upon which might, by the blessing of Providence, ultimately be obtained by his grandson.

There was no remedy for the ten thousand little grievances which must of necessity annoy the private citizen—for the petty distresses, so small in our eyes, so great in the eyes of those who have to endure them. Mr. Wood is a kind, warm-hearted man, as well as an ingeniously intelligent one; and the union of the two qualities suggested and produced the COMPLAINT-BOOK. The public were notified through the press that such a book was opened at the Mayor's office, wherein might be registered complaints of dereliction from duty on the part of any corporation officers, of violated ordinances, of illegal incumbrances, of nuisances, in a word, of any abuse whatever. Soon the broad leaves were covered with complaints. Poor servant-girls told how unjust masters defrauded them of their wages; young sewing-women exposed the cruel cheatery of their employers; policemen were reported for negligence of duty; great merchants for encumbering the thoroughfares with multitudinous boxes; omnibus drivers and cartmen for furious and dangerous driving; hackmen were brought up for overcharges and for insolence; street officials were attacked for leaving streets full of garbage and filth; Mr. Commissioner of Paving got raps on the knuckles for the gullies and displaced curb-stones and unclosed sewer-holes that he neglected to attend to, and frauds of all kinds were exposed; and all these things received the prompt and personal attention of the Mayor, and where it was possible they were remedied.

There were some, however, who sought remedies for wrongs beyond the reach of mayors or other human authorities. Wives wanted cross husbands made amiable; mothers begged that tall daughters might be forced to stay in-doors; poor men asked that rich men might be compelled to give them work; neighbors' quarrels were laid before his perplexed Honor for adjudication. One worthy woman insisted on a personal interview with him, and required him to silence the tongue of her next door neighbor, who used to call her names out of the window; one tailor complained that a policeman would not pay his bill: the officer was called up, plead honest poverty, and Mr. Wood paid the bill from his own pocket, to the great satisfaction of accuser and accused.

The Complaint-Book was so manifestly an admirable invention, that Mayors of various cities came to New-York to see it and to learn its working and effects, and it was set up as an "*institution*" all over the Union. By it, Mr. Wood has been enabled to do an incalculable amount of good, and to secure firm gratitude in thousands of humble hearts, which hitherto had suffered in silence; the voice of whose complaint had hitherto never risen up to the ear of authoritative justice. Children have been restored to their parents; young girls have been rescued from prostitution; right has been done to the oppressed; the rich cheat compelled to make humble compensation; the poor emigrant saved from the brutal runner; the swindler auctioneer to disgorge his ill-gotten gains, and a thousand other benefits resulting from this noble thought of Fernando Wood, and from that decided action of his which that thought entailed upon him, and which entitled him to the gratitude of all this great city. We were grateful for forty hours, and then we forgot all about it. It is the fortieth maxim of Adjutant and Ensign Morgan O'Doherty, that "You may always ascertain whether you are in a city or a village by finding out whether the inhabitants do or do not care for, or speak about, ANY THING, three days after it has happened." In cities they *don't.*

Now, whatsoever good the Mayor has been enabled to accomplish, he has done almost unaided. It is a fact, incredible as it may appear to the inhabitants of other civilized countries, that the Common Council has absolutely neglected to take any action upon the various and important matters laid before them in the message of January 11.

Although the suggestions of that message treated of such vital points as the health of the city, the safety of the citizens, the municipal revenues, the condition of the streets, the public education, and such like, the Hon. Boards of Aldermen and Councilmen have left that message untouched until the day on which these lines are being written—a period of *eight* months; and Mr. Wood has had no assistance from them in the great good already effected, but has been compelled to-day, September 4, to recall their attention to his message in a very peremptory manner.

CHAPTER XIII.

THE POLICE CHAPTER.

BUT one man, though he be chief executive officer, can not *see* all things done, his will carried out, his ideas fulfilled, his thoughts translated into actions, without help. The supreme executive needs sub-executives; the law gives the police corps to the Mayor to fill these positions; and when Mr. Wood came into office he saw, as we have seen, what work there was to be done, and so looked about for some one to help him. He found a sort of civilian body, who did some form of watchman's duty, well or ill according as they were honest men or otherwise.

You saw some of them lounging about upon drinking-house steps, over area-railings, looking on, as calm, uninterested judges of a street-fight; acting according to warrant issued by this or that justice, but without any idea of a duty always imposed upon, and belonging to them by virtue of their office.

But Mr. Wood knew that he had something to do, and that he could not do it alone. This police corps was supposed to belong to him *ex suo officio*, and therefore had his will to carry out as their task in official life. Mr. Wood determined that they should do this, entitling themselves thereby to fair days' wages for their fair days' work, to the respect and confidence of their fellow citizens, to a life of usefulness—a life protective of the life and property of others, their fellow citizens.

The Mayor then — a reading, thinking, and on the whole, unprejudiced man—seeing that the best *city* governments were out of this country and carried on by a military police, resolved to militarize the police of New-York. He began, advanced, and perfected his police reform, with wondrous quickness and with admirable result. New-York was changed as in a moment. To quote from the *Boston Advertiser:*

"Immediately after his inauguration he issued a proclamation which gave New-York 'assurance of a man.' He followed up his words with deeds. The effect of his energetic action was instantly and powerfully felt. The two thousand three hundred drinking-shops, which had poured forth riot and madness into the streets of the city on the Lord's day, were reduced almost at once to less than twenty. Like another Caliph Haroun, Mr. Wood seemed to be ubiquitous. He paralyzed the hand of barkeepers grown bold with long impunity, by the sudden revelation of his name and office, and by the same talisman struck insolent policemen dumb in the moment of their misconduct or their neglect. Wherever his authority clearly extended, he made it felt and respected, and he did not hesitate, wherever that authority was doubtful, to take upon himself the responsibility of decided action, if the public good seemed to demand his interference.

The very stones of New-York bear witness now to his courage and his conduct. The stranger blesses the resolute Mayor when he lands in safety from car or steamboat, unsmitten by the whips, unclutched by the hands of raging Jehus. The 'unprotected female' breathes a sweet wish for him, when the stout arm and quick eye of the polite policeman have cleared for her a passage through the throng of coaches and of omnibuses that make Broadway as turbulent as the rapids of a cataract. There is a fair change come over the face of the great metropolis, and that change is due absolutely and solely to the simple fact that Mayor Wood does his duty like a man; for the charter of New-York is as bad as ever it was. Such is the value of a man."

How he went about this work may best be learned from his own messages and orders.

It was first essential to know precisely under what command this corps of right belonged, and what the duties of its members were. In his communication to the Board of Councilmen of January 1, he expresses his own ideas of these matters thus:

"This department of the City Government is placed more directly under the personal supervision of the Mayor than others; and in assuming its direction, with the restricted power as to appointment and removal, which, after all, constitute the great elements of control, I feel much responsibility and concern; its present condition and discipline is susceptible of improvement.

There is an apparent want of energy and efficiency, which must arise from either defect in the system or want of nerve and vigilance in those who direct it. It shall be my aim to remedy these omissions. I shall require the strictest accountability from the men, and also from the several officers, who shall, in all cases, be made responsible for the conduct of the subordinates under their command.

It was thought that making the police hold office during good behavior would remove it entirely from political influences. It may have had such an effect, to a degree; but whilst the power to appoint, suspend, and remove is political and elective, it will be expecting too much of human nature to suppose that political influence can be excluded altogether.

A perfect police system must be founded upon freedom from all influences except those produced by merit, arising from a faithful and efficient discharge of duty.

When the generals of an army are periodically subjected to change, and in some measure by the votes and influences of the army itself, it will be almost impossible to remove the partisan elements which, *at every election,* are necessarily aroused into activity.

The whole Police Board was elected at the late election, two of the late Board (the Recorder and City Judge) being candidates for reëlection; and *policemen* would have been more or less than men, if they could have remained indifferent spectators of the result.

I am confident the judiciary is not the proper authority for determining police matters; nor are its members qualified, either by habits of life or train of reflection, to make good commissioners. The bench and the service would each be benefited by a separation. My colleagues on the present Police Board fully concur in these opinions.

It shall be my aim to impress all connected with the police, that official merit, and not partisan influence, is what is expected of them; and, so far as my power extends, it shall be exercised for the entire eradication of politics from the department.

On the first of January instant, I issued new orders, a copy of which is annexed, [marked B,] and to which I call your attention as developing the principles upon which I shall administer the department. In connection with this subject, it may be proper for me to add, that there has been opened in the Mayor's office, under my direction, a book for recording complaints against the police, as well as for violations of the ordinances and laws, where charges will be entertained, and acted upon by me in person.

The police are required for several purposes other than the protection of the public interests of the city, for which it should not be obliged to pay.

There is one squad of the reserve corps detailed for the duty of boarding vessels from foreign ports, with emigrant passengers, and other service rendered, before referred to, which should be paid from the fund of the Emigrant Commissioners. Many other policemen are stationed at the several railroad depots and ferries, and at places of public amusement, by request of the proprietors, and for the protection of their private interests, and not for public purposes. This expense should be borne by the parties requiring their services. In London, where the police system is said to be better than our own, such is the practice; and the General Government has adopted the same course with reference to the salaries of its Custom-House officers, when acting for private convenience or safety. About thirty thousand dollars would be thus saved.

The expense of the police force has attracted attention, and it has been properly suggested that it can be used for many public purposes for which the city now pays heavily.

In considering the cost of the police, it should not be forgotten that it is almost entirely made up of salaries. This department disburses little money for any other purpose. It makes no contracts, and procures no supplies; and is confined to the disbursement of such sums, for compensation to the officers and men, as have been fixed by the Common Council. Be it more or less, no officer connected with it is in any way responsible. It is true that much duty, now performed by subordinates under other departments, can be performed by the police, without impairing its efficiency. My direction has already been given to the patrolmen to act as street-inspectors, and to report, through their officers, to me every instance when the contractor fails to clean the streets within his district. They have also been required to report all excavations made under the side-walks or streets, by builders or others—the object of which is to supply information to the Commissioner of Streets, by which he can collect the legal claims of the city for appropriating to private use any portion of the streets.

If my recommendation of consolidating all business appertaining to streets into one department is carried out, many collateral branches can be put under the Police Department, without any detriment to it whatever.

There is no question that the several duties of policemen are entirely too light, in view of the necessity of materially lessening the number of public officers.

It is for you to legislate upon this recommendation,

and you will find me ready to enforce its practical operation."

Nor were the policemen left uninformed as to what was expected from them; for on the same day he instructs them thus:

"I have this day assumed the office of head of the Police Department of this city, and shall expect and require adherence to its rules and regulations. In your hands is placed the care of the property and lives, as well as the order, peace, and outward moral deportment of the whole community.

Though you can not extirpate vice, you can do much to suppress it. Vigilance and an honest discharge of your duties, will not only enable the people to pay more for your protection by reducing the expense which crime produces, but add to the respectability of your position and to the security of its continuance. There is now dissatisfaction in the public mind with the apparent inefficiency of the police. There should be no cause for it! Let there be none! Your duties are light; the pay not illiberal; your social standing good; and the term for which appointed, renders you independent of the contingencies to which the operative and other laboring classes are subjected. You hold positions of trust and honor to which the pride and ambition of any man need not be ashamed to aspire.

It is made my duty to see the laws faithfully executed; you are to be my aids in effecting this. I can not look over the whole city to see that all is right; but you can for me. I rely upon you. You are to be the eyes through which the theatre of my duties is to be observed, and the messengers to convey to me, through your officers, faithful and truthful reports.

In addition to the rules and regulations now in force in the Department, and the several directions therein, you are requested to take note of and comply with the following:

It is hereby made your duty to report every day, when on duty, to your commanding officer, the following information; and an omission to do so, and to conform to every requirement of this circular, will be deemed disobedience, and punished as such.

To report every street uncleaned in your patrol.

Every unlicensed public house for the sale of liquor.

Every public house kept open on the Sabbath.

Every house of prostitution.

Every gambling-house.

Every street not lighted at the proper hour.

Every street or side-walk encumbered, and the party or parties offending.

Every excavation made under the side-walks or streets, by builders or others.

Every nuisance, and the party offending.

Every supposed dereliction by any officer of the Corporation.

Every violation of the city ordinances.

You are further directed to disperse all gatherings of men or boys at the corners of the streets, or other public places, on the Sabbath, where disorder is produced.

To enforce the closing of public houses on the Sabbath day.

To protect the stranger or emigrant from extortion or imposition.

To remove from the streets all beggars, and direct them to the several public and private institutions created for their relief.

To see that the ordinances for the removal of snow and ice from the side-walks and gutters be promptly complied with.

You are further directed to arrest for creating riot or breaches of the peace.

For being intoxicated and disorderly in the street.

For injuring private or public property.

For stopping the free passage of the cross-walks by cartmen, coachmen, or others.

For throwing offal, garbage, vegetables, and rubbish in the streets.

For offences of any kind against the laws.

Your faithful compliance with these directions is requested. Let no consideration induce you to omit one of them.

You have now a determined chief officer, who will not be indifferent to a single dereliction of duty upon the part of those for whose conduct he is responsible to the community.

And further, for the observance of the Sunday laws, he, under date of Feb. 15, bids the captains "continue the utmost vigilance in preserving the quiet, good order, and peace of the Sabbath day. The aid you have rendered me," says he, "so far in accomplishing these great reforms, is appreciated, not only by myself, but by the whole community. Without your hearty coöperation I could do nothing.

In addition to your usual Sunday liquor report, please make returns of any daguerreotype-rooms, clothing-stores, or other business places, illegally open on Sunday, within your district. It is my determination to make this city as distinguished for the orderly, peaceful, and placid character of its streets upon the Sabbath, as it has heretofore been, on that day, for every thing that was objectionable and shocking to the moral sense of the people. To accomplish this improvement, I must have your constant vigilance and faithful obedience to orders."

But Mr. Wood's idea of exclusive control of the police, aroused partisan fear and opposition.

This man is rather too absolute, was the first recalcitory sound heard, dim grumbling in the distance. He has too much power, with this police of his, and *il faut changer tout cela.* Let us get a bill passed by our inspired men at Albany—a new Police Bill, which will strip this on-going man of his authority. And they who grumbled thus went diligently to work and lobbied for that enactment.

But Fernando Wood, courageous, energetic, persistent as he is, nevertheless refused absolutely to fight without arms, to labor without tools. And so he gave the inspired men at Albany to understand that, if they took from him his sword and his bow, he would have the honor of depositing his commission at the feet of that people who gave it to him, respectfully but with characteristic firmness, declining any more to be officer of theirs. To state this clearly, the attempt against him, and his own resolute will in the matter, he, on the 5th of March, 1855, wrote to Lieut.-Governor Raymond the letter here annexed:

Having assumed the office of Mayor with a determination to discharge its duties with a single eye to the public interests, it is impossible for me to remain indifferent to a proposition which, if passed, will strike the death-blow to all my efforts, however feeble, to remove the shocking evils which have grown out of past misgovernment. Though opposed to granting special acts for the benefit of individuals or classes, I am willing to yield almost every thing before giving up the only safeguard we possess for the preservation of the peace and the property and the lives of our people. Give up all, but give us the police. The police, as now organized under its present system, is efficient. As a whole, it not only seconds my efforts, but it has been the main instrument by which nearly every reform projected by me has been carried through. The closing of the liquor shops on the Sabbath has been principally produced by the vigilance of the police in obedience to my orders. To fully comprehend the results of this triumph over one of the greatest sources of vice and crime in this city, it is only necessary to refer to the number of arrests on the Sabbath in 1854, as compared with the arrests on the same day, thus far, in 1855.

The following tabular statement, from official records, is reliable:

ARRESTS ON SUNDAYS, 1854.

Jan. 1,....206	Apr. 2,.... 76	July 2,....162	Oct. 1,.... 95
" 8,.... 63	" 9,....112	" 9,....180	" 8, ...127
" 15,.... 83	" 16,.... 71	" 16,....143	" 15,....123
" 22,.... 85	" 23,....124	" 23,....132	" 22,....120
" 29,.... 70	" 30,....133	" 30,....117	" 29,....118
Feb. 5,....131	May 7,....141	Aug. 6,....164	Nov. 5,....105
" 12,....131	" 14,....136	" 13,....149	" 12,.... 56
" 19,....112	" 21,... 136	" 20,....184	" 19,....133
" 26,.... 77	" 28,....121	" 27,....138	" 26,....110
Mar. 5,.... 97	June 4,... 160	Sept. 3,....168	Dec. 3,.... 71
" 12,....140	" 11, ...139	" 10,....112	" 10,.... 87
" 19,....100	" 18,....130	" 17,....126	" 17,.. .103
" 26,....116	" 25, ...141	" 24,....146	" 24,.... 78
			" 31,....112

ARRESTS ON SUNDAYS, 1855.

Jan. 7,.... 58	Jan. 21,.... 46	Feb. 4,.... 38	Feb. 18,.... 60
" 14,.... 65	" 28,.... 41	" 11,.... 35	" 25,.... 47

By this it will appear, that, in the first eight Sabbaths of 1854, the arrests were 878 as against 338 for the same period in 1855. To appreciate this, under my administration, the increased vigilance and activity of the police must be considered. If, with the lax discipline existing in January and February, 1854, there were arrested on the Sundays in those months, 878 offenders, what would there have been under the new regulations and more stringent administration now existing? But if from any supposed cause other reasons can be found than the closing of the public houses, for so great a difference between the two years, refer to the eight Sundays immediately preceding the commencement of my term, and it will be seen that the arrests were 855 in November and December, 1854, and only, as before stated, 338 for the two following months—January and February, 1855. Comment on these figures is unnecessary. The obvious deductions are, that the abolition of liquor-selling on Sunday, together with the present improved condition of the police, are productive of morality and destructive of disorder, vice and crime; and these results have been mainly effected through the extreme devotion of the police to my orders, and this devotion to my orders is the consequence of its present discipline, produced by the unrestricted power I now hold over it.

Other similar reforms have been effected in the same manner, the consequence of the same cause; but this is sufficient to show conclusively that the police, as now organized and controlled, is rapidly improving, and will soon become second to no similar corps in the world, which is not directly under military rule. This improvement has been accomplished under the present system, which, though not perfect, is far preferable to that now before the Legislature.

That bill proposes that there shall be elected by the people four Commissioners of Police, who, with the Mayor, *ex officio*, shall constitute a Board to sit daily in a room to be provided by the Common Council, and, of course, at an hour when the Mayor can not be present, and who shall, through a President to be selected by themselves, from their own number, have full and unrestricted control over the whole department, even to the issuing of orders, notices, etc., to the police.

The Commissioners are to be elected by the people. It will not do to assume that the members of the Legislature are ignorant of the mode of conducting our primary elections in this city, by dwelling upon the objections to this way of making commissioners who are to be clothed with the important power of appointing, trying, punishing, and removing policemen in whose hands are placed the custody of the peace, order, property, and lives of nearly three quarters of a million of inhabitants. There are some propositions so evident, that no argument or statements are required to elucidate them; that a police system founded upon this principle, deriving its appointment from this source, will be destructive to every semblance of what constitutes police, is one of these. But admitting the elective principle without objection, the withdrawal of power from the Mayor, contemplated by the bill, can not be defended.

The scattering of authority among Fire Commissioners, is of itself bad enough, inasmuch as it destroys that unity of executive authority, without which no good government can exist in this city, with its present hybrid population; but to take from the chief magistrate, whose duty it is made to see the laws executed, and who is responsible to the people, control over the police, is if possible, yet worse.

It is true the bill contains one section that the Mayor shall be "Head of the Police Department," but this is a contemptible falsehood, unworthy of a place in any statute. To declare that any officer shall be the head of a department, when deprived by another section of every thing that constitutes authority over it, is as absurd in theory as it is insulting to the common sense of the people, who it thus seeks to deceive into a belief of its possible practicability.

So far, I have made myself useful in the office of Mayor. My success in removing many evils, and in the introduction of reforms of great benefit, has exceeded my expectations.

I desire to go on unmolested and unrestricted in the use of the weapons by which crime has been punished, vice prevented, and municipal abuses abolished. When these are taken from me, my usefulness is destroyed. Without tools, no mechanic can construct, and without a police, no magistrate can perform his duty.

Pass this bill, and the liquor-shops will soon be again opened on Sunday, and all the other evils which have so long affected us, and from which we are now happily being relieved, will soon be restored, and render this great and beautiful city a disgrace to the American name.

When this comes, the people must find some other occupant for the Mayoralty chair. I shall cease to hold it when deprived of the means to carry out the reforms which I have begun, and, so far, have been successful in accomplishing.

So the inspired men at Albany were good enough not to pass that bill, and Fernando Wood went on.

It also struck New-Yorkers about this time, that possibly the city Police interested them fully as much as it could the member from Cataraugus or the citizens of Desdemona. They begged to have a say in this matter, and on Friday, March 22, 1855, there was convened at the Tabernacle such a meeting as has seldom been seen anywhere. On the platform sat the representatives of at least *fifty millions of dollars;* the oldest and greatest merchants of the city; three of Mr. Wood's predecessors in the Mayoralty, even Mr. Horace Greeley, Editor-Proprietor of the New-York Tribune. All these harmoniously and gratefully thanked Mayor Wood for services already done, and expressed confidence in him for the future.

These were the officers of that meeting:

PRESIDENT.

GEORGE GRISWOLD.

VICE-PRESIDENTS.

Wm. B. Astor,	James Lenox,
Peter Lorillard,	Stephen Whitney,
Wm. B. Crosby,	William Kent,
Thomas Suffern,	Wm. F. Havemeyer,
Cornelius W. Lawrence,	Ambrose C. Kingsland,
Hugh Maxwell,	Jacob A. Westervelt,
Luther Bradish,	Benjamin L. Swan,
George W. Blunt,	John C. Green,
J. Watson Webb,	Horace Greeley,
Wilson G. Hunt,	James W. Barker,
Cyrus Curtis,	Benjamin F. Butler,
Wm. H. Webb,	Shepherd Knapp,
Robert Kelly,	Isaac Newton,
Wm. K. Strong,	Gerard Stuyvesant,
Jonathan I. Coddington,	J. Philips Phœnix,
Wm. W. Evarts,	Samuel B. Ruggles,
James Harper,	John L. Mason,
C. Vanderbilt,	Welcome R. Beebe,
Charles O'Connor,	Thomas B. Stillman,
Gen. Chas. W. Sandford,	Henry A. Smythe,
James W. Gerard,	Charles King,
Daniel Lord,	George J. Cornell,
John Delamater,	Charles H. Russel,
Daniel B. Fearing,	Thomas Tileston,
Zophar Mills,	Walter R. Jones,
J. W. Alsop,	Edwin Hoyt,
Jonathan Sturges,	John A. Stevens,
John J. Palmer,	James Boorman,
Peter Cooper,	Pelatiah Perit,
Robert B. Minturn,	James Brown,
Moses Taylor,	George Douglass,

James Lee.

SECRETARIES.

JOHN L. ASPINWALL,	ROBERT GOODHUE,
JOSHUA J. HENRY,	GEORGE GRISWOLD, JR.,

ROBERT OLYPHANT.

And these were their sentiments:

Mr. R. B. MINTURN said he was glad to enter his protest against any change in the present police system. Our chief magistrate, he said, has thus far discharged his duty nobly. (Applause.) It will be time enough for us to ask a restriction of that power when he abuses it. (Loud applause.) The Mayor ought to be the active head of the police. (Enthusiastic applause.) Why? Because on him is thrown the responsibility of executing the laws. If, therefore, you will not give him power to execute the laws, how can you call upon him and say, why does not the Mayor execute that and that ordinance? The proposed bill creates only four commissioners, but I am told there is already trouble in the camp, for whenever a body of men propose to do wrong there is always a screw geting loose. There are so many political cormorants who want pay, that they have got to increase the commissioners from four to six, and there are now forty aspirants putting forth their claims to the office at $3000 a year. This law cuts off the Mayor's head by providing that the commissioners shall appoint one of their own number to preside over them. Give the Recorder and City Judge a thousand dollars a year extra, and you may depend they will not find their work burdensome. The Mayor does not find it burdensome; he works for eight hours a day, and so far, he has worked well and admirably. (Great cheering.) When I found the Mayor was elected, I wrote him a note tendering my whole service to aid him in executing the law. That's the kind of politician I am. Throughout his whole career I shall give him my support as far as I am able.

Mr. HOXIE said, I speak on behalf of 6756 residents of the First, Second and Third wards. These are the notes of my speech (exhibiting a gigantic roll of names.) These names are only from the First, Second and Third wards, and if we are as successful in the other wards, we will give the Legislature at Albany a hint. They had better pause before they break down the best police system we ever had. I care not for whose benefit this bill is brought forward, and though I have given the strength of my manhood to the Whig party, if the legislators at Albany pass this bill, I have given the last Whig vote I shall ever give in my life. (Loud and long-continued applause.) This paper contains the residences of its signers. They have local habitations as well as names. (The gentleman here unrolled the petition.) The other end of this, I believe, is in the Eighteenth ward. (Laughter and great applause.).

The following is the remonstrance:

REMONSTRANCE, BY THE CITIZENS OF NEW-YORK, AGAINST ANY CHANGE IN THE POLICE SYSTEM.

The undersigned, citizens of New-York, without regard to political distinction, beg leave to represent that we are satisfied with the organization of the police of this city, under the act of 1853, and of its increased respectability and efficiency under the control of the

Mayor, Recorder, and City Judge, our three highest magistrates, and we strongly deprecate any change in the law, by which the safety of our persons and the protection of our property shall be taken away from those responsible magistrates, and placed in the hands of private persons, as commissioners, at large salaries, to be nominated by political committees chosen at packed primary meetings, of which body the Mayor would, by virtue of his office, be but a mere nominal member.

We apprehend that such a change in the law would convert the whole Police Department into a political organization, which would be destructive of its independence and respectability, and of the energies of the officers and men; and that instead of devoting their whole time and attention to the enforcement of the laws, they would become political partisans, and be tempted, by designing politicians, to sell their influence and power to the political party which should offer the strongest inducements for its support.

We respectfully represent, that the members of the Legislature at large are interested with us in the moral character and good government of our city, comprising one fifth of the population of the State, and that their constituents, on their visits to our city on business or pleasure, peculiarly require the protection of a vigilant and energetic police. We, therefore, respectfully beg leave to remonstrate against any change whatever in the present system; but respectfully ask the Legislature to let the Police law of 1853 remain as it is.

NEW-YORK, *March*, 1855.

Mr. PELATIAH PERIT moved the adoption of the following resolution:

Resolved, That the remonstrance which has been circulated extensively by the citizens of New-York, be approved and adopted by this meeting, and that it be transmitted to both Houses of the Legislature by the presiding officer of this meeting.

My only motive, he said, for saying a word, is to bear testimony to the singular unanimity with which the bill at Albany has been resisted. I have found but two individuals who do not unite with us; but they, in a silent way, admitted that party connections tied their hands. There can be no doubt that under the present police system, our condition in New-York has been decidedly improved. Under our present chief magistrate it has been found that the laws can be successfully administered. (Cheers.) Just at this moment we are arrested by a proposition which will effectually remove all that is good in New-York, and substitute what is bad. Let the gentlemen at Albany stand notified, that if all our interests are to be sacrificed, they will lose our adhesion, for we will not follow in their train. (Cheers.)

Mr. STILLMAN, of the Novelty Works, was the next speaker. I rise, he said, to represent the mechanics of New-York, in resisting the bill now before the Legislature. We have at the head of our Police Department a good and efficient man; let us give him proper tools to work with. This is the unanimous sentiment of the mechanics of New-York. (Cheers.)

Three cheers were then given for the Mayor, after which, the meeting dissolved.

It is needless to say that the proposed bill was crushed back into the nothingness from which it had sprung. What further was in the Mayor's mind, he expresses in the following letter to James W. Gerard, Esq.:

MAYOR'S OFFICE, NEW-YORK, *Thursday, April* 5, 1855.

DEAR SIR: Your esteemed favor of 4th inst. is received. I can not conceive that any thing in my messages to the Common Council, which have been referred to, can be construed into an approval of either of the propositions made at Albany, this winter, to amend the present law relating to the police of this city. It is true that in both the inaugural and recommendatory messages, allusion is made to the present police system as defective; but it is as plainly and distinctly sets forth, as well as can be, that the defects lay in the restriction of the powers of the Mayor, as the head of the Police Department, and not that he held too much power, as is the theory of the proposition now before the Senate. In the first of these documents this position is plainly asserted, when I say, "though ostensibly head of the Police Department, he is not so practically, in the essential element of authority—that of controlling the retention or removal of his own subordinates. The Chief of Police holds his place independent of the Mayor, that officer having been appointed during "good behavior," by the late Mayor and Board of Commissioners, under the law of 1853, which they construed to give that authority. He can not, *solus*, appoint or remove the humblest subordinate in the service, nor make the rules and regulations for its governance. Of these requisites of power, so necessary to make an efficient police corps, he is by law deprived. Discipline can only be obtained and maintained by the firm hand of unrestricted power; besides, it is wrong in principle, to make any public officer responsible for the acts of subordinates who are placed beyond his individual power to remove."

Here is a complaint of the want of power of the Mayor over the department; that he should not divide it with others; that he is responsible for the conduct of the police, and hence should govern it; that two commissioners who can outvote him and control the appointments and removals, should not be placed beside him to manage it. To leave no doubt as to these being my views then, as now, I quote again from the recommendatory message of January 11, 1855:

"This department of the city government is placed more directly under the personal supervision of the Mayor than others; and, in assuming its direction, with the restricted power as to appointment and removal, which, after all, constitute the great elements of control, I feel much responsibility and concern."

And again, still carrying out the idea that there should be but one head and one power of appointment and removal, and that the two judges who now form part of the Board of Commissioners should be taken away, and leave *all* to the Mayor, the following passage occurs:

"I am confident the judiciary is not the proper authority for determining police matters; nor are its members qualified, either by habits of life or train of reflection, to make good commissioners. The bench and the service would each be benefited by a separation. My colleagues on the present Police Board fully concur in these opinions."

The whole theory of my views of executive government of every character, so far as this city is concerned, is *one head*. I am satisfied no good government can exist in a city like this, containing so many thousands of the turbulent, the vicious, and the indolent, without a chief officer with necessary power to see to the faithful execution of the laws, for the protection of life, liberty, and the pursuit of happiness. No inconsiderable portion of our population think that republicanism consists in the absence of law and government.

The bill now before the Senate proposes to create three commissioners, who, with the Mayor, *ex officio*, are to form a Board, who are to possess all the powers now held by the present Board. The commissioners are to be elected by the people for the exclusive purpose of making and unmaking policemen. Now, though opposed to dividing the power of the Mayor over the police, with any other officers, still, if the principle is to be tolerated, better that high judicial officers, who are elected judges, and whose duties as commissioners are incident to their duties upon the bench, should be his associates, than men who will be chosen for the purpose under the primary election system now in vogue. Great is the difference between Police Commissioners taken from high judicial positions, and Police Commissioners made by the tools of party, reeking from the stews of sin and iniquity, which at present have so much influence over party machinery. How far the lives and prosperity, and the order and decency of the people of this city will be protected under a Board emanating from a source of this character, there can be no difficulty in divining. The Senate's proposition is to lessen my power over the police, whereas I have asked for its increase. My message can not be construed into any other position. I never used any other language. Instead of giving to the Mayor that strength which a full exercise of the duties of Chief Magistrate of this city should possess, and without which there can not be the necessary vigor and independence, it is proposed by this bill to take away power, to decentralize it, instead of concentrating it in him, by placing three active politicians alongside of him, to annoy and worry him into a compliance with their party behests. It is not too much to add, that the department would soon be filled with men chosen for partisan services and not personal fitness, and the power that placed them in office would protect them against the Mayor afterwards. Not only is the election of Police Commissioners, as such, *exclusively* for this duty, objectionable, but the mode of the election under this bill is yet more so.

It provides that after the expiration of the terms of those named in the act, there are to be chosen two at every election, by taking the two candidates who receive the highest number of votes, in the same manner as the Governors of the Alms-house are selected. The alleged ground for this mode is, to secure a balance of partisan interest in the Board; because, as it is said, each party will be sure to elect a man, and hence parties will be divided. Now, even admitting that such would be its effect—which it will not, as there are at least four political parties in this city—and of course to do this it would be necessary to elect four commissioners. Yet the theory of the mode is wrong, inasmuch as it secures the election of a commissioner who has been rejected by the people. The second highest would be really and in fact discarded, as unfit to be intrusted with the important and delicate duties devolving upon the office. It is proposed to take this repudiated candidate and give him a seat at a Board, with as full powers as the Mayor himself, and in fact to control the action of the Board itself, over the Mayor, even against his efforts to protect the city — it may be from the very interests this commissioner represents.

Suppose the gamblers, lottery men, and houses of prostitution combine to elect Police Commissioners; who can say, that if not successful in electing both, they would not at least secure the second highest, and consequently force upon us an agent to secure the protection of their peculiar interests? Another no less serious objection is the naming of executive officers in a bill by the Legislature. This is a clear encroachment upon the executive by the legislative branch. The Government of this State is separated into the Judicial, Legislative, and Executive. These divisions are defined by the Constitution, not only of New-York, but of the United States, as well as every State in the Union. One branch has no constitutional right to interfere with either of the others. The Legislature, in my judgment, can have no legal authority to perform executive duties, any more than it can judicial duties. And here let me say, that if the liberties of this country are ever betrayed, it will be by legislative assumptions, and not by judicial or executive tyranny. In our own State, the Legislature at Albany brings with it dread and alarm whenever it commences. For years the property of individuals and the rights of municipal corporations have been trampled upon in its acts. Total disregard has been shown to vested rights, and every other safeguard which in former times could procure protection, and so bold has become this innovation, that there is now pending a bill to overrule a recent decision of the Supreme Court. Indeed, the other departments of Government have sunk into a mere inferior condition, from which appeal is had to the Legislature, always with success, if the usual appliances are employed. The people must watch these encroachments. It is not only this city, but every other section of the State removed far from the capital, that is subjected to this wrong. If the city of New-York, within four hours of Albany, and in hourly communication, suffers so much from these legislative frauds how is it with the agricultural and manufacturing interests in the interior, which in some cases are removed far from the danger, and without means to be continually informed of its approach. This bill names persons to do executive duty. If this can be, why not abolish our courts, and name commissions as boards of referees to act instead? Why not, in short, give up all to the two Houses of the Legislature, and permit them to absorb the other branches of government, which by the Constitution are placed independent of the law-making power, as the law-making power is of them. By reference to my message, you will see this evil more fully exposed.

These and other reasons which time will not permit a reference to, will prevent my giving support to the Senate proposition. I am against it in all its length and breadth, and though concurring in some of the provisions of the amendments to the charter proposed, I would reject the whole rather than appear to recognize the fatal principles declared, affecting our police system.

In reply to what is stated of my political proclivities, and the assertion that I am using, or intend to use, the police for personal or partisan purposes, it is scarcely necessary to allude. The position I hold in public estimation is not the result of party machinery. As a magistrate and chief executive officer of this city, I know no party, and recognize no political obligations. The principles which govern my administration are not in keeping with the practices of any party of the day, whatever may be their professions before election. And, though claiming no originality of ideas, yet the practical application of principles of government so long professed, but never practised, is a novel procedure in a public officer, and puzzles the leaders wonderfully. Hence I am at no loss to divine why partisan designs should be attributed to me, by men who can not understand that popular applause can be obtained in any other way than by political trickery, or the declamations of the demagogue. I understand my own position fully. Without egotism, permit me to say that I am fully conscious of a place in public esteem far beyond and above any party, and to add the belief, that if a candidate for the office of Mayor to-morrow, the people would not desert me, if every political organization in the city were to combine in opposition. Therefore, is it necessary for me to act the part of the *mere* politician, and by prostituting the whole Police Department to political purposes, to jeopard this position? Can any party make me so swerve from duty and a proper sense of personal security, as to throw away the good opinion of nearly all my fellow-citizens whose support is worth having? This can never be! The same principles and acts which have given me the confidence of the community, will enable me to hold it down to the close of my administration. Of this I have no fears. The danger to the public lies not in any relaxation or dereliction upon my part, nor in my improper use of the police, but in the passage of this bill. The police has been the main instrument by which I have been enabled to perform the acts which have secured public approval. Take it away, and the horrors of bad government will return upon us fourfold, and it will be difficult then to combat the assertion which will be made, that as head of the Department, (although stripped of the power,) I have been derelict and have deviated from the present policy. Is it uncharitable to add, that some such design may have influenced the projectors of this scheme — that its authors suppose that whilst the people will continue to hold me to a strict accountability for the maintenance of the reforms initiated and sustained, they would at the same time forget that the means by which they have been effected were taken away, and thus demand a continuation of reform after all power of enforcing them had ceased? This opinion of the intelligence of the people, though not very flattering, is consistent with the motives which have evidently dictated this measure.

The warmth of expression of this letter may offend—my language may appear as if emanating from excitement, which is not the fact. It is true, I feel deeply these efforts to deprive me of the means by which any improvement in our city is effected. No man but myself can appreciate the critical state of our social condition, if the authorities are deprived of control of the only means of preventing dangers of a far more serious character than have ever before threatened us. I am no alarmist, but believe me sincere when I tell you that, in my opinion, New-York can only be saved from a rule of corruption engendered by the devotees of the three great vices, namely, intemperance, gaming, and debauchery, but by the strong one-man power, who, with a bold and fearless hand, can command the entire police force without hindrance or molestation. My many pressing duties have not permitted me time to do justice to this subject. This letter is hastily written, and full of imperfections, but without reference to its style or matter, receive it as the honest protest of your friend and fellow-citizen. FERNANDO WOOD.

P. S.—In answer to your request as to the publication of this letter, you may do so, provided you deem my views of sufficient public interest. F. W.

To JAMES W. GERARD, Esq.

The preposterous Police bill was, as we have seen,

thrown out, but the spirit that had given rise to it was still alive here, and strove to work out, by means of small annoyances, the end which the frustrated bill had in view.

Councilmen wanted a list of all detailed policemen, and a history of their missions; Aldermen desired a report of all police appointments since Mr. Wood's election. The first he grants, notifying that eminent body, however, that they are interfering with what is no business of theirs; that they have no right to ask, but are indebted to the information which he gives them simply to his courtesy. But to the Aldermen he says, that they are entirely overstepping their limits, and that he respectfully, but very positively declines to give them that information which they have no right to ask for.

"*To the Honorable the Board of Councilmen:*

GENTLEMEN: I inclose herewith a statement of 'the number of detailed policemen in the city, together with the name of each policeman so detailed, the place or places at which he is detailed, the nature of the service to be performed by him at such place or places, and the length of time per day, and what part of the day such policeman is engaged in his duties,' as called for from the Board of Police Commissioners, by a resolution of the Common Council, emanating in your Board.

This information is furnished by myself, as Mayor, without admitting the right of the Common Council to require it. It is the exclusive privilege of the Mayor, as head of the Police Department, to detail policemen without responsibility to any body, not even to the Board of Police Commissioners itself.

By special laws of the State, and by the charter, the organization and regulating of the police force is placed under the management and control of a Board of Commissioners, consisting of the Mayor, Recorder, and City Judge.

The Common Council of this city is given, by no act of the Legislature, nor by the charter, or any amendment to it, any jurisdiction whatever over the management, direction, or *personnel* of this department.

Beyond the necessary legislation required in voting supplies, such as station-houses, etc, it has nothing whatever to do with it. It can not appoint the Commissioners, nor take any part in the appointment, trial, or removal of policemen, nor interfere with the rules and regulations adopted by them for its government. It has no power over this department whatever, so far as the direction and exercise of its official duties are concerned.

But admitting the right of the Common Council to call for the information asked in the resolution referred to, it has applied to the wrong officers; the detailing of policemen being a prerogative resting exclusively in the Mayor, by State law, the Board of Commissioners, as such, having nothing to do with it whatever. The Mayor makes all the detailments, except officers detailed by the captains, in a few of the wards, who act as dock-masters, etc.

The present Mayor recognizes no authority in the Common Council, or in any other quarter, to supervise his conduct in the discharge of this duty. He will perform it for the public benefit, as he understands it, without being influenced by any action taken elsewhere, having for its object an interference with the course he may adopt with reference to it. The proper efficiency of this corps is dependent upon discipline, which can be obtained and maintained only by the firm hand of unrestricted power, entirely exempt from outside influences.

The Mayor desires to be left unmolested in his exertions to improve this important branch of the public service, which has been wisely placed entirely under him. He is fully conscious of the responsibilities of the trust; and whilst ever ready to impart information to the Common Council, which may be required to enlighten it in the discharge of its legislative duties, he will also protect the department, of which he is the head and over which by law he has (with his associates) sole control, from any efforts to subvert this authority, and thus impair the subordination so essential to the well-being of the police force. Information concerning it can not be required by the Common Council for the purpose of legislation, because it has no power to legislate at all in the premises.

I have deemed it proper to state frankly my position on this subject, that it may not be misunderstood or misconstrued in giving the information now called for.

It is not my wish to refuse any inquiry into the mode of conducting this department. The whole policy of my administration has been to throw all the executive offices open to public scrutiny. Investigation can never prove injurious to a properly conducted public office, though there are many reasons why a large police force, governed by stringent rules affecting its discipline, and under the control of one head, should not be subjected to outside agitating influences, foreign to its command, and unacquainted with the domestic *regime* and the consolidation so necessary to the preservation of proper submission to the recognized authority.

With this brief statement of my views, as to how far the Common Council can interfere in the administration of the Police Department of this city, without any intention of treating your authority with disrespect, I herewith submit the information called for."

And afterwards, for further information to the Board of Aldermen, July 12, he says:

"GENTLEMEN: Your Board passed a resolution on the 12th ultimo, 'that his honor the Mayor be, and he is hereby requested to furnish, for the information of this Board at its next meeting, to-morrow afternoon, the 13th instant, a list of all appointments made in the Police Department since the 1st day of January last, designating them by wards; together with the names of all policemen whose terms of office have expired and were not reäppointed, and also the names of all policemen removed,' which could have been replied to immediately, but for your adjournment until to-day. I now have the honor to reply. It would have been sufficient for me to have said, in response to this resolution, that the appointments and removals in the Police Department are made by the Board of Police Commissioners, and to that body the inquiry should be addressed. But admitting that the power to give the information asked is in my hands, I respectfully decline giving it, inasmuch as it would appear to recognize the right of the Common Council to ask it. The right to call upon the several executive departments for information, is given by the charter to the Mayor and the Common Council, but no authority is given to either Board in its separate capacity, or both Boards jointly, to call upon the Mayor for information respecting the department, of which, by State law, he is made the sole and exclusive head. The object of inquiries of this kind, and, indeed, the only ground upon which they can be maintained, is to procure information for the purpose of legislation, and to furnish to the law-making power data to enable it to arrive at correct conclusions. When these are its objects, it should never be withheld, and would not be by me, even while denying the authority to require it.

In the present instance, however, no such motive can be set up.

The inquiry now made as to the appointment and removal of policemen, can not be required to subserve any legislative objects; because the Common Council have no power to legislate in the premises. It has no jurisdiction over the appointing and removing whatever, and can take no action which will in the least affect them, one way or the other; therefore, to grant this information can serve no good purpose, whilst an admission of the right to ask it, which admits the obligation to give it, would be as detrimental to the interests of the Department as it would be a violation of the charter and laws, which wisely place the police under a Board of Commissioners, who are independent of the Common Council in all respects. The reasons for this regulation are obvious. The police of a city like New-York should be essentially military in its character and discipline; it should possess all the elements of a well-disciplined corps, whose chief duty it is to execute with alacrity and faithfulness the orders issued from head-quarters. It should be consolidated—no one part should be hostile to the other. All influences attempting to interfere with the official *regime*, outside of the immediate command, should be rejected, as much as would be the attempt of the civil authorities in time of war to direct the evolutions of an army. Military command does not divide its authority. However many officers there may be, each possessing commanding powers, they are exercised by gradation, no two having coördinate powers. There is no division of authority—if there were, there would be no efficiency. Our police force is founded upon this principle. It is military in its uniform, in its *personnel*, and in its discipline—in the mode of issuing orders—of individual responsibility, and the nature of its patrol duties. In the city's quiet and peace, each policeman is a sentinel, properly reviewed and conducted by an officer; in time of riot and disorder, it would become an army subject to precisely the same tactics, and commanded precisely upon the same military principles. No outside power, created for duties of an entirely opposite and different character, should be permitted to interpose itself between the commanding general of this army and the army itself. It was a wise provision that the police should be exempt from any interference from the legislative branch of the City Government; that it should be removed from the partisanism, contests and popular influences which are continually agitating your own and all other political deliberative bodies; that there should be one branch of the public service not liable to demoralizing party influences, and tossed to and fro upon the wave of political struggles. With the police no sectional, party or personal interests should be incorporated. It is not difficult to see that in a city like New-York the most stringent government and laws which the nature of our institutions will permit are yet too weak to do the service which may be demanded in the preservation of public order. At any moment the city may be thrown for reliance upon this civil military organization. This body may alone become the stay and corrective of popular violence.

To meet such a calamity no other force should be required. It should always be sufficient to suppress attempts to subvert municipal authority. An armed resistance to an unarmed mob can in no event be necessary if the police is properly organized, disciplined and commanded. It is my aim to do away with the necessity of shedding blood in the preservation of the peace of the city; to bring the police to a condition which will enable it, under my personal command, without military assistance, and without taking life, to put down whatever force may be raised for resistance to the law. I desire to be left alone in these designs, believing myself to be the best judge of what is required, and feeling that the legislative branch of the Government should rather strengthen my power than weaken it by introducing a belief in the Department that there is a higher authority than mine, and a Court of Appeals, to which to apply against the subjection incident to the principle by which I command. These are the motives which bring me to the determination to resist at all hazards any interference with the police by any other power whatever. It is under my command, by State laws, by action of the Commissioners, and by public sentiment, and so long as it remains, all attempts to subvert or lessen this authority shall be resisted to the end. It will be for the people to decide whether I shall be supported in thus upholding their interests; by exercising a firm, honest and impartial administration of the Police Department, and whether the improvement already manifest shall continue and be sustained by the intelligence and virtue of the community."

These men, so well arranged, are exposed to almost every danger; to constant vicissitudes and inclemencies of the climate, and to the wearing effects of fatigue and incessant vigilance. Their sanitary condition is a matter of earnest care to their commander, and he provides for it on this wise. Says he, under date July the 10th:

"The good sanitary condition of the police is essential to its efficiency. Without health, policemen can not properly discharge the required duty. The vigor of body, by which he is to sustain the fatigue, and which generally imparts physical strength and courage, can not be maintained without attention to certain rules regarding regimen, cleanliness, and temperance, and the professional care of experienced medical attendants.

To preserve a healthful condition is a matter of great moment, not only to the policeman himself, but to the people of the city, in whose service he is enlisted. Whether viewed as a humane or as a public economic regulation, attention to this subject is of great importance. The compensation of policemen, though sufficiently liberal to defray the necessary expenses of living, is not enough to provide, in addition, a pecuniary independence, preparatory to the bodily disabilities incident to old age. Therefore, humanity dictates that every precaution should be taken by the authorities to preserve their health.

It is due alike to their faithfulness as well as to the exposures, involving hazard to life and health, to which they are continually subjected.

As a question of money-saving to the city, the proper care of the health of policemen is also of moment. The expense of the whole Department is not far from one million dollars per annum, nearly all of which is for pay alone. Heretofore the average number of sick and disabled has been about fifty per day, out of a force of about eleven hundred, being one in twenty-two. This proportion is too large. There can be no other reason for it than non-attention to sanitary requirements. Every man is selected with care, as to the soundness of his constitution and exemption from physical defects, and is to be presumed enters the corps free from tendency to disease. The interest of the Department is to preserve this condition. The difficulty of discriminating between disease which is the result of exposure, whilst on active duty, and inherent or pulmonary affections, is very great, and it often occurs that services of patrolmen are lost for months, though they are in receipt of pay for the whole period. By law the number is limited. If sick or disabled, substitutes are not permitted, and thus the force is weakened, though the pay is seldom lessened. Hence attention to the healthful state of all connected with the Department is demanded by reasons of economy, as well as by what is due to the officer himself on philanthropic grounds.

With these views, I have carefully devised a plan, having for its object an improvement in the sanitary condition of the whole Department, appertaining to the care of the station-houses, as it regards ventilation, cleanliness of the rooms and sleeping apartments; furnishing a sufficient supply at all times of medicines, surgical instruments, tourniquets, lints, etc.; an immediate attention to all invalids, whether becoming sick in the discharge of duty or not, and constant medical treatment until recovered and fit for duty; the whole to be under the charge of intelligent, experienced practitioners, without any expense to the police whatever.

I propose to divide the whole Department into seven surgical districts, each district to be under the charge of a resident physician. There shall be a surgeon-general, whose station shall be at the office of the Chief of Police, and whose duty it shall be to be at that office every day, at such hours as may be thought necessary by the Mayor, for the purpose of receiving and acting upon reports from the district surgeons, and for the purpose of receiving and giving such directions with reference to the general government of the medical department, as may be necessary.

He shall have full supervision of the whole Department, so far as the health and sanitary condition of the officers and men are concerned.

He shall make written reports to the Mayor at least once in each month, and perform such other duties connected with his department of the Police as may be required.

The city shall be divided into seven surgical districts, as follows:

District	I.—1, 2, 3, 4,	Police Districts.
"	II.—5, 6, 8, 14,	"
"	III.—7, 10, 11,	"
"	IV.—13, 15, 17,	"
"	V.—9, 16, 20,	"
"	VI.—18, 19, 21,	"
"	VII.—12, 22,	"

Each surgical district shall have appointed to it one surgeon, who shall reside in one of the police districts comprehended within his surgical district.

It shall be the duty of the district surgeons to visit each station-house within his district, at least once in every forty-eight hours, to examine into its condition as to cleanliness, ventilation, and the state of the medicine-chest, and to ascertain that every article hereinafter named as being required, shall be supplied, (which shall be done by a requisition on the surgeon-general,) and see that they are fit for use. It shall be his duty to visit at his residence every member of the Department within his district, who is reported as being unable to perform duty, in consequence of physical inability or sickness; to report to the surgeon-general, on or in every forty-eight hours, the specific nature of the malady, whether medicinal or surgical, the probabilities of its having been contracted in actual service, and whether in his judgment the disability is of sufficient magnitude to exempt the patient from duty, and to report the name and numbers of the sick, the convalescent, and the discharged. It shall be his duty to attend and treat professionally every member of the Department, when sick or unable to perform duty, without receiving any compensation from or making charge to the said invalid. This attention shall be constant until the recovery of the patient, without reference to the character of the disease, or how contracted; to be diligent in protecting the Department from simulated sickness, and in no case to report any as having acquired the disability in the course of duty, without conclusive proof of the fact; and to examine into and report all cases where it is supposed intemperate habits, or the use of stimulating drinks, or other vices, are a cause of disease. He shall also examine all applicants for appointment residing within his district, after they shall have passed the examination and approval of the Commissioners. These shall be referred to him immediately after the action of the Commissioners, by the Chief of Police. These examinations shall be careful and critical, and the result be reported promptly in writing to the surgeon-general. The surgeon-general shall then review the examination, and if he approve, it shall be final, whether the applicant be rejected or approved by the surgeon-general. If he do not approve, the Mayor shall determine the result, through outside examination by eminent members of the medical profession.

There will be provided in every station-house, so far as practicable, a room in which to place persons injured by accident or otherwise, and there will be provided medicine-chests, with such medicines and common surgical instruments and appliances as are usually required; also sedan-chairs, tourniquets, lint, bandages, splints, etc., etc.

In cases of injury to persons brought to the station-house, or to prisoners requiring immediate attention, the captains, or other officers in charge, shall notify the district surgeon, whose duty it shall be to attend forthwith, for which he shall be entitled to extra compensation."

Finally, in his grand review of the whole force on May the 26th, he sums up all that he desires to say or that he expects in this way:

"OFFICERS AND MEN: It gives me pleasure to meet you to-day. It is the first time I have had an opportunity to see so large a portion of the whole corps in a body, and indeed it is the first time you have been so called together. This occasion must be as gratifying to yourselves, as I can assure you it is to me. In common with the many distinguished persons present, I have been highly pleased with your officer-like and gentlemanly appearance, with your good condition, your excellent drill, and the general correctness with which you have performed the exercises of the Department.

Gentlemen: I take a deep interest in the way in which your official duties are discharged, nor am I unmindful of what is due to your personal welfare. To enable you to act your part with fidelity, it is indispensable, that you fully appreciate the many advantages of your position and be conscious of what is done for you by the authorities.

You draw from the City Treasury as pay, in the aggregate nearly one million of dollars per annum, besides what is given by individuals as presents, which last year amounted, according to the books in the Mayor's office, to about $15,000, and, so far this year to about $4000, not including many valuable presents, not to be estimated by money.

There is no class of operatives or tradesmen so well paid. You are compensated for every day in the year, rain or shine, duty or no duty, present or absent, the only exception being absence at your own request to be without pay, or sickness not caused by the discharge of duty. And again, the duration of your office adds much to its pecuniary value. It is during good behavior, or, in other words, for life, if you behave yourselves. What other situation, or what other public officer, even to the highest posts of trust and honor, that have the same security against want, or the destitution of old age? With myself, though your commanding officer, a few months will see my place filled by another, who in turn will be replaced by some one else; and as to pecuniary compensation, with a salary which falls far short of the absolute indispensable outlays, consequent upon the office itself, without reference to living expenses at all.

Again, your pay is *certain*. No employer runs off cheating you out of your wages, or making deductions for bad work, or pays you in uncurrent money, liable to heavy discounts, or fails to pay surely and promptly on the promised day. Those of you whose previous avocations have been of a nature to force you to rely upon wages or salaries, will not fail to appreciate this difference in your paymaster.

If vigilant, and attentive to duty, there is the prospect of promotion. The highest posts in the Department are not closed against you; but upon the contrary, merit is the key that will force them open. Many of the most valued officers in the service, entered it in the humblest position, and have won their advancement by good conduct alone.

Again, the attention paid to your sanitary condition is of great value. Your station-houses are well ventilated. Your sleeping apartments cleanly and well cared for, baths are provided, doctors and surgeons gratuitously furnished, and every attention given to your physical well-being and continued health and longevity. If sick, a physician visits you, with the best medical attention, and without expense. In the army or navy a deduction is made from the pay of the men, to defray the expense of this department of the service. There is a fund made up by deductions from the poor pittance they receive, which is devoted to the erection of hospitals, supplying medical stores, surgical instruments, and other material. This is not your case. The city furnishes most of these gratuitously to you. It may not be out of place for me to add, in connection with this point, that I have designs with reference to the better protection of your physical and pecuniary condition, which in due time shall be developed, and which will convince you that I am not your enemy or indifferent to your welfare. The subject has engaged much of my attention and reflection, and I think I can say with truth, that propositions will be made by me, not only to you for your adoption, but to the liberal and philanthropic citizens of New-York, which, if approved, will add to the value of your offices, by fully protecting you against the deprivations and want incident to poverty and old age.

But some complain of hard duty, and many kind-hearted citizens think, that, under my administration, onerous and severe exactions are made. Let us see if this be so. You have every other day off duty from sunrise to sunset, which is your own time, to do with as you please, liable only to duty in case of an extreme emergency, which seldom arises; and when on duty, your labor is exercise in the open air, walking abroad in noble manhood, breathing the free and healthful atmosphere which God has given to us for sustenance, and not imprisoned in the workshop or bending over the work-bench, like the toiling thousands of this metropolis, less favored than yourselves. Contrast this invigorating, healthful, and manly avocation with the operative of any class, and you must agree with me, that yours is far superior, whether viewed as a profitable, a moral, or a physical condition.

Again, the uniform is complained of, and said to be by some a badge of degradation and servitude. How erroneous is this impression. What! a badge of servitude, which is really an emblem of trust and honor! A mark of degradation, to carry upon your person an official insignia, denoting that you have been selected by the Mayor, the Recorder, and the City Judge, (the three highest criminal officers known to our laws,) as worthy to be intrusted with delicate and important duties and prerogatives, involving the care of the life, liberty, and property of the citizen? No sane mind can so construe it, and believe me, fellow-officers, when I tell you that the man who can perpetrate such an absurd theory, is a dangerous companion, who should be avoided as your enemy. There is no degradation in the uniform of a policeman, more than there is in the epaulette of an officer in the regular army; no greater badge of servitude in the *star,* than there is in the *button,* so highly prized by the navy. The degradation is not in the *uniform;* it is in a disregard of duty by him who wears it. The policeman more frequently disgraces the uniform, than the uniform does the policeman. It is a badge of degradation only when made so by the misconduct of the wearer. As the uniform of a military officer is sullied by cowardice or treachery, so can yours be only by conduct unbecoming a policeman and disgraceful to your position as such.

No member of society has a better opportunity to distinguish himself, or to deserve well of his fellow-citizens than yourselves. The line of duty is plain, simple, well defined, and easy of performance. I have no desire to exact too severe labor. I ask no man connected with the corps to devote half as as many hours to its service, as I do myself; and whilst I am ready to demand attention and obedience to orders, I am also willing to recognize and reward meritorious services. The only road to the good opinion of the Head of the Department and of the public, is faithful and vigilant discharge of the trusts confided; this is all that is desired, and is within the power of every man to give. When you assumed the office, it was with full knowledge of this obligation. If these duties are too severe, you should not have undertaken their fulfillment. If they are too onerous and exacting, you should not have agreed to perform them. If they appeared to deprive you of personal rights, you should have so stated, and declined the compacts entered into. Your position as a member of the police is the result of an agreement between yourself and the authorities, voluntarily made by you, in which you agree to give up certain personal privileges and rights to serve the public, as a custodian of their interests. You were not forced to take the post, and are not now forced to retain it; but so long as you do retain it, and draw from the Treasury its compensation, it is my duty to exact the fulfillment of the contract upon your part, or endeavor to fill your place by those who will.

Every public officer yields up personal rights. No man can assume office, whether high or low, without giving up something to the public, if he does his duty. I am simply the agent of the people in the surveillance exercised over your conduct. My position, in relation to yours, is like that of the head of an army actually in battle; for we are always on duty, always in an engagement, our campaign against the enemy is always commencing, always continuing, and never ending. It is a continuous fight against the crime and the wrong-doing of the vicious of this community. Eternal vigilance is the essential requisite of a policeman's duty; and as he relaxes, so does he depart from what shall be required of him, so long as I hold the position of Commanding General.

In conclusion, I can not do better than to call your attention to the prefatory remarks to the Rules and Regulations of the Department, which comprehend what really constitutes your duties and the theory of the Police Department as now organized.

The confidence placed in the Department and its members, and their consequent responsibility, are extreme; their duties and powers, such as demand special and peculiar qualifications in those who compose the force. It is difficult to specify each and every of these duties and powers, although rules and laws may be, and are made to comprehend them; or to designate with precision the manner in which these powers shall be applied, and these duties performed, in each and every case that may arise.

A policeman's duty includes careful attention in its performance, careful industry to acquire an intelligent and correct sense of it, care of bodily health, good habits, habits of neatness and cleanliness, propriety of behavior, of dress and address. It includes a full command of himself, and of his temper, passions, and infirmities, forbearance under provocation, kindness, modesty, and civility of deportment, the avoidance of harshness, ill temper, or bad language, and the example of orderly and moral conversation and behavior. It includes obedience to all lawful orders, respect for the officers and fellow members of the Department, and unwavering fidelity, integrity, and truth.

In action he should be firm, fearless, calm, and intrepid, discriminating, discreet, and judicious, employing resolutely all the force that is necessary, and prompt in its application, yet employing it with decision, wisdom, and skill, and only to the extent required; unyielding, though quiet and energetic in the performance of his task. In case of emergency and where personal conflict is inevitable, he must be brave without rashness, courageous and persevering without needless temerity, and employ that degree of judgment which denotes chastened and invincible valor.

On post he should be ever vigilant, active, and in motion, avoiding all habits of listlessness, of lounging or idle conversation, and every thing by which his incessant attention to his duty may even for a moment be impaired; and when on duty he is a sentinel, whose whole mind and abilities should be directed to the task imposed on him.

When on duty, the emblems now prescribed for both officers and men will be expected to be worn without any exception, and that they will be kept neat and becomingly fitted to the person; for the taste and tidiness with which a policeman attires himself is a material accessory to the esteem and respect in which he is held by the public.

The officers of the Department are all emphatically enjoined, not only to accomplish themselves in a full knowledge of their duties, and of the rules and laws which relate to them, but by every proper means in their power to instruct those under their command in their respective duties.

A correct and exemplary moral conduct and efficient performance of duty, on the part of the respective members of the force, will not only justify the confidence reposed in it by the public, but must elevate the Department to the highest degree of respectability.

And now, gentlemen, I must repeat the expression of my gratification with the proceedings of this day. It has been no empty pageant—no holiday, in which to show you to the crowds of citizens here assembled. Its designs were to give me an opportunity to inspect your appearance—to observe your improvement in the drill exercise, and to see and converse with you on the important subject of your duties.

I have no doubt the result will be advantageous to you, as it is most agreeable to me. I take my leave with an increased admiration for you as an efficient protective corps, and with a confident belief that if ever your entire force shall be required for the preservation of the peace, it will be found entirely able to meet and overwhelm any antagonistic body, however great in number or desperate in character."

Now, the result of all this has been the formation of a body of some thousand men; chosen men, well equipped, well disciplined, well drilled. The city is free from riots; the calendar of crime decreased; accidents now occur once a week where before they happened a dozen times a day; and instead of a lounging, slouching constable, you find a well-dressed, soldierly-looking man; kind, gentle, civil, and yet thoroughly effective. And this work is Mayor Wood's alone.

No regiment is composed of angels. There are bad men still in the police force. Let the pessimists quote and gloat.

CHAPTER XIV.

WHAT WE SHALL LEGALLY HAVE TO DRINK.

THERE is, we presume, but one opinion in the world about the vice of intemperance, and the horrid evils which it produces. All men, drunkards included, shudder when they think of the ruin of health, life, intellect, fortune, traceable to this debasing vice. To destroy it is the desire of all, or nearly all; for temperance above all other virtues is admired—temperance in all things.

On account of the public ills arising from drunkenness—breaches of peace, murders, pauperism, fires, etc. —governments have been obliged to give their attention to this question, and to make laws calculated to lessen the amount of intoxication, if not to do away with it altogether. The drunkard openly reeling through the streets has always been held a fair subject for arrest, and it is questioned nowadays whether that is not the limit of legislative power. Some go for more, saying that legislatures may have power to declare not only, "Thou shalt not be publicly drunken," but this also and absolutely, "Thou shalt not drink."

Be this as it may, the inspired men who sate in the House and Senate Chamber at Albany, in the year of our Lord 1855, being greatly moved by the excess of drunkenness in this Empire State, created and passed a law entitled, "An Act for the Prevention of Intemperance, Pauperism, and Crime," all of which excellent results were to be obtained by total prohibition of all beverages but Croton and ginger-beer.

Then there arose men who said: "We will not obey this law;" some of them using expletives and *quasi*-profane language, in their utterance of that disobedient resolve. Well, so far as New-York was concerned, the favorers of the law looked to the Chief Executive to enforce and compulse obedience to its dictates, clamored to him about it, called on him by endearing and other epithets to come up to their help against the evil dealers in wine, cider, and gin. On the other hand, Mr. Coleman of the Astor House asked His Honor what course was to be taken in the matter; whether existing city laws were not severe enough without such a thorough whirlwind, offsweeping all things potable, and the reply, under date of January 24th, exhibited these views:

"This evil in our midst," says Mayor Wood, "appears to me to result rather from the non-execution of present laws, than from the character of the laws themselves. It is a popular error to mistake feeble administrative enforcements for defects in the statutes. This mistake has been productive of continual and never-ending legislation upon all subjects, until the books are so full of laws, that none but the most astute and studious lawyers can tell what is and what is not law. I regret that it is impossible for me at this time, to go at length into the subject of the suppression of intemperance, and the proper mode to effect it, as your letter calls for. I can say, however, with truth, that the reform effected by me in the Sabbath dram-drinking, has not been by coërcion. Until yesterday, *no licenses have been revoked* through my orders, *no arrests* have been made, *no penalty or punishment* inflicted; and *yet out of nearly six thousand* licenses, the number of places *open* for the sale of liquor has been reduced from two thousand three hundred before the commencement of my administration, to twenty-six last Sunday."

But the act having once fairly passed, it became his duty to state to the people of the city wherein his duty lay, and what he, for his part, intended to do in this matter. This he did in the two following

PROCLAMATIONS:

The Legislature of this State having passed an act entitled, "An Act for the Suppression of Intemperance, Pauperism, and Crime," known as the Prohibitory Liquor Law, and as my position with reference to its enforcement in this city, so far as that duty may devolve upon my office, should be declared at an early day, to leave no doubt as to its character, I hereby present, for public consideration, the principles which control my conduct as a public officer, alike applicable to matters of great or small import.

That the people govern — not in their primary capacity, but through representatives freely and fairly chosen—is the theory of American government. The people are the source of political power. They make the laws; and the great safeguard of American liberty is general compliance. As the statutes thus created for the better protection of life and property, and the pursuit of happiness, are but the reflection of the popular will for the time being, so are they binding upon the body politic — the minority as well as the majority—who are alike parties to the compact, the obligations of which it is dishonorable to disregard. And though these elements of self-government present the distinguishing features between our own and the governments of Europe, still our success has been owing more to acquiescence in the will of the majority than in the character of the government itself.

Other republics have failed, even when founded upon our forms and constitution, only because of the resistance of the vanquished contestants for rule, by rebellion against the laws and the executive power appointed to enforce them. We understand Republicanism differently, and hence have no such struggles. The generally pervading common-school educational system — the rigid principle of obedience instilled into the child by the parent, and the scholar by the teacher—the enlarged human progress, leading onward to the expansion of the heart and intellect, all founded upon an enlightened, unproscriptive, religious sentiment, furnish the platform upon which American liberty stands, and from which no calamity, save forcible resistance to the laws, can ever remove it.

It is not contended that minorities have not grievances, and that their grievances must remain unredressed. Their rights are fully protected. The same fundamental law that binds minorities to submit, points out clearly the road to relief against an illegal or improper exercise of authority upon the part of the majority. Even whenever fanaticism rules the hour and covers the country with its baneful influence, to the exclusion of reason and justice, public opinion will soon correct the error, and restore the calm sense of mature conservative judgment. What if the law-maker proves recreant, and betrays the constituent he was chosen to represent? The wrong inflicted is not irremediable, though it may be a proper chastisement for a negligent or corrupt use of the franchise. Time repairs all the errors of legislation. Its evils and wrongs, however great, invariably recoil before public opinion and the decisions of the courts. Redress and relief can thus always be obtained. The legal tribunals and the ballot-box are never approached in vain for the maintenance of a good, or the overthrow of a bad cause. These are the only constitutional resorts—all others are treason or rebellion.

Another marked characteristic of the American people is the universal submission to the governmental forms restricting the powers and duties of the three components of government, namely, the Legislative, the Judicial, and the Executive. The first can only make the laws, the second can only expound them, and the third has no discretion but to see them faithfully executed. It is my province to act as agent for the people in one of these departments. I am an executive officer. I aid in the execution of the laws, and have sworn to do so "to the best of my ability." With no part or responsibility in their creation, so far as State legislation is concerned, I have no option but compliance, as an instrument for their enforcement, and to require a compliance in others, as far as I have the ability. It is my duty to exact obedience, and yours to obey. The officer of the law is not accountable for the making of the law; he is bound to execute it, pursuant to his oath of office, though the responsibility of the people, as the source of all political power, can not be so easily denied. As Mayor, I have endeavored to fulfill this duty. Though sometimes painful, yet it has been performed diligently and impartially. I hope to continue without relaxation. The act relating to the prohibition of the liquor traffic and consumption is now a law, holding the same position as any other law, and, until decided invalid by the courts, or amended or repealed by the Legislature, should command the same obedience. So far as its execution depends upon me, I have no discretion but to exercise all my power to enforce it. It is unnecessary for me to express an opinion in regard to legislation of this character, or of this law; for whatever that opinion may be, I can not, without dishonor, shrink from a faithful discharge of the trust confided, whatever shall be the personal consequences to myself. I now call upon the friends of law and order to aid in the performance of this obligation, and in sustaining the laws—a principle upon which rests the corner-stone of all our national prosperity and greatness.

Deeming my course, with reference to this subject, of interest to those whose occupations are to be affected, and especially to those whose licenses will expire with the year ending the first of May ensuing, I have felt it incumbent upon me to indicate it frankly. I have availed myself of the first moment after the adjournment of the Legislature, when all expectations of repeal or modification were hopeless, to thus make public my position, without having had time to examine it, or to receive counsel as to my duties under it, and without knowing whether I am called upon or have power as Mayor to take any part in its execution. I shall inform myself on these points without delay, and announce my conclusions to the public with the same candor that prompts this communication.

FERNANDO WOOD.

MAYOR'S OFFICE, NEW-YORK, *Friday, April* 27, 1855.

To the Citizens of New-York:

MY late communication to the people of this city respecting the Prohibitory Liquor Law, recently passed by the Legislature, closed as follows:

"I have availed myself of the first moment after the adjournment of the Legislature, when all expectations of repeal or modification were hopeless, to thus make public my position, without having had time to examine it, or to receive counsel as to my duties under it, and without knowing whether I am called upon or have power as Mayor to take any part in its execution. I shall inform myself on these points without delay, and announce my conclusion to the public with the same candor that prompts this communication."

The opinions of my legal advisers before the public, and their conclusions need but brief reïteration at my hands. In my capacity as Mayor, the Corporation Counsel is by the Charter constituted my guide; in my functions as Magistrate, the District-Attorney becomes my coöperator. These gentlemen sustain the same relations to me as are held by Attorney-Generals to the President or the Governor. To act contrary to their direction, until it is superseded by absolute judicial declaration, would be an illegal assumption, for doubtful powers are thus made certain. I have no discretion to take any other line of conduct, without doing what could be properly charged as an illegal assumption of power unauthorized by law. Therefore, while standing ever ready to execute all laws faithfully and diligently, to the extent of the means placed at my command, I am, like other executive officers, confined within the boundaries prescribed by the legal advisers of my office; to act contrary would be to violate the law, or what I am obliged to consider the law, until decided to be otherwise by the courts.

The reply made by Mr. Hall the District-Attorney, is dated three days succeeding the publication of my views; that of Mr. Dillon is dated the following day. My inquiry to Mr. Hall was confined to what would be the law governing the sale of liquor in this city after the expiration of existing licenses (May 1) until July 4, when the penalties of prohibition will go into effect, and as to the laws governing Sunday selling during the same period. He replied that the old license system is superseded by the new, with its own appropriate penalties; that the old penalties were not only specific to the old system, but are inapplicable to the new system, as well because penalties can not be extended by implication, as because the new system had *its own* specific penalties. That by an oversight of the Legislature the new penalties are superseded until that part of the act creating them becomes operative. That from May 1, when existing licenses expire, until July 4, no obstacle exists to the free sale of liquor in this city, and that it can be sold the same as any other commodity. And that for Sunday selling there is no penalty save the old civil penalty of two dollars and fifty cents for a whole day's traffic, and which is to be prosecuted and collected in a civil action by the Corporation Attorney.

The inquiries to Mr. Dillon were more general, applying to the whole scope of the Prohibitory section.

In reply he says, that the Mayor is not empowered to hear and determine the charges and punish offenses arising under any part of its provisions. That the Mayor is not authorized to perform any other duty under the act than to require policemen to perform the duties enjoined upon them, but that in his direction to the police he must caution them against any infraction of that section of the law which declares it shall not apply to liquors, the right to sell which in this State is given by any law or treaty of the United States, and which are exempt from seizure, for the selling of which there is no penalty, and that policemen will not be warranted in seizing any such liquors, or the vessels in which they are contained. The Counsel more particularly describes these liquors as being all those which are permitted to be imported by act of Congress, namely, which pay duty; thus comprehending all that are imported. He also thinks that the Mayor has been appropriately advised by the District-Attorney on other branches of the law before referred to.

And now an experiment is to be tried in this city, whether in the absence of legal compulsory authority, there is sufficient moral force in the community to prevent unlimited indulgence in intoxicating drinks. Under these opinions of the law officers the coërcive principle recently adopted by the Legislature, being in effect almost entirely nullified, shall we by general license and unbridled indulgence prove that coërcion is necessary? Shall we thus admit the force of the prohibitory argument by showing our inability of self-restraint; our incompetency for social self-government? If so disqualified we are totally unfit for the blessing of political self-government.

It is unnecessary to descant upon the evils of intemperance. Its results are too indelibly stamped upon the condition of a very large portion of this community, to require any allusion from me. Any man who walks abroad, or who visits the garrets and cellars of this metropolis, filled with indigence, wretchedness, and disease, or who takes a glance into our prisons, hospitals, or Alms-House, will be more or less than man if he does not turn away with a painful and humiliating consciousness of the crime, misery, and degradation to which alcohol reduces all who yield to its temptation. Nor is it here alone where these sad results are exhibited. The same developments are often found among the opulent, the educated, and the refined. And can we be surprised that as the philanthropist surveys this dreadful but not over-colored picture, he should resort to remedies as violent as the evil sought to be removed appears extreme and destructive?

I apprehend all will agree with me in the existence of this great injury to society in our midst, and let us so restrain ourselves by moral force alone, that penal enactments may be unnecessary to enforce its prohibition. The best coërcion is voluntary determination. The human will should have force enough to counteract the social evils of this kind of over-indulgence. When the mental has become subservient to the animal propensities, all distinctions from the brute are removed, and man is debased indeed.

And especially with reference to the Sabbath, let us unite these principles, with a reverence for a day hallowed and blest by divine institutions throughout the civilized world. Do not again place that day in jeopardy. It has been my constant effort to give New-York quiet, peaceful Sabbaths, consistent with the calmness and devotion which characterize a time dedicated to such sacred objects. The closing of the liquor-shops, and it may be said almost total abstinence has been obtained. A disposition has been manifested to comply with my wishes and with the law, in this matter, highly creditable to those engaged in the trade, and which in no small degree has served to allay much hostility to the traffic generally, besides raising the moral position of the trade itself.

Though I look into the future with some fear in view of my present restricted legal power over this subject, still there shall be no change in my efforts to maintain intact the present cessation of liquor-selling and other employments on that day, and in this the liquor-dealers themselves should continue to coöperate. It is their duty as well as their interest to comply. Even those who defend the occupation as an abstract, inherent right to deal in any article of merchandise, can not but admit that none but the evil-minded, who are not creditable members of any profession or society, can maintain a position so antagonistic to public sentiment and morals. I look upon liquor-selling upon the Sabbath day as a degrading occupation, from which any man, as he values his reputation, should fly as from a contagion.

Let me urge, therefore, upon all to show that the citizens of New-York have within their own breasts a higher law, which governs their appetites without penal punishments, and that having tasted the sweets of quiet Sabbath; of one day's rest and repose from the toils, strifes, and wickedness of the weekly contests incident to city life, we will not again relax into what is little better than bestial indulgence on a day devoted, throughout the Christian world, to the worship of the "only true and ever-living God."

FERNANDO WOOD.

But the much good already done in the city of New-York by this one energetic man, had spread his reputation far and wide over the country, and even solid men of Boston must needs come to him for advice upon the matter of "strong potations," and laws prohibitory thereof.

No less imposing a body than the "Massachusetts Temperance Society" write to him to know what is to be done by their executive officers in their towns and villages. And he replies: "That the duty of a mayor with reference to the execution of any law depends upon the law itself. There are laws the enforcement of which rests entirely with other functionaries, and with which municipal officers have nothing to do; therefore of the duties of mayors in the execution of your prohibitory law in the cities of Massachusetts I can not speak, never having read that law, and without knowledge as to the magisterial prerogatives of their offices in your State.

"By a singular oversight the Legislature of New-York has passed a prohibitory law which imposes no duty upon the mayor of this city whatever. That officer is not only not named in the act, but its execution depends entirely upon other officers who are designated therein. Had our Legislature passed a law for the suppression of intemperance, and it became my duty as Mayor of this city to enforce its provisions, the effort would have been made by me at all hazards, and with a determined use of the whole power of my office. An executive officer has nothing to do but to administer the laws as far as their enforcement devolves upon him, taking care, however, to receive the advice of the law officers of his office, as to his power and duties; and especially is legal advice necessary with reference to the execution of laws like the Maine Law, which directs the seizure and destruction of property; otherwise serious personal liability would be assumed, sufficient to ruin the wealthiest man in the community. Were I to attempt the execution of our Prohibitory Law, and seize and destroy liquors after having received the official assurances of the legal advisers of my office that such seizure and interference would be illegal, I would subject myself to personal liability, inasmuch as the execution of the law did not devolve upon my office at all, and I should be assuming a responsibility not justified by any public considerations whatever."

Already he has seen to the enforcement of such city laws as do exist. He has issued a kind and courteous circular to the liquor-dealers, begging them to coöperate with him in this matter. He has said that the sale of liquors upon Sunday shall be stopped; that open drunkenness shall be punished according to the law in such case made and provided. He has given his instructions to the Police Department, and now, in the end, he defines what power he has under this new "Act to Prevent Intemperance, Pauperism, and Crime," as follows, on June the 25th.

After quoting from his counsel, Mr. Dillon, as follows: "That the Mayor is not empowered to hear and determine the charges and punish offenses arising under any part of its provisions. That the Mayor is not authorized to perform any other duty under the act, than to require policemen to perform the duties enjoined upon them, but that in his direction to the Police he must caution them against any infraction of that section of the law, which declares it shall not apply to liquors, the right to sell which in this State is given by any law or treaty of the United States, and which are exempt from seizure, for the selling of which there is no penalty, and that policemen will not be warranted in seizing any such liquors, or the vessels in which they are contained. The Counsel more particularly describes these liquors as being those which are permitted to be imported by act of Congress, namely, which pay duty, thus comprehending all that are imported. He also thinks that the Mayor has been appropriately advised by the District-Attorney, on other branches of the law above referred to." He proceeds to say:

"Subsequently, I have examined this law with great care, being sincerely desirous of arriving at correct conclusions, as to my whole duty under it.

It is undeniable that the Executive officer must assume every act of the Legislature to be valid. This assumption, however, in the present case, must be adopted with some reference to the doubts expressed as to some branches of this law. In assuming the law valid, I am not to give up the duty of administering it according to those views concerning its practical execution which I have concluded have the highest legal authority. Whilst assuming an act valid, it is also imperative upon the public officer to ascertain what is really required of him, and in case of doubt as to any particular provision—the enforcing of which will incur personal responsibility, by the infliction of injuries upon the persons and property of the citizens—to exercise extreme caution. For whilst the people have a right to call upon a public officer to enforce the laws, they have no right to require him to seize property and arrest persons, if there be any well-founded doubt as to the subsequent maintenance of this authority by the courts. It would not do to tell the citizen, after the courts had decided that his property had been illegally seized and his person illegally imprisoned, that the magistrate had believed himself authorized to order it under the law, and that there is no redress.

The presumption is, that the officer assumes no illegal powers; that he is careful to avoid the exercise of such powers, especially if they are oppressive in their character and incur personal liability. No public officer can be called upon to do this, and it matters little whether the liability falls upon the officer personally, or the damages are to be reïmbursed by taxation upon the property of the whole people.

It is self-evident, therefore, that whilst it is my duty to execute this law, yet its peculiar character, connected with the doubts thrown around its true interpretation and its constitutionality, justifies me in giving it what I believe to be the most accurate legal construction, so far as my office has any thing to do with it. This I have determined to do, and refer to the accompanying order to the Police as declaring what that construction is.

It will be seen that this order applies exclusively to those duties put upon the Police by *the act in which they are clothed with the power of seizing property and arresting persons merely upon their own motion, without warrants or complaint.* It does not interfere with their duty in the serving of process, or in executing warrants based upon the complaint of others. It leaves any citizen the right, who is willing and able to assume the responsibility, to test the law in the courts by attempting its enforcement. In my opinion, no time should be lost in giving it this direction, that judicial decision may be obtained to dispel all doubts, and ascertain fully whether every apparent condition shall be carried out. It is scarcely necessary for me to add, that if adverse to the views which I have considered it my duty to adopt, I shall acquiesce and use every power at my command to give force and effect to that decision whatever it may be.

It is to be regretted that, so far as this city is concerned, some other and more practical means had not been adopted for the suppression of intemperance. No citizen will go farther or do more to accomplish so great a good than myself. I look upon intoxication, and the habitual use of intoxicating liquor, as a vice more destructive in its effects, and more debasing in its character, than any other extant in this community. My own practice and precepts have always been in accordance with these opinions; and since holding my present official relations to the people of this city, I have been active and determined in thus treating it. But, as a public officer, I can not act upon theories of ethics. The law must be my guide, to be construed according to the best lights presented."

The doctrine being settled, the practice becomes a

question to be decided. The aids of the Executive are the officers of police. Therefore instructions must be issued to them, and on June the 25th, a couple of weeks before the law should have its effect, he details to them their powers, duties, and responsibilities, on this wise:

"Herewith is furnished a copy of an Act entitled 'An Act for the Prevention of Intemperance, Pauperism, and Crime,' passed April 9th, 1855. I call your attention especially to the 1st, 7th, and 12th sections, which more directly refer to such duties as are imposed upon you by its provisions. The first section declares that intoxicating liquors, except as are hereinafter provided,

"Shall not be sold or *kept* for sale, or with *intent* to be sold, by any person, for himself or any other person, in any place whatsoever; nor shall it be given away, (except as a medicine, by physicians pursuing the practice of medicine as a business, or for sacramental purposes,) nor be kept with intent to be given away in any place whatsoever, except in a dwelling-house in which, or in any part of which, no tavern, store, grocery, shop, boarding or victualling house, or room for gambling, dancing, or other public amusement or recreation of any kind is kept; nor shall it be kept or deposited in any place whatsoever, except in such dwelling-house, as above described, or in a church, or place of worship, for sacramental purposes, or in a place where either some chemical, mechanical, or medicinal art, requiring the use of liquor, is carried on as a regular branch of business; or while in actual transportation from one place to another, or stored in a warehouse prior to its reaching the place of its destination. This section shall not apply to liquor, the right to sell which in this State is given by any law or treaty of the United States."

The seventh section declares the duty of the officer after the seizure of the liquor, pursuant to the twelfth section, with reference to giving notice to the owner, etc., etc. The twelfth section declares that

> "It shall be the duty of every sheriff, under-sheriff, deputy-sheriff, constable, marshal, or policeman, to serve all processes to be issued by virtue of this act, to arrest any person whom he shall *see* actually engaged in the commission of any offense in violation of the first section of this act, and to seize all liquors kept in violation of said section, at the time and place of the commission of such offense, together with the vessels in which the same is contained, and forthwith to convey such person before any magistrate of the same city or town, to be dealt with according to law, and to store the liquor and vessels so seized in some convenient place, to be disposed of as hereinafter provided. It shall be the duty of every officer, by whom any arrest and seizure shall be made under this section, to make complaint, on oath, against the person or persons arrested, and to prosecute such complaint to judgment and execution. It shall be the duty of every such officer, whenever he shall see any intoxicated person in any store, hotel, street, alley, highway or place, or disturbing the public peace and quiet, to apprehend such person, and take him before some magistrate, and if said magistrate shall, after due examination, deem him too much intoxicated to be examined, or to answer upon oath correctly, he shall direct said officer to keep him in some jail, lock-up, or other safe and convenient place, to be designated by said magistrate until he shall become sober, and thereupon forthwith to take him before said magistrate, or if he can not be found, before some other magistrate."

Now, whilst it is clearly obligatory upon you to enforce all laws passed by the Legislature, which impose duties on your office, and to assume them valid until decided otherwise by the courts, yet, as your commanding officer, and responsible for your acts, if pursuant to orders, I feel it incumbent upon me to state, what is the interpretation to be put upon this law, so far as it imposes any duties upon you, and what are the limits of your powers under it.

You will not be authorized to seize any foreign liquors, or in arresting for the sale of the same, except upon warrant issued by a competent magistrate upon testimony other than your own. Whether liquors exhibited in your presence, either for sale or otherwise, are intoxicating liquors, (as designated in section 22,) or of foreign manufacture or not, you must judge with great circumspection, and be careful to avoid seizing any thus exempt.

An error in this regard may lay you liable to severe personal responsibility, inasmuch as you are hereby expressly enjoined to seize no such liquors.

Your principal duties arise under the 12th section. The duties under other sections are merely to serve processes of magistrates. The 12th section requires you,

First, To arrest any person *seen* in the violation of the 1st section.

Second, To seize all liquors *kept* in violation of the 1st section, at the time and place of the commission of the offense.

Third, When an arrest or seizure is made, to make a complaint before a proper magistrate under the Act.

Fourth, To arrest any intoxicated person, in a store, hotel, public place, or disturbing the peace, and take him before a magistrate.

The first and second items thus referred to in this section are of vital importance, and require to be executed with great judgment. They require the *arrest* of persons and the *seizure* of property, in the *visible* violation of the Act. You will therefore be careful that when an arrest or seizure is to be made *on view*—that is, merely as the result of your own observation—that it must be such a violation as *the eye itself can fully disclose*, and can not embrace offenses, where the whole of the offense does not fall under your own eye: as thus, a sale of liquor in your presence not in any of the excepted places, or by one of the licensed persons, and not dutiable, is an absolute violation of the law, calling for arrest of the person, seizure of the liquor and complaint to the magistrate. But *keeping* with *intent to sell* or give away, is not an offense fully within the scope of the eye; the keeping is, but the *intent* is a matter of which the eye alone is not, and can not be a sufficient judge. You can not *see* the violation of this clause, for an intent can not be *seen;* it is only to be made out from many circumstances which are to prove it to the judgment, and not to the sight. These violations, therefore, do not come within this section, (12th,) so as to compel you to arrest or seize without complaints.

As to the third item, it is consequent upon the first and second. It is important to be followed up; because the conviction under the complaint is essential for your own protection.

The fourth item, as to the arrest of intoxicated persons, etc., is already required of you by the laws and the rules and regulations of the Police Department, as far as the streets are concerned.

I can not too seriously impress upon you the discreet exercise of your duties, under this law. The power of seizing property at will, and arresting persons by no other authority than your own volition, is one which has heretofore never been conferred on police officers, and should be carefully guarded, so as to avoid oppression of the citizen.

It is one of the dearest rights of American citizens to be secure in person and property. Neither should be touched, without the strongest and most conclusive proof that the act is fully warranted: and in the exercise of this important discretion, too much caution and judgment can not be adopted. I shall hold you to severe accountability, and trust that while the law is faithfully executed, sustained, and carried out on the one hand, no oppressive acts on the other will be perpetrated against the rights of the citizen, in the performance of the duties which are thus devolved upon you."

So that matter is ended, and the "Act for the Prevention of Intemperance, Pauperism, and Crime," passed by the inspired men convened at Albany, now obtains in the city of New-York all the respectful obedience to which perhaps it was entitled. It is, however, a subject of sincere regret with Mayor Wood that all his well-directed and successful efforts to close the liquor-shops on the Sabbath day have been paralyzed and destroyed by the construction which his official legal advisers have put upon this law.

Previous to its operation, he had entirely succeeded in that wonderful work with the laws as they then stood, but as this act repealed all former acts relating to liquor, (including those forbidding the sale of liquor on

Sunday) he had no law by which to punish for the sale on that day, and consequently could not enforce obedience. Persons who either do not understand the subject, or will not, have essayed censure upon the authorities, because Sunday dram-drinking is not suppressed as before the law was changed. The evil is not chargeable to Mayor Wood. It is to the law, or the want of law; or it may be the erroneous impressions of it by those who are placed by him as expounders of it. *He* has done *his* whole duty in the premises, and challenges criticism upon his course without any fear of the result.

CHAPTER XV.

ABOUT EMIGRANTS.

SINCE the establishment of the United States, as a nation, the vast extent of territory ruled over by that government has served as a home and place of refuge for the oppressed, the poor, the Europeans with republican tendencies and the political exile of every grade. These were welcomed kindly, particularly in New-York, where hospitals and alms-houses, and emigrant societies exist to an immense extent and where a fabulous amount of money is expended for the amelioration of the condition of these poor people.

But when the Powers on the other side, observed that their poor and suffering were so well received in this city, they conceived the idea of making it a sort of Cave of Adullum or New Rome, whither all their outlaws, felons, rogues and diseased beggars might be sent for *their* country's good.

Now this idea was put into execution, and we soon had a foreign population of a nature which would induce a thoughtful man to vote *against* the abolition of capital punishment. Well, our worthy rulers dozed and grunted over this sorrow, and the sorrow waxed. Then

Mr. Wood being called to the chair of the Mayoralty, and keeping his weather-eye open, as is his custom, at last spied an opportunty to attempt a reform of this evil.

He first endeavored to interest the general government, whose natural business it was, in the matter, and with that intention, addressed the following letter to President Pierce:

MAYOR'S OFFICE, NEW-YORK, *January* 2, 1855.

HIS EXCELLENCY FRANKLIN PIERCE,
President of the United States.

DEAR SIR: There can be no doubt that, for many years, this port has been a sort of penal colony for felons and paupers, by the local authorities of several of the continental European nations. The desperate character of a portion of the people arriving here from those countries, together with the increase of crime and misery among that class of our population, with other facts before us, prove conclusively, that such is the case.

It is unnecessary to refer to the gross wrong thus perpetrated upon this city. It requires from me no allusion to the jeopardy of our lives and property from this cause. Men who, by a long career of crime and destitution have learned to recognize no laws, either civil or natural, can not fail to produce feelings of terror at their approach.

The inherent right of every community to protect itself from dangers arising from such emigration, can not be questioned. New-York has submitted to it long enough. The disease and pauperism arriving here almost daily from abroad, is of itself a sufficient evil; but when to it is added crime, we must be permitted to remonstrate. We ask the interference of the general government; as it is its duty to protect us from foreign aggression, with ball and cannon, so it is its duty to protect us against an enemy more insidious and destructive, though coming in another form.

I call your attention to this subject, hoping it will receive from you that action which its very great importance to the whole country demands. I am very truly yours, etc.,

FERNANDO WOOD, *Mayor.*

This letter producing no effect upon the elevated official to whom it was addressed, the Mayor wrote upon the 26th of February, to a Member of Congress from New-York, Hon. John Wheeler. This letter exhibits an intimate knowledge of the abominable system of the Swiss republic with regard to their paupers; from which country and Germany there came to this port last year 186,000 immigrants, of whom many were transferred directly from the ship to the Alms-House. Mr. Wood shows the exceeding peril of all this, and proves the necessity for national legislation to prevent it:

DEAR SIR: In reply to your inquiries respecting the Belgians lately in confinement in this city, I have the honor to advise, that they are now at liberty, and beyond the control of the authorities, except so far as they may become amenable to our laws hereafter. Judge Roosevelt of the Supreme Court released them on the 24th instant, and they are now at large, whether for weal or woe remains to be seen.

I *resisted* this proceeding, and hence am conscious of having discharged my duty. However much crime or destitution may be increased among us in consequence, *I shall feel no self-reproach.* I can not nevertheless but express regret that they should have been released so summarily at this time. I never counseled their detention in prison, but advised that they should be returned to Antwerp, and but for this application to the Courts, they would have now been on their way thither. Their discharge in this manner will, I fear, nullify my efforts to prevent the immigration of criminals and paupers into this country. It appears to establish the fact, that the courts defend their introduction. Any action of the municipal authorities hereafter to counteract this, will be looked upon as illegal, and will be entirely futile. *An order that they shall not land will be met by smuggling them on shore, when if arrested and imprisoned, a writ of habeas corpus sets them at liberty* to depredate upon our lives and property.

It may not be known to you, that very extensive preparations are now being made in Germany and Belgium and other nations of Europe, for further exportation of the same class of people.

In Switzerland, the preparatory movements have been so extensive, that the cantonal governments are now legislating as to the cheapest and best mode of getting them away.

A singular fact, in connection with the public property of the towns and villages of Switzerland adds an additional inducement to the banishment of their paupers and criminals. The lands and forests belong to the commune, and in many instances would amount in value to 500 to 700 francs per individual. The local authorities therefore have a double object in getting rid of the poor. The expense of their support and the evils of their crime are not only removed for ever, but the proprietory interest of those remaining is increased by getting rid of so large a portion of the population. Official statements show that in some of the districts one sixth of the population subsists by public alms.

The principles of self-preservation from the evils of criminal and pauper immigration recommended by me are fully understood in Switzerland. These villages and communes are far more jealous of their own local interest, even against each other, than we have shown ourselves against foreign nations.

A pauper resident in one canton is not permitted to become a resident of another canton. Every one visiting into another canton, even under a plea of looking for work, is closely watched, and the passports and papers with which they must always be provided, closely examined. The same, and even to a greater extent, is the case in Germany. None dare venture into a neighboring State, without a passport and other requisite papers, and if he is found to be destitute, (for on the borders of a country one must show a certain sum of money,) he is immediately ordered back, and if necessary, transferred forcibly back by the police, fearful that by entering he will become a public charge.

This appears to be the domestic policy of those countries towards each other, but who, however, have no compunctions of conscience or regard for our rights, in transferring these outcasts to our care. However contending with each other as to the care of these unfortunates, they appear to make common cause in saddling them upon us. Therefore, in not receiving them, and in forcibly sending them back, we but follow the policy of the countries from whence they came. I regret we have not in this instance followed so good an example. The inherent right of every community to protect itself from the ingress of dangerous persons, can not be questioned. "Self-preservation is the first law of nature." Why is it that quarantine regulations are adopted, but to prevent the introduction of contagion into cities? And if it is right to exclude contagion, why is it not right to exclude what is equally fatal and destructive? Do we protect ourselves from this evil? Does this decision protect us from it? Are not the efforts of the city authorities worthy of some support from the courts in a matter of such paramount importance to the people of this city? The late Grand-Jury of this city say in their presentment: "In connection with the subject, the Grand-Jury would call the public attention to the sources of our crime and pauperism. They found that in the institutions visited by them, fully three fourths of the inmates were of foreign birth. While the city must maintain those now upon its hands, it is no part of its duty to bear the burden of the crime, lunacy, and pauperism of foreign countries. If we had to maintain only that which originates among us, the burden would be comparatively light. While we would extend welcome and encouragement to the industrious and well-disposed emigrant from every country, we should, so far as possible, prevent the entrance among us of those who must become a public charge."

The number of alien passengers who arrived at this port last year was 319,223, of which 185,869 were from Germany and Switzerland.

My observation and experience within the past three months have forced me to the conclusion, that it is in a portion of the emigration from these countries that our institutions are to receive their greatest shock, our morality the severest taints, and our local taxation its largest addition.

I do not wish to be understood as asserting that this emigration is detrimental as a whole. Among them are many honest, industrious, and thrifty people, whose presence here may be called a blessing to the country; but it is to that portion that I allude who, like the Belgians, have been sent out of their own country as either paupers or criminals.

If nearly two hundred thousand found their way here in 1854, (many being transferred directly from the ship to the Alms-House,) when it was a doubtful question whether our authorities had not the power to expel or imprison them, how many may we not look for, when it is known abroad that a simple application of a writ of habeas corpus will place them at large, in defiance of all municipal regulations?

The process of filling our prisons and alms-houses has now become simplified. The foreign government who desires to rid itself of this burden, has but to instruct its minister or consul to engage the services of some attorney at the port in this country where it is to be sent, and a writ is taken out, and "the deed is done."

In view of these facts, I need not add, that legislation is demanded without delay to put a stop to it. I hope Congress will do something for us. The country can be served in no better or more effectual manner, as far as it respects the welfare of the people.

Very respectfully yours,

FERNANDO WOOD, *Mayor.*

Fears were then entertained by some of the foreign governments that emigration itself was to be opposed here, and Mr. Fay, Chargé d'Affaires at Berne, wrote to the Mayor. His answer, which follows, succinctly and clearly shows the exact position of this country towards the emigrant, and sets forth clearly the real evils complained of, and the duty of the general government to cure them.

NEW-YORK, *May* 8, 1855.

SIR: I am in receipt of a letter from you without date, received per the last European mail. I had before been advised of the desire manifested by you, to protect this country from the evil, and our naturalized citizens from the odium, of the immigration to our shores of certain classes who are detrimental to the morals and well-being of our people.

The authorities, and particularly our foreign population from the German States, should thank you, for your exertions to this end, so far as your influence upon the government of Switzerland is concerned, and that government has commended itself to our good opinion, by its promptness in complying with your request.

In reply to what is stated in your letter now before me, relating to the reception of emigrants, and asking "due forbearance with regard to too sudden application of severe rules, and that such regulations, when suddenly adopted, may not be put in force against Swiss citizens without timely notice," I have the honor to say, that, so far as is known to me, there is no disposition in this country to resort to injurious or oppressive measures against the Swiss, or any other emigrant. No change is contemplated, except it be for the better protection of his interests or welfare. And if no change is made by the authorities to his disadvantage, you will agree with me, that every right or favor which hospitality or humanity can dictate is well secured to him.

Indeed, our own native citizens, when reaching this city from distant sections of the Union, do not receive the kindly aid which is constantly and diligently exercised for the foreign emigrant. A large number of our City Police, at great expense, have been detailed especially for their protection, without the treasury deriving one dollar in return from any quarter whatever. The State has organized a Board of Commissioners, whose exclusive duty it is to look after his welfare, without any pecuniary consideration to the gentlemen comprising it. Numerous private and public institutions not only watch over and shield them, but provide employment and information, with no other reward than what philanthropy furnishes; and no inconsiderable portion of my own time is devoted to the same objects. No country has thrown around the exile the same safeguards, or offered to him the same advantages.

As the United States is the most favored nation, so has the foreign emigrant become its most favored people. And, so far as his reception and protection when arriving here are concerned, I apprehend there is no disposition to alter this course towards him. It is proper, however, to add, that whilst this is our policy generally, we are not indifferent to the conduct of those governments, who, in defiance of all principles of courtesy and gratitude, force upon us their *convicts* and *paupers.* This we condemn and denounce, and at this port shall not be longer tolerated. If outcasts from their own countries, disqualified either by crime, disease, or destitution, from the rights of citizenship there, we do not want them here. If unfit for the less enlightened and intelligent countries of Continental Europe, they are unworthy of our reception. If too degraded for European morality, they have sunk too low for American association. It is not against the honest and industrious stranger, who voluntarily seeks our land as a refuge from oppression, or as developing better rewards for his industry, that we feel repugnance; but it is to the depraved, the vicious, the indolent, and the diseased mendicant, who, from a policy as inhuman as it is narrow-minded and selfish, are driven in upon us, through motives of mistaken political economy.

It is this practice, which, if continued, will lead not only to the stringent measures you fear, but to more serious results. It will become a source of national difficulty. In my opinion, the central government at Washington must take more emphatic cognizance of the subject. No government can long resist the public sentiment now forming antagonistic to it. It is at Washington that the States have centred the control of their foreign interests; and it is there that the people naturally look for relief from foreign aggression. Nor does it, in my judgment, call even for congressional action. The Executive, it appears to me, has ample power to reach the evil. A decided remonstrance, clothed in language which could not be misunderstood, would command respect, and accomplish its abolition. The moral power of this nation, if energetically and determinedly exercised, can not be disregarded. If in my humble sphere, confined to the narrow limits of a municipal office, restricted and hampered by charters and laws, and deprived of any real control over the matter, I have been enabled to check in any degree the sending of these people here, to how much greater extent it could have been accomplished, provided a similar policy had been adopted by those possessing actual power over our foreign relations.

The disregard of a diplomatic technicality, or the unhappy turning of a period in diplomatic correspondence, is often made the grounds of complaint, and sometimes produces war. How then should it be, when suffering under the infliction of a positive wrong, so injurious to our national welfare, and so insulting to our national pride?

I am glad that the government of Switzerland evinces so considerate a feeling and high sense of honor on this question, and it can rest assured it will not be disadvantageous to its citizens, when reaching this hospitable but much-abused city.

I have the honor to be, with much consideration, your fellow-citizen,

FERNANDO WOOD.

The Belgian and Sardinian governments having on hand a number of convicted felons and incurable paupers, and not happening to be in immediate need of them, generously resolved to bestow them, for our education, upon us. Our Mayor, however, appears to have seen this proposed kindness in a different light from the amiable governments which originated it. He received the Belgians and put them into the city prison; as for the Sardinians, he stopped them out at sea. Then followed a hint to United States Consuls abroad to the following effect, "That an ounce of prevention is worth a pound of cure," and that if they would nip such emigrations in the bud, they would save the rulers here much trouble and the paternal governments over there the expense of the voyage.

The subjoined letters will show more distinctly the exact features of this case.

MAYOR'S OFFICE, NEW-YORK, *February* 14, 1855.

H. W. T. MALI, Esq., Belgian Consul, *New-York*.

AFTER mature deliberation and examination of the testimony taken before Justice Bogart, together with additional information from the American consul at Antwerp, just received, I am reluctantly forced to the conclusion, that the persons now in the city prison, who came as emigrant passengers by the ship Rochambeau, from Antwerp, are not of a character to be permitted to go at large in this city or in this country, and while we can not set them at liberty, we can not longer retain them in custody. Some measures must be adopted at once, to relieve the city from the expense of providing for them, and at the same time to secure us from the danger of their presence abroad in the country. Therefore as it is beyond question, from the evidence before me, and which is open to your examination, that they were embarked at Antwerp by the order and at the expense of the Belgian local authorities, I suggest that they be returned to their own country at the cost of the Belgian government, whose agent you are in this city. I see no other recourse. Humanity and justice require, that they should no longer be retained in prison in this city, where they have committed no offense; and self-preservation requires that we should prevent them being set at liberty here, with a belief that their presence would be dangerous to our property.

From your high character in this city, and knowledge and appreciation of our institutions, I am confident you will comprehend the necessity which forces me to take this position, and promptly respond to the request that these people be reëmbarked for Antwerp without delay.

I am with great respect your obedient servant,

FERNANDO WOOD, *Mayor*.

P. S.—The ship Henry Read, which arrived at this port from Antwerp, 10th instant, had on board six or eight of the same class of emigrants, sent by the Belgian authorities, under the same circumstances as those now referred to per Rochambeau; but my information of the fact, which is official, did not reach me until the 13th instant, when too late to take action, and they are now in our midst to add to the crime and destitution which surround me on all sides. F. W.

MAYOR'S OFFICE, NEW-YORK, *January* 26, 1855.

C. FABBRICOTTI,

Vice-Consul of Sardinia.

SIR: On the 19th December last, the Sardinian frigate, Des Geneys, commanded by the Chevalier Mantica, sailed from Genoa for this port, having on board over sixty persons intended to be landed on arrival, who are represented by competent authority through our Department of State at Washington to have been objectionable or dangerous citizens, some of whom had been in prison in Turin and elsewhere. There is no doubt that the emigrants alluded to are intended to be cast upon our shores like others have been under similar circumstances, to find their way into our prisons or alms-houses, to become a burden or a pest upon this hospitable but much-abused land. It is my duty as the chief-magistrate of this city to inform you, the representative of the Sardinian government here, that if the representations in this case are true, these outcasts from your country shall not be permitted a landing at this port. And it is the object of this letter to advise you, as you will probably have immediate communication with the commander of the frigate, that I propose to institute a rigid inquiry on board of the vessel as to the past life and present circumstances and condition of each of these persons before they can come on shore, and all who had been convicts or paupers, whom it is reasonable to suppose will be dangerous citizens, will be excluded entirely, and for the remainder bonds must be given that they will not become a charge upon this country.

Upon the arrival of the Des Geneys, I shall be pleased to confer with you or the commander, as to the mode of conducting the proposed examination. Very respectfully yours,

(Signed,) FERNANDO WOOD, *Mayor*.

CIRCULAR FORWARDED TO UNITED STATES CONSULS IN EUROPE.

MAYOR'S OFFICE, NEW-YORK, *April* 12, 1855.

SIR: It has long been the practice of many of the local authorities of several of the continental European nations, not only to encourage the emigration to this country of their indigent and destitute, but to send here, at their own expense, paupers and convicts.

This city has been made the great *entrepot* for the delivery of these outcasts and banished mendicants. The authorities here have determined to submit to this no longer, and are resolved to use every means at their command to prevent it entirely, if possible.

There is no doubt that Congress will at its next session adopt some preventives which will prove perfectly effectual to this end. Until then, however, we must guard against it as best we may.

You will confer a great favor upon this city and upon the country you represent by aiding us. This can be done by promptly communicating to me all the information in your possession at any time, relative to the intention of the authorities of the city to which you are accredited as consul, or any other which you may have reason to think intend to send this class of people to this country.

Please furnish me the names and description of these persons, the vessel by which sent, the port of destination, and, if possible, evidence sufficient to fix the character of the emigrant.

In thus coöperating with the authorities of this city to prevent an evil which has afflicted us for many years, and which has heretofore been remonstrated against in vain, I am confident you will but second an earnest wish of the general government at Washington.

Very respectfully yours,

FERNANDO WOOD, *Mayor*.

CHAPTER XVI.

REFORMS DEMANDED — DIFFICULTIES IN THE MAYOR'S WAY — REFORMS OBTAINED—DAY IN THE MAYOR'S OFFICE.

OUR task is nearly ended. We have shown in our chapter on the Mayoralty, page 156, what was the condition of the city when Fernando Wood was elected, over three other candidates, to its chief-magistracy. We have endeavored in our first chapter to show the radical causes of such a municipal condition, and the difficulties in the way of reform, and have now but to sum up the contents of this volume, add a few pages, and so lay down the pen.

On the first day of January, 1855, Mayor Wood took his first official survey of the city he had been called to govern. He found the public moneys shamefully wasted, broken contracts paid for, ordinances violated for bribes or favoritism. He found the streets of this great metropolis ill-paved, broken by carts and omnibuses into ruts and perilous gullies, obstructed by boxes and sign-boards, impassable by reason of thronging vehicles, and filled with filth and garbage, which was left where it had been thrown, to rot and send out its pestiferous fumes, breeding fever and cholera, and a host of diseases all over the city. He found hacks, carts, and omnibuses choking the thoroughfares, their Jehu drivers dashing through the crowd furiously, reckless of life; women and children were knocked down and trampled on, and the ruffians drove on uncaught; hackmen overcharged and were insolent to their passengers; baggage-smashers haunted the docks, tearing one's baggage about, stealing it sometimes, and demanding from timid women and stranger men unnumbered fees for doing mischief, or for doing nothing; emigrant runners, half-bull-dog and half-leech, burst in crowds upon the decks of arriving ships, carried off the poor foreign people, fleeced them, and set them adrift upon the town; rowdyism seemed to rule the city; it was at the risk of your life that you walked the streets late at night; the club, the knife, the slung-shot, and revolver were in constant activity; the Sunday low dram-shops polluted the Sabbath air, disturbed its sacred stillness, and in the afternoon and night sent forth their crowds of wretches infuriate with bad liquor, to howl out blasphemies, to fight, or to lie prone, swine-like, on the side-walks and in the gutters. Prostitution, grown bold by impunity, polluted the public highway, brazenly insolent to modesty and common decency; and idle policemen, undistinguished from other citizens, lounged about, gaped, gossipped, drank, and smoked, inactively useless upon street-corners and in porter-houses.

Mr. Wood had this complicated disease to cure.

Not an easy task; for were there not by charter *nine* different, independent, sovereign departments to rule the city? Yes; and to the legislative municipal powers he looked in vain for aid: they were too busy with their contracts, with their inquiries about the birth-place of city officers, with researches into matters of no consequence to the people, and they left the chief-magistrate's first prayer for help unnoticed on their table for *eight months.* Besides all this, his powers were undefined, he knew not what he was authorized to do; he must take the responsibility of assuming doubtful powers, if he were to purify this pestilential establishment. But, if he did not know his powers, his duties were carefully set before him. He is to do manifold labor besides this work of reform, for he is one of the highest criminal Magistrates in the city, the Chief of the Police Department, President of the Board of Supervisors, President of the Sinking Fund Commissioners, President of the Police Commissioners, President of the Leake & Watts' Orphan Asylum, *ex-officio* member of Commissioners of Emigration, President of the Board of Trustees of the Sailors' Snug Harbor, President of the Board of Health Commissioners, *ex-officio* Director of the New-York Juvenile Asylum, *ex-officio* member of the Board of Trustees of the Astor Library, and *ex-officio* Trustee of the Eastern Dispensary.

All this does not dismay him; he will fulfill punctually all the duties of these offices, and will do more—he will accomplish his work of reform and give good government to this city; if he can not get aid from the Common Council, then, with the help of God and his own determined will. So he established his Complaint-Book. Those thousand little iniquities practised upon the poor should also come up before him, and he would have justice done.

He began his work, and if he has not arrived at perfection, let us remember he has worked alone. But not before, in our time, have the streets been clean and unobstructed as now; the records of the Health Commissioners' office show an unexampled improvement in the sanitary condition of the city; the Complaint-Book has taught the hackman to be legal in his charges and civil to his passengers; the cartman and omnibus man have learned to stop racing, and to drive without running over pedestrians; he has placed policemen at the most frequented crossings, to stop from time to time the torrent of vehicles until the pedestrians gathered on the sidewalks can cross; he has smashed the baggage-smasher, and rescued the poor emigrant from the clutches of the brutal runner; he has seen the wronged sewing-woman and poor servant-girl righted; he has made at least the more frequented streets as safe by night as in the day-time; he closed the vile Sunday dram-shops till the Legislature at Albany took his power away, and threw them open again; and he has done all this by the help of the Police which he has re-created—of which he has made a splendid regiment of uniformed, disciplined, military, and useful men, his own glory and the pride of the city.

Nothing has been too small to attract his notice and action; nothing so great as not to claim his attention to the utmost limit of his power; he has shown that whenever a law exists it can be executed; he has proved that abuses can be reformed; he has convinced despairing New-Yorkers that their great and beautiful city can be well governed; he has taught the Common Council by stern, peremptory vetoes, that the public moneys shall not be wasted; and he has gained for himself the resolute good opinion, admiration, and lasting respect of the moral and religious world, of the truly temperate, of the protection-seeking owner of vast property, and of the poor man, whose interests he has so carefully considered. But he has mortally and, I trust, irremediably offended the professor of rowdyism, cheatery, and violence, as well as the ultra-fanatic and the small politician, who has been crazed and blinded by an unreasoning partisanship.

We will close this chapter with an extract from the New-York *Courier & Enquirer*, which gives an admirable idea of "A Day in the Mayor's Office:"

We saw the Mayor on the 5th day of February, 1855, in the City Hall, and we now give a faithful chronicle of all that there occurred during the regular hours of his sitting to listen to the complaints and petitions of citizens, and issue his orders for the government of the city.

Although quite early in the morning, and the Mayor had but just arrived, a crowd is waiting for him in the passage of the City Hall leading to the apartments allotted to his use. It is a motley crowd, mostly men, a few women, and representing fairly, in almost every grade, the varied population of the city. With a part of the crowd we enter, and are within what is called the Mayor's office. No grandeur meets the eye—nothing but two rooms, plain in architecture and furniture, but with lofty ceilings—the one large and spacious, the other half the size of the first—the greater part of the first railed off, leaving an open space on a line with the outer door—within the rail, full of desks and clerks—without the rail, the crowd seeking an interview with the Mayor. At the outer door, police officers with shining stars; at the door of the rail, more stars; and at the door of the smaller room, another star, to usher you into the municipal sanctum—clerks all polite and attentive, stars very benignant—all very orderly and noiseless in their movements, but brisk and prompt—a spirit, in fact, of orderly and noiseless energy in the outer room, marking a ruling spirit of the same character beyond in the inner chamber. Such are all the pomp and grandeur of the Mayor's office in its various appointments. But we are within the inner chamber, and in the presence of the Mayor.

A slight figure of a man with features pale but strongly marked, particularly about the mouth, on the compressed lips of which great firmness is legibly written, is seated in a plain oak chair, covered with green silk velvet, before an equally plain mahogany counting-house table.

Thus sat the Hon. Fernando Wood, Mayor of the City of New-York, President of the Board of Supervisors, President of the Board of Sinking-Fund Commissioners, President of the Board of Police Commissioners, President of the Leake & Watts' Orphan Asylum, *ex-officio* Member of the Board of Emigrant Commissioners, Member of the Board of Trustees of Sailors' Snug Harbor, Director of the New-York Juvenile Asylum, Member of the Board of Trustees of the Astor Library, in his chair of state, in the inner chamber of his office in the City Hall.

"Mr. H., I wish to know when the taxes on this property were paid, or whether they were paid at all. I wish to know all about it. Can you inform me?"

These words of the Mayor, in a business-like and yet polite tone, were addressed to a gentlemanly-looking little man, who, taking the slips of paper which the Mayor held out to him, answered in the same prompt manner in which he had been addressed, that he thought he could get the information of another official whom he named, and then disappeared.

At the same moment the police star shone at the door, and an elderly man, tall in person and dignified in appearance, was ushered in. He held in his hand a small bundle of slips of paper, the peculiar form of the printing and writing on which would strongly suggest to any one conversant with financial matters, the idea of bank-checks. And bank-checks they were, signed by one city official, and wanting only the signature of another to raise their real value to that represented by the figures on their faces. The signature wanting was the Mayor's. He took them from the hand of the elderly man, but he did not take it for granted that they were all right, and place his signature upon them as if it was a matter of mere form. He examined them carefully one by one, and after a few questions, satisfied that all was correct, placed his name upon them. The checks were connected with the payment of street commissioners, which led to a brief conversation on the street department of the city government generally, in which the Mayor spoke openly of the crying abuses in that department, in the way of the sinecures enjoyed by many street-inspectors, and the loose manner in which it was customary to pay street commissioners before the work was done. He expressed his determination to do all in his power to remedy the evil, and declared he would not sign any warrant for payment in certain cases, until every requirement of the law was complied with from the beginning to the end, no matter what had been the custom, and no matter what any other official or other branch of the city government said to the contrary. His tone was firm although pleasant, and the elderly gentleman with the checks, evidently thinking the Mayor was right and knew what he was about, departed.

The foot of the elderly gentleman had not yet crossed the threshold, when there was another entrance, and this time it was a captain of police. There was a complaint about the removal of some men detailed at his office, to duty in a different direction, and the Mayor said :

"Altogether too many detailed men, sir, about the Department, weakening the strength of the force that should be on active duty in the wards ; 170 men detailed about the courts, for instance, besides those detailed for private interests. I shall endeavor to remedy it. If railroads, or any other interests, want policemen for their special benefit, let them pay the city for it. I could throw $40,000 a year into the City Treasury by this means, whereas now the city loses by the operation of these private detailed policemen." And the Mayor, after saying more on this subject, arranged the matter in hand with the captain of police apparently to his satisfaction, and the latter also took his leave.

Two policemen now entered the room, and it was evident that something of an unusual occurrence was on hand. It was soon developed. A complaint had been made against the two policemen for an offense of a very aggravated character. The Mayor had sent for them, and they were now present.

"Tell your story, sir," said the Mayor; and the man told it in a straightforward manner. The Mayor looked keenly on him during the recital, and frequently interrupted him to put some searching questions.

"This case is one of the gravest importance," said the Mayor when the man had finished, "and shall be thoroughly investigated. I refer it over to the Commissioners of Police."

There was next ushered in an individual whose general appearance might be described as one of the "unwashed." On his hands and face, black seemed to be contending with flesh-color for the possession of the ground, and the contest was of such an equal nature as to leave the spectator in doubt as to which had the mastery. The glance of the man's eye, which shone out from the dirt of his thick, heavy features, was restless and uneasy, and fell beneath the gaze of the Mayor.

"Here again, sir," said the latter; "I thought I gave you sufficient warning. I am determined to put down all these junk-shops, which are nothing but the nurseries of young thieves. Mr. Ming!"

"Sure your Honor I kape a respictable shop," interrupted the man in a rapid voice; but the Mayor's hand had struck a small bell on the table before him, and Mr. Ming was in the room in an instant.

"Revoke that man's license!" said the Mayor; and at the same time a star shone at the side of him of the "unwashed," and the star lighted him from the presence of the Mayor.

"I come, Mr. Mayor, to complain of a den of thieves in —— street. It professes to be a public-house, and has, I am informed, a license; but it is the resort of burglars, and from it they issue on the roofs of the houses on the same block, and come down through the scuttles to rob them. One was robbed last night, and one a night or two ago."

Such was the address of a middle-aged gentleman to the Mayor, the moment the junk-shop delinquent had left. The Mayor touched the bell.

"Mr. Hinchman," said he, to the gentleman who answered the summons, "ascertain, if you please, if the house in —— street has a license, and in the mean time, send for the captain of the —— Ward Police. Have the goodness to wait a moment, Mr. ——;" and the complainant of the resort of thieves gave place to a short, thick-set man, with an immense pair of black whiskers, who, pulling a pawn-ticket from his pocket, said:

"I have been cheated, your Honor, by this pawnbroker;" and the man then told a long story about his pawning a cap for six shillings, and pawning other articles, and getting no ticket nor money for the cap. The Mayor listened attentively, took the ticket, looked at it, and then handed it over to one of his clerks, with the direction that he would inquire into the matter, as there must be some mistake about it, for the pawnbroker complained of was one of the most respectable of his class.

The next visitors to the Mayor, who were ushered into his presence, were two gentlemen, one of whom took from his pocket a formidable-looking document, and made known his business as follows:

"Mr. Mayor, I have been appointed an auctioneer, and my securities live in —— county, and are not here to justify. I wish for some advice how I shall proceed."

"Go by the law, my friend," answered the Mayor, pleasantly; "I can not help you in that particular; the law points out the course for you to pursue, and you have only to take legal advice and follow it;" and the newly-appointed auctioneer, with his friend, bowed and retired.

"Please, sir, I hire a house of Mr. —— for —— dollars. I pay him one month's advance—I can not pay him this month in advance, the times is hard—I agree to pay him in advance, but I can not pay him for this month until next month. But he says I must go out; what shall I do?"

Thus spoke, in a slightly foreign accent, a man dressed very plainly, and apparently belonging to the working classes. He had stood ready with a friend who accompanied him, to occupy the attention of the Mayor as soon as the auctioneer left. In order that the Mayor should not fail to be fully informed of all the particulars of the case, his friend repeated, with a few additions, the story of the rent, and then awaited an answer with eager looks.

"My friend," said the Mayor, "I can not help you; you must keep your contract, I see no other help for you."

The rent man, with a disappointed air, retired with his friend. He evidently had expected something like an order from the Mayor commanding the landlord to suffer him to remain in the house whether he paid or not.

At this moment, the captain of —— Ward Police, who had been sent for in reference to the house in —— street, where the thieves resorted, made his appearance before the Mayor.

"Do you know any thing of this house, and the character of its inmates?" said the Mayor.

"Yes, sir, I believe it has a license as a public house, but it has a bad character." A clerk here entered and informed the Mayor that the house was licensed.

"Revoke the license," said the Mayor to the clerk, "and you, Captain, will please to attend to this house at once. Send some one there immediately. I expect you will do what is necessary in the premises, and for the protection of that block of houses which seems now to be so exposed;" and thus the Mayor disposed of the "Resort of Thieves" in —— street for the present.

"Dis voman's huspan peen in jail 'leven day—no preat—no money —no noting—and have five leetle chiltren—speak no English, and vants her huspan pe let from ter jail."

These words were addressed to the Mayor by his next visitor, a short, fat German, coarsely clad, who held his hat respectfully in one hand, while with the other he motioned to a woman who accompanied him to step up nearer to the table, as if he wanted the Mayor to have a better view of her.

"And her hand is no goot," he continued, as the woman complied with his request and stepped up in fuller view of the Mayor.

A curious little figure was the poor German woman who came to beg her husband from the prison. Short and thick-set, as wide as she was long, and not much shape in breadth or width, repulsively plain in feature, and yet the repulsion softened by the tears which streamed down her eyes turned imploringly on the Mayor. One of her hands was bound up in a dirty cloth, and rested in a sling formed of a still dirtier handkerchief.

"What is her husband's name?" asked the Mayor.

"Conrad—and there ish another man vat has got a woman vat is in te jail too."

"Ah! I recollect—the bone-boilers in —— street, to whom I gave warning; well, I'll send for them, and see if they have had punishment enough;" and the Mayor touched his bell, and gave orders to have the men brought from the prison.

The German wife and her friend were then escorted by the star to the outer room, and an ex-Senator and a member of the Assembly of the State of New-York, were then introduced.

The ex-Senator called, he said, simply to pay his respects to the Mayor, and thank him for the manly and energetic manner in which he was enforcing the laws for the benefit of the city of New-York, and he was happy to pay his tribute of respect. The Assemblyman called also to pay his respects. A brief conversation followed, in which the Mayor said he was determined to enforce all the laws, and make New-York as distinguished for order as it has been for disorder. As for shutting up the liquor places on Sunday, he should pursue it to the very end of the law, make it a personal matter, if necessary, and indict every place disobeying, if he could not reach them in any other way. But he was happy to say that, in most instances, he had been successful, and most all had yielded. The Fourth and Sixth Wards gave him the most trouble, for their representatives in the Common Council would not coöperate with him. But he should go on to the end undeterred. Something was said concerning the change for the better which had taken place in the police since he came into power. The Mayor observed that he considered the police his right arm, but he must have control of them. A movement was now on foot in the Legislature to render him a blank either in their appointment or control, and if it should prevail, it would deprive him of one of his strongest aids to introduce and keep good order in the city. The movement is to have four Commissioners of Police elective by the people, making him the fifth Commissioner. The Mayor considers it an effort to palsy his arm of power, and that the practical workings of such a law would produce such a result.

The two bone-boilers now arrived in charge of policemen, and the visitors took their leave.

Shaggy and wild looked the two bone-boilers as they stood before the Mayor, twirling their caps, while meekly beside them stood the little, broad wife, with the tears rolling down her brown, coarse cheeks, and falling on the bound-up hand in the sling.

The Mayor touched his bell. "Call Mr. Semlar," he said, and Mr. Semlar, of the Emigrant Department of the Mayor's office, was before him almost instantly.

"Mr. Semlar, ask them if they have had enough of the prison."

Mr. Semlar put the question in German, and two hearty *yaws* were heard, which were only exceeded in emphatic accent by an energetic and rapid bobbing of two heads, which showed that the whole souls of the two bone-boilers were in the *yaws* and the bobs,

"Now ask them whether they will ever repeat the offense."

Two *neins*, and the shaking of two heads, characterized by the same heartiness and energy as the *yaws* and the bobbings, were the answer, and the broad, little wife, locked the only arm she had at command in that of her husband, and escorted him away in joy, followed by the other German whose wife had not honored the Mayor with her presence.

The next visitor was the Chief of Police. He came dressed in full police uniform, and after respectfully saluting the Mayor was seen in a deep consultation with him, which was conducted in a low tone, but with great earnestness on both sides. It had reference to the arrest of two prize-fighters, and the next day developed the evidence how watchful and prompt the Mayor had been in preventing a most disgraceful and brutal scene taking place in the neighborhood of New-York. The prize-fight between John Leese and Frank McIntyre, which was to come off that day at Parker's Island, in the East River, was effectually stopped, and Leese safely locked up in a prison.

A lady and two gentlemen entered immediately on the departure of the Chief.

"This lady has been most shamefully defrauded and robbed by those who pretended to be her friends," commenced one of the gentlemen, "but perhaps she had better tell the story herself."

The lady was on the point of speaking, when the Mayor waved his hand.

"With all respect," he said pleasantly, "I would suggest that the gentleman tell the story; you ladies, in such matters, are apt, sometimes, to go a good way around before you get at the point."

And the gentleman told the story. The lady's father was dead, and had left her heir to a gun, an invention of his own. It had eleven barrels, could be loaded at the breech, and would fire one hundred and twenty shots a minute. Two pretended friends had obtained from her possession of this gun, by false representations, and she came for redress. Such in brief was her story.

"Write out an affidavit, and bring it to me, properly executed, and I will order their arrest at once: the case seems an aggravated one," promptly said the Mayor; and the parties departed to follow his directions.

There were several other complaints made during the Mayor's sitting, but we have given the principal features of the day. Among the last persons who claimed the attention of his Honor, was a man bearing a beautiful white satin flag, with the arms of the city embroidered on it in blue and silver. It is a flag which he intends using in boarding, whenever he sees fit, vessels entering the harbor.

As the clock struck two, the Mayor ordered the doors to be closed, and of course we closed our "Day at the Mayor's Office."

CHAPTER XVII.

FERNANDO WOOD.

THE personal appearance of the Mayor of the city of New-York is considerably indicative of his character. He is about five feet eleven in height, spare, but wiry and strong in build, and very erect, rather military indeed, in carriage. The head, not large but distinctly characterized, shows strong will, perceptiveness, combination, and decision; the well-opened blue eye is calm, except for an occasional sparkle of fun; the forehead is rather high than broad, giving the imaginative qualities less room than the more purely rational ones. The mouth is straight and firm, and the lips apt to be compressed; and the under jaw, in which, with the mouth, the great character of the face lies, is massive and of iron strength; eloquent of will, energy, and great capacity of endurance.

His voice is kind and well-toned, but lacks all impulsive intonations—is rather a grave voice, denoting either lack of quick passions, or great and habitual control over them. His manner is suave and courteous; in business hours you are struck with the courtesy with which he gives you his closest attention, but when your business with him is over, he turns away at once and unaffectedly to other occupations. He does not bow when he speaks to you, but standing perfectly erect puts out his hand to you, looking fully though kindly into your eyes. While you are stating your case, he does not weigh the matter as you proceed, but is altogether absorbed in listening, and when you have finished speaking he keeps silence for a moment and then decides. To that decision, if you adduce no new contra-arguments, he remains inflexibly firm.

This physique and manner reveal his predominant moral qualities, which are, great self-command, physical and moral courage, quick appreciation and decision, prodigious energy, and a resolute unshakenness of will that nearly approaches to obstinacy. To relieve these sterner traits, he has an intense love for children and a quick and genial though not much practised sense of humor and relish of fun.

Politically, Mr. Wood is a Democrat. The struggle which has existed for years between the sections of that party in the State of New-York is well known. It is unnecessary to allude to the causes here. The antagonism has been violent, the acrimony bitter: it reached every member of the party who was forced to participate to some extent in the strife. No man of any consequence could avoid becoming embroiled in it. Mr. Wood had always been identified with the Democratic party, was its candidate for Congress in 1840, and for the Mayoralty in 1850. He did not, however, sympathize with the violent men of either of the contending factions; nor has he been identified with a clique nor known as a mere hanger-on to greater men. He has been the follower of no aspirant after the Presidency, but has contented himself by giving a consistent support to the regular nominees of his party, as they were duly put forth by the regular National Convention.

In 1848, he supported Lewis Cass as the Democratic candidate for President. But in the conflicts of his party he took little part, believing that so far as regards the principles for which this party was distinguished, there was no distinction nor division of opinion. He could not really be called "Hard" or "Soft," though a member of the latter organization and in full communion with it. The confidence which both sections placed in him was evinced upon the occasion of his last nomination for Mayor. Although each had a separate nominating convention, and though each held a hostile attitude towards the other, yet both concurred in nominating him their candidate without any effort or solicitation upon his part.

No greater mark of confidence could have been given, nor is there another man in the party who could have commanded it. It was a compliment to his personal character and eminent abilities rather than to his identity with the strifes of either faction, although no doubt, the leaders on both sides saw in his, an available name which they desired to secure to aid their candidates for other offices.

In national politics, Mr. Wood's opinions are purely republican, inclining more towards those of Washington as gathered from the writings of that great man, than towards those of any other statesman of this country. He is withal a strict Constitutionalist, believing in no latitudinarian experiments upon the meaning of the Constitution; and he would maintain with rigid firmness, the rights, prerogatives, and local political individualities of the States. He is thoroughly a State Rights man. On the old party issues, National Bank, Tariff, Distribution of the proceeds of sales of Public Lands, Sub-Treasury, etc., he has not changed his opinion, but still adheres to the position of the Democratic party in 1840. As for the Tariff, he not only looks on protection as unconstitutional but looks upon absolute free-trade as essential to the continued prosperity of the country; without it, indeed, he believes that the city of New-York can not continue her present advance towards greatness and power, while with it he believes that not the city only will prosper in a far greater progressive ratio than heretofore.

Therefore he would desire an immediate material reduction of the Tariff and a gradual abolition of it altogether. In foreign affairs he would not only maintain the Monroe doctrine of non-intervention, but would, without waiting for exchange of diplomatic courtesies, resent any affront to the flag or honor of his country. He would carry no grievance to the footstool of king or queen, but by a bold, instant, armed resentment, would let the demand for explanation come from the offended dignity of the other side. He could defend an act of reprisal better than he could ask from royalty reparation for an injury to American commerce or honor.

In the maintenance of a nation's interests, he can see no other principles of government than those acted upon by him in commanding the observance of municipal laws. In both is required the exercise of a firm power, a strong will, a manly spirit, and an invariable official fidelity.

The characteristics and principles of the Mayor, and the determined action which has been guided by him, have not been without their reward. There are those who still blame him for not doing what the Legislature has taken away his power to do; and for what the Common Council will not give him its necessary help in; but throughout the city and country we do not fear to believe that there is nowhere a more completely popular man. It is a mistake to judge of a man's popularity by what the noisy classes say; the deep heart of the people is still, impressions remain on it, judgment is not guided by partisan feeling, observation is unprejudiced, and therefore quiet and close. And such men and women have given their admiration and respect to Mr. Wood.

All classes, political, social, religious, moral, contribute to swell this host of his admirers. Municipal and other officers have come or sent from every part of the Union to ask the secret of his government and to imitate it, and his immense executive ability has been generally recognized.

Nay, even in Europe he is spoken of. Various Continental papers have contained eulogistic articles on the man who has done so much for New-York. A distinguished American artist, just returned from Rome, says, that Fernando Wood is become a household word in the mouths of the citizens of this country now living in the Eternal City. Ex-President Van Buren, in his late journey through the wild mountain region of Wales, was asked in a little wayside inn, by the landlord, particulars of the appearance and manner and peculiarities of the man whom they had learned to venerate.

In the Mayor's late journey westward through a portion of the State, this quiet popular feeling had an opportunity to evince itself. Mr. Wood was thoroughly worn out with the multitudinous duties of his office, and determined to seek repose for a few days at Saratoga, Lake George, etc. At the Springs, where throngs of people from every part of the United States were found, he was received with the utmost enthusiasm; public dinners were tendered to him, congratulations offered, and public thanks given for his great services in the cause of municipal reform.

On his road to Lake George, whither he went (by invitation from a committee of gentlemen from that region) partly in the cars and partly in a carriage, his progress was a sort of triumphal march. The people came out from their houses to cheer him, and at every little village he found a huzzaing crowd. At Fort Edward, Sandy Hill, Glen's Falls, and other towns, refreshments had been prepared, and the citizens were gathered to pay him their respects. His arrival at Lake George was announced by the roar of artillery, the waving of flags, and the peal of military music. A splendid dinner was prepared, and in the speeches made thereat he was greeted as a model magistrate, as a public reformer and benefactor. A ball and supper followed in the evening, when he spoke, in answer to a sentiment in his honor, of the "field of grounded arms," and of the many points of historical interest peculiar to that section of country.

These attentions continued during his stay, and followed him on his journey to Auburn and back to the city of New-York. From these exhibitions of respect, from the murmured or outspoken praises of his fellow-citizens, from the compliments of municipal authorities throughout the Union, and the commendations of the press from Maine to California, Mr. Wood's popularity may be reckoned as not inferior to that of any man in the country. All the way from far Iowa came a proposal to nominate him for the Presidency. The letter and its answer we will give here, without remark upon either.

DAVENPORT, *March* 10, 1855.

HON. FERNANDO WOOD, *New-York*:

It is, I think, quite apparent that at the next presidential election, the people of the United States will demand, as a condition precedent to their vote, that the candidate shall be a positive and not a negative character.

The old stock is gone. Especially in the Democratic party, is there no man of the ancient "regime" upon whom public attention is or can be fixed; the next President will, it seems to me, be a young man.

It is not at all probable that I am the first man to propose, or rather to suggest to you that, as a matter of fact, the *thing* which will be demanded is found in you.

The fact that a man is found capable of governing the city of New-York, is thought to be evidence that one can be found who will properly discharge the duties of President.

It is my opinion that the people want such a man as you; as one of them, I inquire whether to that end any thing has been done or can be, and whether it is best to take any steps, and when to place this matter before them, and to secure, if possible, a nomination (if that is best) by the party. Allow me to say, that I should be glad to aid in whatever way possible to secure so desirable a result.

You do not know me. Warren G. Brown, Esq., Wall street, does, and L. A. Fuller, Esq., Broadway.

If now, or at some future time, any steps shall be taken, I shall be glad to coöperate with your friends.

Yours with much respect,

GEO. S. C. DOW.

MAYOR'S OFFICE, NEW-YORK, *March* 17, 1855.

DEAR SIR: In reply to your kind letter of the 10th inst., I beg to assure you, that my aspirations have not been directed to any higher position than to discharge the duties of my present office in such a manner as to deserve and receive the applause of my fellow-citizens. If I can accomplish this, it will be all that is aimed at by me. Rest assured that at no time has a higher official position passed my thoughts, nor have my exertions in this office been dictated by any such motive. It is true, that I am not insensible to the fact that many friends desire my promotion; but if I entered into their views and feelings, it would detract materially from the independence of all personal considerations, which so far has alone enabled me to succeed. Besides, my dear sir, what more exalted station can any man reach than the almost universal approbation of the people of a city like New-York? Fully appreciating your kind partiality, and assuring you in all sincerity that I know of no organized intent among my friends with reference to the use of my name for the station to which you allude, I am very truly yours,

FERNANDO WOOD.

GEO. S. C. DOW, Davenport, Iowa.

And now our task is done. During the course of the printing and publication of this volume, many new illustrations of the Mayor's character will of necessity be made public. This work is thought to be up to this date as nearly perfect as possible. For the present writer, he has no further observation to make. Let the reader judge of the subject of this biography, of his merits, his aspirations, and his future career.

APPENDIX.

LETTERS AND MESSAGES.

VERY much of the peculiar character of Mr. Wood may be learned from the veto messages. There is a singular distinctness of vision about the man; and a great directness in going to his point. What he has to say is clearly settled in his own mind, and then outspoken with such simple precision that he who runs may read.

Another lesson is to be learned here; to wit, that a veto power in this good city of New-York, can in no wise safely be dispensed with.

MAYOR'S OFFICE, NEW-YORK, *March* 23, 1855.

To the Honorable the Board of Councilmen:

GENTLEMEN: The Board of Councilmen passed, April 3, 1853, a resolution, memorializing the Legislature to curtail the dimensions of the proposed Central Park. This resolution was introduced by a lengthy report, from the then Committee on Lands and Places, the statements and arguments of which, no doubt, influenced its passage. The subject remained without further action during the whole of the term of the late Common Council, and until the 15th March, instant, when the Board of Aldermen, without awaiting your decision on the same subject, now under deliberation, passed the proposition of the Councilmen of last year.

This resolution has been laid before me for my approval, which, after deliberation, and a careful examination of the facts and arguments set forth in the report, I find it impossible to give, consistent with my own convictions of duty.

Though it proposes only to take from the Central Park a portion of the area agreed upon, still it will be, in effect, a blow at the whole.

Any proposition having for its aim an interference with the work as originally devised, and which will encourage delay, and retard the proceedings of the commission, already too long protracted, will, in my opinion, jeopard the success of the most intelligent, philanthropic, and patriotic public enterprise, which has been undertaken by the people of this city since the introduction of the waters of the Croton river.

I had supposed that the necessity for defending the Central Park had ceased; that the opposition before raised had subsided, and that time and reflection had enabled all to appreciate its advantages, not only to the present, but to all succeeding generations. In my second message to the Common Council, of January 11th last, in alluding to the subject, I say: "There can be no doubt as to the necessity of some such park, conveniently located on this island.

In my opinion, future generations who are to pay the expense, will have good reasons for reflecting upon us, if we permitted the entire island to be taken possession of by population, without some spot like this, devoted to rural beauty, healthful recreation, and pure atmosphere."

These views have been confirmed by subsequent observation. The opportunities which the duties of my office give for a survey of this great city, its vast financial, commercial, and manufacturing advantages, the inherent seeds it contains of a growth far beyond the comprehension of the most visionary enthusiast, all force upon me the necessity of some such reservation.

We will be derelict, if by any narrow or selfish feeling of present saving, we deprive the teeming millions yet to inhabit and toil upon this island, of one place not given up to mammon, where they can, even if but one day in the year, observe and worship nature, untarnished by conflict with art. To admit the necessity of a great park, and to assert that this will be too large, is, in my opinion, an exceedingly limited view of the question, and entirely unworthy of even the present position of this metropolis, to say nothing of a destiny now opening so brilliantly before us.

Let us not follow our Dutch ancestors in their views of municipal prudence, who considered cow-paths as proper sites for streets and avenues, inasmuch as they saved the necessary expenses of surveys, etc. To have suggested to the original Knickerbockers the propriety of laying out and regulating wide and evenly-graded streets, commensurate to the wants of the city as it now is, would have been met by the wise fathers of that day, with arguments derived from the same principles and views as are now used with reference to this subject, by its opponents.

Let New-York follow up the noble spirit asserted so boldly in the introduction of the Croton water. The aforethought and comprehensive policy embodied in that masterly proposition, is now universally respected and admired, as will be, at no distant day, that to open Central Park. Being imbued with these sentiments, I can never give my consent to any measure which will throw an obstacle in its way, much less to abolish or curtail it.

But admitting the park too large, and that it should be diminished, this resolution proposes to do it in an improper manner, inasmuch as it asks that the only portion of it that can be accessible to the foot-passenger now shall be lopped off, and, in fact, remove it nearly a mile further off from the present densely-populated part of the city. This resolution asks, that instead of Fifty-ninth street, Seventy-second street shall be the lower boundary, or, in other words, that the park shall be removed thirteen blocks further into the interior, and, at present, almost uninhabited part of the island. If there is to be a curtailment, let it be rather from the other end. Instead of lopping off the lower and most accessible part, take it from the upper portion.

Besides these objections, there are others entitled to weight. Many lots, comprehended within the part to be cut off, were purchased of the Corporation, under its sales, at auction, anterior to the passage of the act for this park. These have been relinquished to the city, the purchase-money repaid to the buyers, by order of the Common Council. And again, owners of lots within the area proposed to be taken, would, in my opinion, have just claim against the city, for any damages that they may have suffered, in consequence of closing to them all opportunities for improvements, enjoyment, or favorable sales, by the existing act, to take possession of their lots for public purposes. The damages arising from the passage of this resolution, may amount to nearly as much as the expense to the city of the land to be taken by it.

Inasmuch as the action of the Board of Aldermen was based upon the report referred to, without any report of their own Committee, it may not be improper for me to correct some of its errors of facts; I am the more induced to this, as it is evident that the public have been misled by this report. It states that the area of the park, excluding the State Arsenal and the Reservoir, will be 750 acres, that the number of building-lots comprehended will be 13,521, and that the total cost can not be less than fifteen millions of dollars. These statements are erroneous, as will be shown by the following extracts from my message, before referred to, which contains reliable and authentic data and information upon these points.

"It will be remembered that this park is to be bounded south by Fifty-ninth street; north, by One Hundred and Sixth street; east, by the Fifth avenue; and west, by the Eighth avenue, and will comprehend an area of seven hundred and seventy-six acres, say, 776

From which deduct		State Arsenal, say, ...	14	
"	"	Croton Reservoir,................	38	
"	"	Proposed "	112	
"	"	Streets and avenues,..............	190	
"	"	belonging to the city,............	34	—388
Leaving to be paid for, acres,.................				388

Which, by estimating at sixteen lots per acre, makes six thousand two hundred and eight lots to be paid for by the city, and by assessments upon contiguous property. The important question of the valuation of these lots has not as yet been positively fixed by the Commissioners. The subject is now before them, and I advise all who are interested to appear at their office. Another question of much public interest, in connection with this matter, is the territorial limit to which the Commissioners shall extend their assessments upon property of individuals, and what proportion of the whole cost shall be made a tax upon the city."

"These questions are entirely under the control of the Commissioners. I am informed, unofficially, that the disposition of the Board is to extend the area of assessment three blocks east and west, and a greater distance north and south, and to make two thirds of the whole cost payable by the city. If this be the determination, it can be easily ascertained about what sum the park will cost. Estimating the average value of the land at five hundred dollars per lot, a liberal estimate, the whole cost would be three millions one hundred and four thousand dollars; deduct one third to be paid by individuals whose property is supposed to be benefited, it will leave two millions sixty-nine thousand dollars to be paid for by the city."

Much surprise is manifested at the apparent delay of the Commissioners. I am without any official information as to their proceedings. The whole scope of their duties appears to me to be very simple, and easily accomplished. I do not see any reason why they should consume so long a time, As far as my inquiry has extended, I have been unable to discover, in any quarter, information of what has been done, or is being done by them, beyond what is contained in this extract from my message of January 11.

The Council to the Corporation has volunteered his services to the Board without compensation, and has, with commendable liberality, furnished gratuitously much valuable information, tending to facilitate the work and give the people speedy possession of its promised advantages. Had all interested evinced as much enthusiasm in its favor, I am quite certain many hundred workmen and laborers would now be employed towards its completion.

For these reasons, herein briefly and imperfectly set forth, I can not sign this resolution; it appears to me to have been passed under a misapprehension of the facts.

With respect for the opinion of others who differ from me, and with a repugnance to the position of apparent hostility to the action of the Common Council, which my duty forces upon me, I beg leave to return the resolution to decrease the size of Central Park, without my approval. Very respectfully,

FERNANDO WOOD, *Mayor*.

STATEN ISLAND FERRY LEASE.

MAYOR'S OFFICE, NEW-YORK, *May* 18, 1855.

To the Honorable the Board of Councilmen:

GENTLEMEN: A resolution defining the conditions upon which the Staten-Island Ferry should be leased, passed the Board of Aldermen on the evening of the 11th inst. It came to me on the afternoon of Saturday, 12th inst., and was taken up for examination on the 14th inst. The sale of the ferries, including the Staten-Island Ferry, had been fixed, by a previous resolution of the Common Council, for the 15th inst., thus leaving me too short a time to examine a subject of so much importance. I found it impossible to approve it in time for the sale of that date, consistent with several objections, which presented themselves on the first reading of the document. Subsequent examination of it has fully satisfied me that this resolution, if adopted, would have resulted in loss to the city, in consequence of its effect in excluding bidders at the sale.

By its terms the lessees were *compelled* to run boats to the Quarantine Dock and to Stapleton, though these points are exclusively the property of individuals, who could or could not, at their own option, permit the privilege, there being no power in the Common Council, or the lessees, to prevent.

Another and a more serious objection, was the privilege proposed to be given of using and occupying the water on the westerly side of the pier lying west of pier No. 1, East River, and running ferry-boats to and from the same, as aforesaid, *until such use or occupation shall be interfered with by the operations of the contractor for the Battery enlargement.* It requires little sagacity to see that this privilege could be made of more detriment to the public interest, and of far greater advantage to the lessees, than could be accomplished in almost any other way. Its value would be almost incalculable. The waters of this privileged space could be extended for five hundred feet along and around the Battery front, and provide room for a dozen ferries, which, under these conditions, could be run to as many contiguous points as it is desirable to have ferry communication. If this privilege should have been given, and the lessees have acted in collusion with the contractor of the Battery enlargement, the city would find, when too late, that it had parted with privileges without any equivalent, of exceeding value to the parties interested, and serious injury to the public interest.

There were other objections which, though of less importance, yet of themselves would have been sufficient to induce me to withhold my assent to this proposition. Permit me respectfully to deprecate the haste with which important measures are sometimes passed by the Common Council. These conditions, involving consequences of such magnitude to the city, proposing to part with valuable privileges, and which really should have received great consideration, and have been adopted only upon the official opinion of the Counsel to the Corporation as to the legal rights of all parties, passed the Board of Councilmen on the 9th inst., and the Board of Aldermen on the 11th inst., apparently without any deliberation or examination whatever. I herewith return the resolution without my approval.

Very respectfully,

FERNANDO WOOD, *Mayor.*

GRADING OF FIFTY-SECOND STREET.

MAYOR'S OFFICE, NEW-YORK, *May* 17, 1855.

To the Honorable the Board of Councilmen:

GENTLEMEN: I return herewith a resolution to grade Fifty-second street from Tenth to Eleventh avenues, which originated in your

Board, without my signature. It appears that this proposition emanated from a member of the Board of Councilmen, without the request or knowledge of any of the parties in interest, who are to be affected by the proposed improvement, and that nearly all of said interest remonstrated against it. Now, as it is all settled that the majority of owners in all such matters have an undoubted right to control, and as in this particular case the improvement was not asked for by any person really interested, I must withhold my assent. I herewith return the resolution without my signature. All of which is respectfully submitted.

FERNANDO WOOD, *Mayor*.

THE REYNOLDS' JOB.

MAYOR'S OFFICE, NEW-YORK, *June* 14, 1855.

To the Honorable the Board of Councilmen:

GENTLEMEN: I return without my approval the resolution directing the Comptroller to pay Wm. B. Reynolds forty-six thousand seven hundred and forty-five dollars and fifty-one cents, for the purchase of certain property enumerated therein, and appropriating that sum for that purpose.

I am compelled to this course for the following among other reasons:

The resolution in question, among other property, specifies the following: "The right and title to Barren Island, including all the leases, contracts, and conveyances held by Wm. B. Reynolds for any part or portion of the Island and its appurtenances, the sum of $10,000, copy of the leases and deeds which are hereunto annexed, and the originals of which are to be transferred to the city on the payment of the aforesaid sum."

Among the papers is a deed from Wm. B. Reynolds to the Corporation, conveying two acres of land on Barren Island for the nominal sum of one dollar, and an assignment of a lease of other property in which the consideration is fixed at $10,000. The resolution above referred to includes the leasehold and the fee in one mass, as the property to be purchased for $10,000, and I am therefore to disregard the application made of this sum by the seller, by which only a nominal portion of the $10,000 is applied to the fee property. But even assuming that it is a purchase made for the consideration of only one dollar, it is yet a purchase of land ; and, as Barren Island is in Kings county, a purchase of land outside of the jurisdiction of the city. This presents to me the first objection, whether any such power has been devolved upon the authorities of the city. I confess this question has caused me much concern, and no little investigation.

The Montgomery Charter authorizes the city to take and hold land, but it expressly limits the amount which may be thus held to property of the yearly rent or value of three thousand pounds. In the edition just published of the laws of the State, applicable to the city, there is a note to this clause of the charter, stating that this limitation does not prevent the holding of land, which, when purchased, was not of greater annual value, but which afterwards rose beyond it, showing that this limitation was considered still in force.

I have not been able to find any general act which has extended this power of purchase, although the statute-book is dotted with laws authorizing particular purchases by the city from time to time, for various public objects. I infer that this limitation still stands, except as it has been enlarged by the special acts, authorizing particular purchases.

There is no question but that the city now holds property of a much greater annual value than the charter authorizes, and this being the case, I am brought to the conclusion that there is an entire absence of power to make the purchase in question. The rule of law applicable to municipal corporations, as laid down by the highest judicial authorities in this State, is this : "That they take only the special powers granted to them by their charter or by subsequent laws." Authority must be shown for this purchase before it becomes lawful. The only power known to me is the one which is fettered with the limitation expressed. If the power to purchase land were unlimited, whether in or out of our local jurisdiction, the discretion of the two Boards and of the Mayor would be the only safeguard of tax-payers against the most extensive purchases at extravagant prices, a safeguard that might not at all times be sufficient. The community do not rely entirely on protection of this character, and hence in charters and constitutions it is common to interpose checks over the exercise of dangerous powers. For the first time since my accession to office has this important question been presented to me, whether the city can purchase land outside of our jurisdiction, and I have examined it with the care which such a question demands, in view of its becoming a precedent and an example for other and more important cases. It is a power likely to lead to great abuse, and I withhold my assent to the resolution, not only because the charter requires it, but also because I am satisfied that unlimited power of that character would be highly dangerous. The amendments to the charter, adopted in 1830, 1849, and 1853, clearly show that no such unlimited authority was left in our local legislation. The amendments of 1853 provide that *all supplies* to be furnished, embracing an expenditure of over $250, shall be by contract, for which estimates and bids shall be furnished after due publication. All that is not real estate or leasehold property, comprehended in this proposed purchase from Mr. Reynolds, is personal property—the tools and implements of conducting his business as a contractor for removal of offal, etc., and for its manufacture into articles of use — boats, shovels, carts, etc. These are supplies furnished to the city without the formalities required by the charter. I can not suppose that it was intended to fetter the public authorities in this respect so completely, and yet leave a power to purchase any amount of land anywhere at any price in the discretion of those whose action heretofore had made checks and guards highly necessary. An amendment to the charter adopted in 1849 provides, that neither the Common Council nor any member thereof shall perform any executive business whatever. This restriction, I understand, was intended among other things to prevent the purchase of articles or the making of contracts by this branch of the city government, leaving such duties to be performed by the heads of departments. This resolution, in effect, dispenses with all the executive officers, and specifies the things to be purchased, the prices to be paid, and the person from whom purchased; and this is not compatible with the theory upon which the local government was then formed in dividing the executive and legislative departments. The resolution in this case appears to me to be an infraction of the amendment calculated to defeat the object which governed the Legislature in establishing it. I have other grounds of objection, to which it is unnecessary to allude. They refer more particularly to matters of detail. The principles involved I have deemed of great importance, and upon them alone I have considered it sufficient to stand in the discussion of this subject. Had the Common Council followed the practice with reference to ferry leases, etc., of making it incumbent upon the successor of Mr. Reynolds in the offal contract to take the property here alluded to instead of the city, many of the objections which I see to this proposition would have been avoided.

With distrust in my own knowledge of law generally, but confident in the soundness of the position herein assumed, I beg to return the resolution without my approval.

Very respectfully, FERNANDO WOOD, *Mayor.*

THE BULKHEAD CONTRACT.

MAYOR'S OFFICE, NEW-YORK, *June* 30, 1855.

To the Honorable the Board of Councilmen:

GENTLEMEN: I return herewith the preamble and resolution directing the discontinuance of the contract to build a bulkhead at Manhattanville, by the present contractor, and to direct the Street Commissioner to receive proposals for a contract for building a new bulkhead, to rest upon the work already made, and that the contractor for the new work shall take the old work at an appraisement to be made by two persons, to be selected by the old contractor and the Street Commissioner.

My objections to this proposition are many. It is sufficient to state only the most prominent.

Without referring to the many attempts made to comply with the reasonable wishes of the people of Manhattanville for suitable dock accommodations at that point, and the several contracts which have been made, and large sums of money already fruitlessly expended for that purpose, and which by a strange fatality have not as yet succeeded in yielding any thing but disappointments, I shall only deal with the present proposition now before me. It appears that previous to this resolution by the Common Council, a contract was entered into, 14th September, 1854, with David Hunt, to build a rip-rap wall and bulkhead extending from 130th to 131st street, Manhattanville, the conditions of which were that the work should be of the most substantial and durable character, and to be of certain ornamental material and style of construction, for the sum of forty-six thousand four hundred and fifty dollars, to be completed in five months from date of contract, under a penalty of $20 for each day that it should remain uncompleted after the time had expired.

Fifteen thousand dollars of this sum have been paid. That Mr. Hunt or assigns have failed to perform this contract is evident, otherwise we would not have the proposition to release him, and to construct another and far more expensive work. The report and resolutions now before me for approval admit in effect that Mr. Hunt has forfeited his contract, but give as a reason that " since the commencement of the work it has been discovered that the bottom under the rip-rap wall is so steep and rocky, as to render the foundation insecure, and to expose the whole work to slide off, and that a portion of it already built had slid about 90 feet into the rear, and there rests upon a solid bottom well fitted for the foundation of a permanent work. Therefore," continues the preamble, " it has become inexpedient to go on with the building of the bulkhead as heretofore ordered, and it is necessary to build a bulkhead at a further distance from the shore ;" and these are all the reasons for releasing Mr. Hunt or his assigns, and ordering the construction of another work, far more extensive, and it is to be presumed far more expensive. By what means the committee arrived at their conclusions does not appear. No evidence is furnished me that scientific or practical men were employed to make soundings and examine the bottom with the necessary caution for the erection of this new work, and I am forced to the conclusion that none were employed. Certainly, if the many attempts made to build bulkheads, rip-rap walls, and piers at that point have all failed in consequence of some unusual impediment of the bottom or other physical defects, it behoves us to examine the whole matter with care before venturing another contract; and expressly is this necessary before building upon that part of Mr. Hunt's work that has slid out into the river, as this resolution proposes, without knowing whether it lies, as represented, on a solid bottom, and is well secured and safe from further slidings. It would be an inexcusable waste of the people's money to go on with further experiments in such a blind manner, with every probability of another failure, and another similar proposition as the present. But, admitting that these examinations have been made, and that the proposed work will be substantial, and in all respects answer the purpose, still it furnishes no grounds for releasing Mr. Hunt from his contract, which the Corporation made with him in good faith, and to which it would have been held with great tenacity, if it had failed in any particular. He contracted to build this work, gave sufficient security to perform the agreement, has received a large sum of money on account, and should be compelled to finish it. It is no answer to say the work slid out into the river and he could not. When he agreed to receive from the Corporation $46,450 for its construction, he took the hazard of all accidents and all contingencies. It was, in short, a contract by which he assumed, not only the expense, but the risk of every other kind from the elements, from physical obstructions at the bottom of the river, and of every other nature. And he should be made to perform his agreement, or respond to the city in any damage that it suffers in consequence of failure. If this position be thought too severe and exacting as between the city and an individual, a compromise might be effected, in which it should be stipulated that the Corporation should be allowed to retain the work which has slid out (and which by the way may be worthless for the purposes of a new contract such as may be required) and Mr. Hunt retain the $15,000 already paid. This would be a fair and liberal arrangement to which among individuals not the slightest objection would be made.

I am aware that the idea of compromising matters of this kind in which the city is a party, upon principles of exact equity, is entirely novel, and that the practice has been to hold the Corporation to a rigid fulfillment when the bargain has been against its interest, (as is the case ninety-nine times out of a hundred,) and to release the individual from loss or responsibility when the bargain has been against him; but we now hope for fairer dealings, and a little protection for the rights and interests of the people. But admitting that it be right to contract this new work as proposed, and that it be right to build on the work that has slid out, without examination as to its fitness for that purpose, and that it be right to release Mr. Hunt from his contract, can it be right not only to release, but also to pay him for the work done, which is of no value to the city as it now remains? In my opinion, such a course can not be justified. It looks to me like giving a premium for forfeiting contracts; like the game of "Heads I win, tails you lose." The city is to lose in any event; for it requires no sagacity to see that the sum paid for this old work to Mr. Hunt or assigns will be put upon the cost of the new work, and of course merged in the price charged to the city. It will then have lost the $15,000 paid Mr. Hunt or assigns beside the hazard of having the same game played over again under another name, and perhaps involving a much greater loss. Admitting that it be right to pay Mr. Hunt for this work, (supposing the city has not yet paid its value,) I object to the mode of appraisement. It should be appraised in some other way in which the interests of the city should be represented upon one side, the interests of the new contractor (after he had made the new contract) upon the other. This will be equitable, admitting the objections urged by me to such a proceeding are without force.

With these views, thus hurriedly expressed, it will be impossible for me to concur with the Common Council in this resolution. I am forced to this conclusion much against my predisposition in the premises, because I am sincerely desirous of offering no obstacle to the speedy construction of sufficient dockage at Manhattanville. The people of that ancient locality are distinguished for industry and probity, and it is incumbent upon the Corporation to afford every facility for the better protection of their interests, and for the development of their industrial capacities. I think the immediate expenditure of an existing appropriation made to improve the present pier and the northerly portion of the bulkhead north of it, could be made to answer all the present business wants. These improvements could be made without delay, and in the mean time thorough examination by competent engineers can be obtained so as to proceed in the erection of suitable works, with a sure knowledge and reliable data upon which to make new contracts.

This course would secure us against further failures, and be more compatible with the true interests of the city and of the people of Manhattanville. Very respectfully,

FERNANDO WOOD, *Mayor*.

PIER AT FOOT OF THIRTY-FOURTH STREET.

MAYOR'S OFFICE, NEW-YORK, *July* 11, 1855.

To the Honorable the Board of Councilmen :

GENTLEMEN : I return the resolution to build a pier 350 feet long and 40 feet wide at the foot of Thirty-fourth street, North River, without my approval.

At the last session of the Legislature an Act was passed for the appointment of a Commission to ascertain and clearly define the water-line of the Corporation limits of this city, and other duties appertaining to this harbor. This Commission was duly appointed, and is now in session. It has made some progress, and will soon complete its work.

Section 2 of the Act referred to provides that " No grants of land under the waters, in respect to which the said Commissioners are herein required to report, shall be made by the Commissioners of the Land Office, or by the Common Council of the City of New-York, or by any board, officer, or corporation, until the further direction of the Legislature in the premises. And the said Commissioners may, by their order in writing, restrain and stay all proceedings until the further direction of the Legislature, by virtue of any grant of land under the said waters heretofore made, and all permanent erections in or obstructions of the said waters, which, in their judgment, may interfere with or embarrass the establishment of such exterior lines as they shall deem proper to recommend to the Legislature, which order shall be enforced, and disobedience thereof shall be punished by the Supreme Court in the Second Judicial District, at any special or general term thereof, in the same manner and to the same extent as in cases of injunction issued out of said Court. *And any permanent erection or obstructions made contrary to any such order, may be removed and abated by the said Commissioners.*"

Until the Harbor Commission have completed their labors and the Legislature have acted thereon, it will, in my opinion, be impolitic to undertake the construction of a pier of this extent, or indeed to attempt any permanent erection in our harbor.

At present the water-line is undefined on the west side of the city. We do not know the extent of our boundaries there, and inasmuch as this law gives to these Commissioners power to restrain our action in the erection of such works, I submit whether it is prudent to undertake them.

If this resolution passes, and the Street Commissioner makes a contract in pursuance of it, the city will become liable in damages to the contractor, if he is prevented from building the pier by the interference of the Harbor Commission.

We have already suffered largely from similar causes, and it is best to guard the future as far as possible.

As soon as the water-line is established, and the grounds of objection referred to by me are removed, I shall make no opposition to the construction of a pier at foot of Thirty-fourth street, if legally and properly undertaken. Very respectfully,

FERNANDO WOOD, *Mayor.*

CITY CONTRACTS.

MAYOR'S OFFICE, NEW-YORK, *July* 14, 1855.

To the Honorable the Board of Councilmen:

GENTLEMEN: The resolution emanating in your Board, directing the Commissioner of Streets and Lamps to withdraw the advertisement, inviting proposals for cleaning the streets of the city, until the further action of the Common Council, is returned herewith without approval.

As the charter and ordinances compel that officer to clean the streets by contract, I do not see how this proposition to dispense with contracts can be adopted. Besides, it is now too late for this resolution to have any effect upon the action of the Commissioner, as he has already advertised the required ten days, received and opened the bids, and, as I am advised, awarded the contracts, under the advice of the Counsel to the Corporation.

Very respectfully,

FERNANDO WOOD, *Mayor.*

MAYOR'S OFFICE, NEW-YORK, *July* 14, 1855.

To the Honorable Board of Councilmen:

GENTLEMEN: I return, without approval, the ordinance proposing to further amend the ordinance regulating the making of contracts, passed May 30, 1849.

In my opinion, if adopted, this amendment may in effect materially conflict with that section of the charter which provides that all contracts "shall be given to the lowest bidder." As the ordinance now stands, the lowest bidder is entitled to the contract, and the Head of the Department is authorized to award it to him, if the bid be regular in form, adequate security be given; all bids are opened in the presence of the Comptroller, and an appropriation has been made for the purpose. It appears to me that these conditions are about all that the charter seems to require; indeed, to go farther may defeat the object of the charter altogether.

This subject of making contracts, and the many difficulties surrounding it, has not escaped my attention. It is full of difficulties, under the very best regulations which human wisdom can devise. In the message submitted by me, January 11th last, I alluded to it in this language: "The present mode of making contracts is defective. Notwithstanding the improvement of late years, in exacting more publicity, in opening bids, and in guarding against favoritism in granting contracts, yet it is supposed much wrong still exists. There is no doubt that frauds are still perpetrated in this branch of the public service. Bids are frequently put in in the name of fictitious persons, ranging from a high to a low estimate—speculators standing ready to take advantage of any embarrassment to the Department owing to the non-appearance of the false bidder, and to get the contract at the highest possible limits. Again, it is the practice to put in estimates, not with the expectation of making and performing a contract, but to be bought off by some more responsible party, who has been underbid. Various other ways, the details of which are known only to the initiated, are in vogue, by which to defraud the treasury. If the head of a department acts in collusion with these outsiders, it is next to impossible to prevent frauds under the present system."

Subsequent experience in the office of Mayor has confirmed these views; but I am satisfied, that great caution is required in the adoption of any plan for the better protection of the public interests in this matter, lest we open the door still wider for wrong-doing.

One of the features of the proposition now presented is, that no contract shall be made, although all the requirements of the charters be complied with, *until the Common Council confirm it.*

With respect, permit me to say, that in my judgment this alteration will be unwise, inasmuch as it may practically defeat the charter itself. Its operation will be, that "the lowest bidder," after undergoing a competition with other bidders, as to price, and the scrutiny of his bid, by the head of the Department and the Comptroller, and in case of doubt, also by the Counsel to the Corporation, he must, in addition, "run the gauntlet" of the Common Council, where the result may depend upon other considerations than those appertaining to the bid itself.

I submit whether such additional requirements are demanded by the public interests, and whether they may not be productive of great injury, not only to the individual bidder, but to the public treasury. Besides, it requires no stretch of imagination to see, that the wise safeguards of the charter could thus be entirely disregarded. An unsuccessful bidder, of wealth and influence, could have little difficulty in defeating the confirmation of a contract in the Common Council, which, in cases of urgent necessity, would give the Head of the Department an excuse for going into the open market, without any contract whatever, or the Head of the Department himself could, in the exercise of the influence which the patronage of his position necessarily gives, accomplish that purpose, and thus make all the agreements himself, without contracts. It would be creating a Board of Appeals to which unsuccessful bidders would have recourse, when disappointed. Instead of resorting to the courts, the proper recourse of those who are dissatisfied with the action of the officers who have charge of deciding upon the bids, it will send them to your lobbies, and no inconsiderable portion of your time will be taken up in listening to these complaints.

The charter places these matters in the departments, where they should be permitted to remain, subject of course to such regulations as the Common Council may direct, having for their object the maintenance of the principles of the charter, which must govern us at all times.

We should not forget that contractors and bidders have rights, as well as the Corporation, which are equally entitled to protection from the frauds which too often govern the making of contracts. I can see no equity in forcing a man into the Common Council, for the award of a contract, after he has honorably complied with the charter and the ordinance; has shown himself fairly and honestly the lowest bidder, and been awarded the contract by the Comptroller, and the Head of the Department. Whilst such a regulation will be oppressive to the individual, it will inure to the disadvantage of the Corporation, by compelling bidders to make provision in their estimates, for the cost and trouble attending such a proceeding, and the expense to the bidder can be no inconsiderable sum, inasmuch as it frequently occurs, that obscure men with limited influence, are obliged to procure the aid of counsel to get measures through, even where the merits of the measures themselves are entirely sufficient, and beyond any doubt. These expenses will, of course, be added to the cost of the work to the Corporation, and thus materially increase the expenses of the City Government, already too onerous.

For this reason it is impossible for me to approve of the amendment proposed.

I am aware that an improvement can be made upon the present mode of giving out contracts, but do not think that this will be an *improvement*. I fear that it will subject us to still further evils, and add to the already existing difficulties surrounding the whole matter of giving contracts to the lowest *bonâ-fide* bidder.

Very respectfully, FERNANDO WOOD, *Mayor*.

DIAMOND REEF.

MAYOR'S OFFICE, NEW-YORK, *August* 7, 1855.

To the Honorable the Board of Councilmen:

GENTLEMEN: I return, without approval, the resolution directing the Street Commissioner to award to Husted & Kroehl the contract for removing Diamond Reef.

In January last, the Common Council passed a resolution with my concurrence, directing the Street Commissioner to advertise for estimates to blast Diamond Reef, and to report to them the bids; the object being, as I supposed, to ascertain about what the work would cost before deciding upon its execution.

The Street Commissioner proceeded accordingly to advertise; but, by a strange mistake, worded his specifications in such a manner as to leave it doubtful whether estimates were to be put in to blast the rock by the cubic yard, or in the gross for the whole quantity to be removed.

This error occurred by requiring bidders to state their "lowest terms," without declaring whether it was meant the lowest terms for the entire rock, or the lowest terms per cubic yard. As could be foretold, estimators construed this advertisement differently; some bidding by the yard, and others by the gross. Thirteen bids were received; ten offering by the cubic yard, and three for the whole; Husted & Kroehl being for the former. The Street Commissioner marked all the yard bidders as informal and irregular, declaring the lowest sum in gross as the lowest bidder, and consequently as entitled to the contract. This, if confirmed by the Common Council, would have given the contract to Cornelius Smith, whose bid was forty thousand dollars, as the sum for which he would remove the rock.

It is unnecessary to inquire whether the Street Commissioner was right in rejecting any bids as informal, upon the ground of irregularity, for the Common Council appear to have taken from him all such discretion. He was directed to report the bids, and under that direction he was deprived of all control or supervision over them. He, therefore, duly reported every bid to the Common Council, who took them into consideration, called the bidders before its Committee, went into an examination of the whole matter, and adopted the resolution now before me for approval, directing the Street Commissioner to make a contract with Husted & Kroehl, who had bid by the yard, but who subsequently altered their bid to make it in gross sum.

I do not think it necessary to go into any investigation as to who are the lowest bidders. The error in the form of the advertisement, and the consequent ignorance of the bidders, as to what was meant by *the lowest terms* by the Department, are sufficient grounds upon which to set aside any award made either by the Street Commissioner or the Common Council. There should be no ambiguity in the advertisements to receive proposals for doing Corporation work. If there were, the charter, which requires all work to be done by contract to be given to the lowest bidder, with adequate security, could be easily disregarded and rendered inoperative. An ingeniously-worded advertisement would exclude any bid. The object of public advertisements is to invite competition, but there can be no competition if impediments are thrown in the way of the uninitiated and honest bidders.

Any friend of a head of a department, who is acquainted with the intention of those who are to decide upon the regularity or irregularity of the estimates, would have great advantage, and could in all cases obtain the contract at his own price. Therefore, it is obvious that ambiguity or uncertainty, in so important a matter as this, is of itself sufficient to warrant a reädvertisement, and should prevent my approval of any award to any party bidding under it.

In the present instance, the greatest uncertainty existed in the minds of bidders; and, in my opinion, every bid put in was regular, none could be excluded, and the lowest bid for the gross and the lowest bid for the cubic yard were each "the lowest bidder"—an anomaly never before existing to my knowledge.

But there are other objections. The Common Council by this proceeding is virtually "doing executive business." It is awarding and making contracts. No other construction can be fairly put upon this transaction. It takes from the head of an executive department, the power of deciding who is the lowest bidder, (actually reversing his decision;) in whom, in my judgment, the charter and the ordinance of 1849 expressly place it. It is no answer to say that the Street Commissioner is left the power to make the award and to execute the contract, because he is deprived of all discretion in the premises, and is made the mere machine of the Common Council, under whose exclusive direction he is forced to act. If the legislative department of the city government can designate the parties by whom work shall be done, against the decision of a head of a department, it can name the parties by whom supplies shall be furnished, and by a further slight encroachment can fix the price and order the money paid, all under the plea that it is simply making an appropriation and confirming a contract.

As I have stated upon another occasion, the government of this city, like all American governments, is divided into the legislative, the executive, and the judicial. The first can merely *make laws*, the second executes, and the last expounds them. With the Common Council of New-York all power beyond legislation is cut off entirely by the amended charter. It is left less of executive prerogative than any other legislative body in the country. The restriction is extremely stringent. The Legislature appears to have been jealous of the exercise of this authority by those bodies, seeing less danger in the executive than in the legislative branches of our city government. Whether there be less danger or not can not be considered now; the only question is, how far it is competent for the Common Council to go into the transaction of other than strictly law-making business; my own views are clear on this point; the limit is decided, and so long as the power is placed in my hands, I shall interpose every legal obstacle in the way of any transgression.

There are other points of objection appertaining more particularly to details, to which it will be unnecessary to allude. I do not see how we are to surmount those already enumerated. If, however, you do not concur with me, permit me to suggest that before making any contract for this work, careful surveys be made by competent and honest engineers, and that the money to pay for it be placed in the tax bill, and authority be procured from the Legislature to raise it for this purpose. Very respectfully,

FERNANDO WOOD, *Mayor.*

INDICTMENT OF ALDERMEN.

MAYOR'S OFFICE, NEW-YORK, *Sept. 24th,* 1855.

To the Honorable the Board of Aldermen:

GENTLEMEN: I inclose a copy of a communication made to me this day by A. Oakey Hall, Esq., District-Attorney of the city, stating that indictments have been found by the Grand-Jury against certain members of your body for corrupt practices in the discharge of their official duties. However painful and humiliating it is to me to make this announcement, and for you to receive it, still we owe a duty to the public from which we must not shrink, affect whom it may. Your body should not only be purged of every corrupt member who may hold a place among you, but the utmost penalty of the law should be inflicted against every man thus guilty. This community has struggled against its own officials long enough. Its repeated efforts to reduce the expenditures, to raise the standard of the incumbents of office, and to improve the character of the government of the city, will continue futile so long as the legislative branch is impure and unfaithful. From a corrupt fountain nothing but contamination can flow. A Common Council without integrity, be the source and origin of the ordinances, will not fail to impart its own spirit to those who are to execute its proceedings, until the whole machinery of government will speedily become rotten and demoralized. It is the conviction of honest men, that in the management of our public affairs we are fast progressing to this lamentable state of degradation. In my opinion, public indignation can not be much longer suppressed. We are approaching a crisis when the general cry will be, "Reformation or revolution." New-York, so strong, so proud, so eminent in all that constitutes commercial honor, hard-earned wealth, and exalted social position, can not, with all her greatness, long resist the gnawings of this foul canker, working thus steadily at her municipal heart. It behoves us, therefore, to make common cause in a common effort, without reference to party predilections or personal animosities, to redeem, if possible, the fair fame of our city from the load of official ignominy which is now bearing it down.

Very respectfully,

FERNANDO WOOD, *Mayor.*

AMENDED CHARTER.

MAYOR'S OFFICE, NEW-YORK, *Sept.* 24, 1855.

To the Honorable the Board of Councilmen:

GENTLEMEN: I return you herewith a preamble and resolutions presented to me for approval, which proposes to create a Joint Committee of the two Boards of the Common Council for the purpose of devising a new charter for the city.

By the fourth section of the amendments to the Charter, passed April 2, 1849, it is provided that "the two Boards shall have concurrent powers, and a negative on each other's proceedings, and shall, in all cases, act as separate bodies, *and shall not appoint Joint Committees, except a Committee on Accounts.*" Therefore, the Common Council have not the power to create Joint Committees for this or any other purpose, except only as it relates to accounts.

I am aware that this resolution, by calling first for the appointment of a Committee by your Board, and then a similar Committee to "confer with it," by the Board of Aldermen, seeks to avoid what is termed a *Joint Committee;* but the wording of the second resolution, in stating that the two committees may "jointly" make application to the Legislature after having "jointly" agreed upon a charter, fixes its character clearly within the restriction of the amended charter referred to.

But, admitting that this objection has been avoided, there are others of sufficient weight to prevent my approval.

One of the peculiar and suspicious features of this proceeding is the last clause of the second resolution, which gives to this Joint Committee power to "make application to the Legislature, at its next session, for the enactment of the Charter," which it is thus empowered to devise, without any submission of it to the Common Council, or to the people of the city. I can not consent to delegate such a power to any committee, however unexceptionable as to ability or character. Ten men, to be selected by the two presiding officers of the present Common Council, should not be intrusted with such an important duty, to be performed without check, without supervision, or even without accountability.

Another objection, not much less forcible, is that this Committee is authorized to proceed to a Legislature yet to be chosen, when the body it purports to represent must have ceased to have an official existence. The Legislature does not convene before January next, when an entire new Board of Councilmen and new members for one half of the Board of Aldermen will be sitting in the places now filled by the bodies which get up this proceeding. How then could this Joint Committee with propriety represent the Mayor and Commonality of New-York, at the time its influence is to be exercised?

It is not necessary to state the many difficulties which present themselves to me in the way of the measure. That the Charter should be amended all admit; that it is exceedingly defective and susceptible of great improvement, we all know. This subject was alluded to in the first communication submitted to the Common Council on the 1st of January last. A portion of the intervening months could have been profitably passed in devising a proper Charter, which after due deliberation and general consultation would be ready to be presented to the next Legislature for adoption.

It is now too late for *this* Common Council to take up the subject.

The next Common Council will be "fresh from the people," and probably command public confidence to a greater extent. Let the duty of amending the Charter be left with your successors.

Very respectfully,

FERNANDO WOOD, *Mayor.*

APROPOS OF PAUPER AND FELON EMIGRANTS.

OFFICE OF CITY INFIRMARY, CINCINNATI, *Oct.* 23, 1855.

Hon. Fernando Wood, Mayor of the City of New York:

DEAR SIR: Having heard and read frequent reports of the vigor you exercise in regard to the importations of foreign paupers into your city, by the aid and sanction of foreign governments, we would respectfully call your attention to facts which have been made manifest to us for some time back, in relation to the trans-shipment of foreign paupers to the West, by aid of the Emigration Societies, and, as is alleged, by your city authorities. Of this last, however, we know nothing certain, having only the words of the paupers arriving here. But this much is certain, that we have almost weekly arrivals of batches of from three to twelve paupers, who are sent here from your city, and are landed amongst us without money or friends, many of whom are sick when landed, whose expenses to this place are paid by the Emigration Societies of your city, or by the city authorities themselves. These, if not sent back, would soon become a public charge upon us. Many are in a sickly condition, and can not be sent back; others linger along for a while until they become fastened upon us, and finally become a public charge for life.

We ask you if this is right—well knowing, from the estimate we have formed of your character, that your response will be emphatically "No." We therefore call upon you to aid us in putting a stop to this nefarious practice, by all the power you can bring to your aid, as soon as possible. We are informed that by your laws you compel each and every foreigner arriving at your port, to pay two dollars towards a fund, from which to pay the expenses of any foreigners who may hereafter become a charge on your poor fund. This fund, from the great number of emigrants arriving at your port, must necessarily be very large, and ought to be sufficient to keep them, without sending them away to be maintained at the expense of our and other cities, who have no such fund.

We have come to the determination to send all back, as fast as they come, hereafter; and, as a matter of justice to us, we call upon you to use your authority to stay the evil, or, if you have no power in the premises, at least to expose the matter, so that we may know where the blame rests, and apply the proper remedy.

Respectfully yours, A. S. Hornung,
Clerk Board City Infirmary.

By order of Adam Hornung,
William Crossman,
Geo. A. Peter,
} *Directors City Infirmary.*

Mayor's Office, New-York, *Nov.* 3, 1855.

Dear Sirs: Your letter of the 23d ult., respecting the supposed trans-shipment of foreign criminals and paupers from this city to the West, by the authorities and emigrant societies of New-York, would have been replied to sooner but for pressing public duties. I have now the pleasure to advise that such is not the fact, and that I am confident no such violation of the common principles of justice and courtesy has ever taken place in this city.

You are quite right in supposing that my own feelings and views would be hostile to practices of this character, upon the part of the authorities and others here. The stand taken by me with reference to the shipment to our port of these unfortunates, by the local authorities of European governments, would preclude me from countenancing the perpetration of the same wrong upon the people of your city. It would be impossible for me to do that which I have so often denounced in others. But it is very certain, there have been no such trans-shipments. The emigrant paupers and criminals to whom you allude, as having been forwarded to Cincinnati, were no doubt sent thither direct from the prisons of their own country. This has been the practice for several years. The stringency of my own course, in objecting to the reception and incorporation of this outcast population into our own community, has no doubt had the effect to increase this practice, in supposed avoidance of the grounds upon which we refuse to receive them. I am happy to advise, however, that it has had no such tendency. I feel it incumbent upon me not only to protect New-York, but the whole country, from so great an evil, so far as I have the power, and reject and return forthwith every such person known to me, whether intended to be domiciled in this city or sent to the West. My policy and practice has been to return them forthwith, if possible by the vessel that brought them. The Hamburgh ship Deutschland, from Hamburgh, which arrived at this port on the 17th September, brought four criminals, sent out by the order and at the expense of the authorities of Güstrow, Duchy of Mecklenburg, direct from the prison at that place. These persons were provided with through-tickets from New-York to Milwaukee. These tickets were purchased from the agents in Hamburgh. All the principal forwarding lines have agencies in the leading European cities, for the sale of through-tickets into the interior of this country.

Thus you will see that although the foreign emigrants, alluded to by you, may properly represent themselves as from this city, they have merely passed through it, *en route* from some workhouse or poorhouse in other lands; and instead of being sent by our own authorities, have been forwarded, even to your very doors, by the inhumane and inhospitable governors and overseers of their own country.

I fully appreciate the sentiments expressed in your letter, on this subject. In my judgment, the evil is becoming of sufficient magnitude to call for the action of the General Government. Our whole country is more or less interested. Its effect upon society and taxation is no longer insignificant, and must soon attract the thoughtful concern of the statesman and patriot. Very respectfully,

FERNANDO WOOD, *Mayor.*

To Messrs. ADAM HORNUNG,
WILLIAM CROSSMAN,
GEO. A. PETER,
Directors City Infirmary.

Donald Macleod's Works.

LIFE OF SIR WALTER SCOTT.

BY DONALD MACLEOD.

1 vol., 12mo., cloth, with portrait. Price $1.

"This is a model biography. The author has delineated the character of him once styled the Great Unknown, so that all who read these pages may know him, and cherish for him a personal attachment."—*Christian Intelligencer.*

"This is a most delightful and even fascinating volume. Its fascination consists in the clear flow of its narration, warm with a glowing love for its subject, and all over gemmed with racy and sparkling anecdote.

"It tells the story of the great wizard's life with simple directness, condensing the more elaborate narratives of others, and culling from them only the more salient and spicy facts of his biography, thus making it one of the agreeable books of the season."—*Watchman and Observer.*

"We can but commend this work to our readers as one of unflagging interest, from the beginning to the end; written in language simple but often exceedingly picturesque, and always in keeping with the particular theme in hand."—*Knickerbocker Magazine.*

"A fresher, pleasanter, more vivacious biography we have seldom read."—*Temp. Courier.*

"We should not be surprised if this Life of the 'Author of Waverley' finds as many readers as anything which has before been written about the true 'Wizard of the North.'" —*The Presbyterian.*

"It is written with great care and judgment, and portrays the remarkable career of the great novelist with an exactness and fidelity that renders it as valuable as a work of reference, as it is interesting in its subject."—*Home Gazette.*

"With a loving, reverential spirit, and a fair power of discernment, he has drawn a graceful outline of the personal life and character of Sir Walter. It is peculiarly a book for the people, and as such has its charms; and yet no one, however familiar he may be with the Great Magician of the North, will read it without pleasure."—*New York Courier and Enquirer.*

THE IDLER OF THE ALPS,

OR, PYNNSHURST AND HIS WANDERINGS.

BY DONALD MACLEOD.

1 vol., 12mo., cloth, Price $1 25.

"We have certainly, since Thackeray, had no such pleasant tourist; incidents, adventures, comic as well as serious, anecdotes, descriptions, poetry, and satire, are most happily intermingled, and the result is as delightful a volume for a summer day or a winter evening, as we have seen for a long time."—*Philadelphia Evening Bulletin.*

"This is an eminently clever and readable work, which, we venture to predict, will at once secure its author a distinguished place among American writers. It is a fine tissue of humor, wit, and adventure, pathos and description, woven into just enough of acting and moving story to create a lively interest."—*Graham's Magazine.*

O. F. PARSONS'

CATALOGUE OF

BOOKS, MAPS, AND CHARTS,

ADAPTED ESPECIALLY TO THE WANTS OF AGENTS,

140 NASSAU STREET,

Between the Times and the Tribune Offices, Office of the Monthly Trade Gazette, } NEW-YORK.

	Retail Prices.
Battles of the Crimea, including a complete **Historical Summary of the Russian War,** from the commencement (giving an account of the origin) to the present time. Embellished with eight splendid full-page Engravings, illustrating the Stirring Scenes in the Crimea, and a superb Map of the CRIMEA, BLACK SEA, DANUBIAN PROVINCES, TURKEY IN ASIA, a Ground Plan of ST. PETERSBURGH and CRONSTADT, a Ground Plan of SIEGE OPERATIONS BEFORE SEBASTOPOL, and a PLAN OF SEBASTOPOL, showing its Fortifications, Siege Works, Batteries, Position of Contending Forces, etc. Octavo, 128 pages,	$ 0 50
WELLS' Lawyer and United States Form Book, containing Legal Information, Forms, Laws, etc. Adapted to every part of the United States. 12mo. Full bound,	1 00
Half bound,	0 75
The American Lawyer and Business Man's Form Book, containing Legal information, meeting almost every possible circumstance in the ordinary transactions of business in any part of the United States. It also contains a new and beautiful Map and Seal of each State, with the County Lines delineated, besides a Map of the United States. 12mo. Full bound,	1 00
Half bound,	0 75
In German. Half bound,	0 75
do. Cloth,	1 00
Pronouncing Gazetteer of the World, or Geographical Dictionary, containing a greater amount of matter than any single volume in the English language,	6 00
PHELPS' One Hundred Cities and Large Towns of America. Being a description of One Hundred Cities and Towns, giving the Population at the various Censuses for the past Thirty Years; together with the principal Railroad and Steamboat Routes and Distances; with Maps of Fourteen of the principal Cities; Bird's eye View of New-York; View of Crystal Palace, etc., etc. Those having Colored Maps,	0 38
Those having Plain Maps,	0 25

	Retail Prices.
Book of the World,	2 00
FANNING'S Illustrated Gazetteer of the United States. Census of 1850. Illustrated with Maps of all the States, and the largest Cities. 8vo. Full bound,	1 75
Do. Do. Do. with Map of the United States,	2 00
Do. Do. Do. Half bound,	1 50
Do. Do. Do. " with Map,	1 75
Illustrated Biography of all Nations,	2 50
Danger in the Dark,	1 00
HOGAN on Popery,	1 25
Stanhope Burleigh,	1 00
Paul and Julia. Gilt,	1 00
Plain,	0 75
Traditions of De-coo-dah, and Antiquarian Researches, relating to a Race of Inhabitants in America before the Indians. 8vo.,	2 00
Lives of the Presidents of the United States,	0 25
Wedding Gift,	0 31
Farmers' Guide in the Management of Domestic Animals,	0 25
Frugal Housewife's Kitchen Companion,	0 25
Family Doctor,	0 25
Family Receipt Book,	0 25
Book of the United States,	0 25
The Lions of New-York, being a Guide to Objects of Interest in and around the Great Metropolis. By H. PHELPS,	0 25
The Art of Pleasing; or, the American Lady and Gentleman's Book of Etiquette. A Work for every Parent, Teacher, and Guardian, as well as every young person about entering Society. This book is bound in gilt binding, and sold at the low price of...	0 35
MRS. BRADLEY'S Housekeeper's Guide, Family Receipt and Cook Book. A Book for every Mother, Wife, and Daughter,	0 38
Life of Henry Clay, illustrated with his Portrait, and a Picture of his Birth-place, in Pamphlet Form,	0 38
The Fair Rebel; a Tale of Colonial Times. By EMMERSON BENNETT. In Pamphlet Form, Illustrated,	0 31
Do. Do. Do. Not Illustrated,	0 25
Adalaska; or, the Strange and Mysterious Family of the Cave of Genreva. By GEORGE W. L. BICKLEY, M.D., Author of "Tazewell Co.," etc.,	0 25
New-York; Its Upper Ten and Lower Million. The last and best Work ever written by GEORGE LIPPARD. In Muslin Binding,	1 00
Do Do. Do. Thick Paper "	0 75
The Medical Light-House. By H. K. ROOT,	2 00
A Variety of 32 Page PAMPHLETS, with Circulars, at	0 12½
" 48 " " " at	0 15
" 64 " " " at	0 18¾
" 96 to 112 " " " at	0 25
Life of Horace Greeley,	1 25
" **P. T Barnum,**	1 25
" **James Gordon Bennett,**	1 25
" **Wm. H. Seward,**	1 00

	Retail Prices.
Life of Sam Houston,	1 25
" **George Law,**	1 25
Ida May. By MARY LANGDON,	1 25
The May-Flower. By MRS. STOWE,	1 25
Star Papers. By H. W. BEECHER,	1 25
Woman of the 19th Century,	1 00
The Marines,	1 25
Which—The Right or the Left?	1 25

POCKET MAPS AND GUIDES.

	Retail Prices.
WELLS' New Map of the Seat of War, including the Crimea, Black Sea, Danubian Provinces, Russia, Turkey in Asia, a Ground Plan of Cronstadt, St. Petersburgh, and Siege Operations before Sebastopol,	0 25
WELLS' New Plan of Sebastopol, showing the City of Sebastopol, its Fortifications, Batteries, Siege Works, Position of Contending Forces, etc.,	0 25
RANNEY'S New Map of the United States, exhibiting all the New Territorial Boundaries extending through to the Pacific Coast, with the Principal Completed and Projected Railroad Routes, including the various Routes to the Pacific; Census of the United States; Wealth; Number of Representatives, etc. Printed in Three Colors, and Colored in States,	0 50
The Teacher's Present, being the Grammatical Tree, neatly put up	0 50
in Pocket form. Bound in Red Muslin. Gilt,	0 50
MORSE'S New Railroad and Township Map of Illinois. The most correct Map extant,	0 50
Guide Book through the United States, etc. Travellers' and Tourists' Guide Book through the United States of America and the Canadas. Containing the Routes and Distances on all the great lines of travel by Railroads, Canals, Stage Roads and Steamboats; together with Descriptions of the several States, and the principal Cities, Towns, and Villages in each; accompanied with a large and accurate Map,	1 00
Western Portraiture, and Emigrants' Guide. A Description of Wisconsin, Illinois, and Iowa, with Remarks on Minnesota and other Territories. By DANIEL S. CURTISS. In 1 vol., 12mo, pp. 360. Illustrated with a Township Map,	1 00
The Western Tourist, and Emigrants' Guide through the States of Ohio, Michigan, Indiana, Illinois, Missouri, Iowa, and Wisconsin, and the Territories of Minnesota, Missouri, and Nebraska, being an accurate and concise description of each State and Territory; and containing the Routes and Distances on the great lines of travel; accompanied with a large and minute Map exhibiting the Township Lines of the United States' Surveys, the Boundaries of Counties, and the Position of Cities, Villages, and Settlements, etc.,	0 75

	Retail Prices.
Route Book through the United States, etc. Travellers' and Tourists' Route Book through the United States of America and the Canadas. Containing the Routes and Distances on all the great lines of travel by Railroads, Stage Roads, Canals, Rivers, and Lakes, etc.; accompanied with a large and accurate Map, ...	0 75
Map of the State of New-York. With the Stations and Distances on Railroads in and running out of the State,....................	0 50
Township Map of Pennsylvania, ...	0 50
" " **Ohio,**	0 50
" " **Massachusetts, Connecticut, & Rhode-Island,**	0 50
Pocket Map of New-York City, showing the entire Island, with **Brooklyn and Williamsburgh,**	0 50
Map of the City of New-York, with Street Directory, ...	0 31¼
PHELPS' New-York City Guide and Conductor to Environs, Muslin. Gilt, ...	0 37½
Do. Do. Do. Paper Covers,....	0 25
Guide Book through the New-England and Middle States. Travellers' and Tourists' Guide Book through the New-England and Middle States, and the Canadas. Containing the Routes and Distances on all the great lines of travel by Railroads, Canals, Stage Roads, and Steamboats, together with descriptions of the several States, and the principal Cities, Towns, and Villages in each; accompanied with a large and accurate Map,......................	0 75
PHELPS' Travellers' Guide through the United States. Containing nearly Eight Hundred Railroad, Steamboat, Canal, and Stage Routes. Revised Edition,...............................	0 75
ENSIGN & THAYER'S Guide through the Western States. With a List of all the Railroad, Steamboat, Canal, and Stage Routes therein, ...	0 75
Railroad and Township Map of Ohio. A large and elegant Map. Just published. Colored in Towns, ...	1 25
Do. Do. Do. Colored in Counties,....	1 00
Map of Canada, East and West, ...	0 75
COLTON'S New Series of Maps for Travellers. This Series embraces Maps of each of the United States, of the several British Provinces, and of Mexico, Central America, and the West-Indies; exhibiting, with accuracy, the Railroads, Canals, Stage Routes, etc.; also, the principal Cities, and other objects of interest, in appended Diagrams.	

	Retail.		Retail.		
Alabama, ...	$0 38	Maine, ...	$0 38	Pennsylvania,..	0 38
Arkansas,.........	0 38	Massachusetts	0 38	Rhode-Island,..	0 38
Canada East,......	0 38	and Rhode I.,....	0 38	South-Carolina,.	0 38
Canada West, ...	0 38	Michigan, N'h.....	0 38	Texas,.........	0 38
Connecticut, ...	0 38	Michigan, S'h.....	0 38	Vermont,......	0 38
Delaware and	0 38	Minnesota,........	0 38	Virginia, ...	0 38
Maryland,.........	0 38	Mississippi, ...	0 38	Wisconsin,.....	0 38
Florida, ...	0 38	Missouri,.........	0 38	West-Indies, .	0 50
Georgia, ...	0 38	N. Brunswick,....	0 38	California, ...	0 50
Illinois,...........	0 38	Nova Scotia,....	0 38	Central Amer.,.	0 50
Indiana, ...	0 38	etc., ...	0 38	Mexico, ...	0 50
Iowa, ...	0 38	N. Hampshire,....	0 38	N w-Mexico .	
Kentucky and	0 38	New-Jersey, ...	0 38	and Utah,.....	0 50
Tennessee,.......	0 38	New-York, ...	0 38	Oregon and .	
Lake Superior,....	0 38	N'th-Carolina,....	0 38	Washington .	
Louisiana, ...	0 38	Ohio, ...	0 38	Territory,.....	0 50

CHARTS,

IN SHEETS, COLORED, SIZE 23 BY 31 INCHES, AND LARGER.

The following will be found the most useful, as well as the most salable List of Charts ever offered to the Public.

	Retail Prices.
WELLS' New Map of the Seat of War and Plan of Sebastopol Combined, showing the City of Sebastopol, its Fortifications, Batteries, Position of Contending Forces, and a superb Map of the Crimea, Black Sea, Danubian Provinces, Russia, Turkey in Asia, a Plan of Cronstadt, St. Petersburgh, and a Ground Plan of Siege Operations before Sebastopol—25 by 38 inches,	0 25
WELLS' New Plan of Sebastopol,	0 12½
" " Map of the Seat of War,	0 12½
Europe and her Sovereigns,	0 37
War in Europe,	0 25
Maps of Wisconsin, Iowa, and Minnesota,	0 37
World's Progress,	0 25
A New and Beautiful Map of the United States, exhibiting all the new Territorial Boundaries, extending through to the Pacific Coast, with the principal Completed and Projected Railroad Routes, including the various Routes to the Pacific; Census of the United States; Wealth; Number of Representatives, etc. Printed in Three Colors, and Colored also in States,	0 25
MORSE'S New Railroad and Township Map of Illinois. This is the latest and best Map of Illinois ever published, much pains having been taken to obtain the most reliable information from each County in the State,	0 25
BLANCHARD's Grammatical Tree, showing the Classification and Properties of English Parts of Speech. Neatly Colored. A useful ornament,	0 25
A New Chart, containing the Portraits of the Presidents, with a brief Sketch of their Lives,	0 25
Declaration of Independence,	0 25
Do. Do. in German,	0 25
Costumes of all Nations,	0 25
United States at One View,	0 25
World " "	0 25
Tree of Liberty, containing the Seals of all the States,	0 25
A New Chart the Constitution of the United States, with National Flag,	0 25
Township Map of Pennsylvania, with Population for 1840 and 1850,	0 25
Railroad and Township Map of Ohio, with Population for 1840 and 1850,	0 25
Railroad and Township Map of Massachusetts, Connecticut, and Rhode Island,	0 25
Map of New-York State, with Population for 1840 and 1850,	0 25
Map of New-York City, with Census at various periods, from 1653 to 1850,	0 25
New-York and Vicinity, embracing 30 miles around the City,	0 25

	Retail Prices.
Map of the New-England States, ...	0 25
World at One View, Costumes of all Nations, etc., ...	0 25
Map of Ireland, Colored in Counties, ...	0 25
Morse's World, ...	0 37
New R. R. Map, ...	0 83

MOUNTED MAPS AND CHARTS.

	Retail Prices.
CHAPIN'S Large Ornamental Map of the United States, with Portraits of all the Presidents, on steel. Size 5 ft. 1 in. by 4 ft. 4 in.,	5 00
Map of North-America, Europe, and the North-Atlantic Ocean, showing the Lines of Communication between the Continents. Size 5 ft. 4 in. by 3 ft., ...	5 00
JOHNSON'S Map and Chart of the New World, Illustrated and Embellished, showing the British Possessions on the Western Continent, the United States and Territories, West-India Islands, Central and South-America, with the Pacific Coast. From the latest authorities. Size, 3 ft. 6 in. by 4 ft. 9 in., ...	4 00
JOHNSON'S Four-Sheet Map of the New World, recently improved. Size 4 ft. 4 in. by 4 ft., ...	4 50
Four-Sheet Map of the United States, showing the Counties of the United States, with a Plan of its Territories, from the latest authorities, and a splendid Ornamental Border. Size 3 ft. 10 in. by 3 ft. 3 in., ...Colored in Counties,	3 00
Do. Do. Do. " States,...	2 50
Map of the Great West, embracing the States of Illinois, Missouri, Wisconsin, Iowa, and Territory of Minnesota. A large and splendid Map. Size, 3 ft. 2 in. by 4 ft. 2 in., ...	3 00
Map of the World, on Mercator's Projection, with the Flags of all Nations, colored. Size, 3 ft. 10 in. by 2 ft. 9 in., ...	2 50
Do. Do. **Do., improved,** showing the Western Continent in the centre of the map, and embellished with Engravings. Size, 3 ft. 10 in. by 2 ft. 10 in., ...	3 00
Large Township Map of the State of New-York, most beautifully and distinctly Engraved. Size, 3 ft. 8 in. by 2 ft. 11 in., Colored in Towns,..	2 50
Do. Do. Do. " Counties,..	2 00
Large Township Map of the State of Ohio, Size, 3 ft. by 3 ft. 3 in., Colored in Towns,..	2 50
Do. Do. Do. " Counties...	2 00
Map of the United States and Territories, with Mexico and the West-Indies, showing the California Steamship Routes, Distances, etc. Size, 3 ft. by 3 ft. 3 in.	1 75
BLANCHARD'S Grammatical Tree, showing the Classification and Properties of English Parts of Speech. For the use of Schools. "*The Chart will be an Aid and Ornament in the School Room.*"—Joseph McKeen, Superintendent of Common Schools, New-York, ...	1 00

	Retail Prices.
Pictorial Map of the United States and Territories, with many beautiful Engravings. A very salable Map. Size, 3 ft. 7 in. by 2 ft. 8 in.,	1 50
Map of Canada, East and West. A new Edittion, vastly improved. Size 3 ft. 8 in. by 2 ft. 9 in.,	2 00
Portraits of the Presidents of the United States, with the Declaration of Independence, all on one large sheet, beautifully Colored and Mounted. Size, 2 ft. 8 in. by 3 ft. 7 in.,	1 50
JOHNSON'S Map of Europe. Size, 2 ft. 6 in. by 2 ft. 10 in.,	2 00
Map of the City and County of New-York, showing also a portion of Brooklyn, Williamsburgh, and Jersey City. Size, 5 ft. by 2 ft. 4 in.,	2 00
Map of Massachusetts, Connecticut, and Rhode-Island. Colored in Towns. Size, 3 ft. 8 in. by 2 ft. 6 in.,	1 50
Map of the Seven Western States, comprising Michigan, Ohio, Indiana, Illinois, Missouri, Wisconsin, and Iowa. Colored in Counties. Size, 2 ft. 7 in. by 2 ft. 2 in.,	1 25
Map of Pennsylvania. Colored in Counties. Size, 3 ft. by 2 ft. 1 in.,	1 25
Map of New-York State. Colored in Counties. Size, 2 ft. 8 in. by 2 ft. 1 in.,	1 00
Map of New-Jersey. Colored in Counties. Size, 2 ft. 1 in. by 2 ft. 8 in.	1 00
Plate of the Last Supper of our Lord, beautifully Ornamented and Colored. Size, 2 ft. 10 in. by 2 ft. 4 in.,	1 25
Do. Do. Do. Plain,	1 00
Plate of the Crucifixion of Christ. Colored. Size, 2 ft. 8 in. by 2 ft. 2 in.,	1 00
Plate of the Resurrection of Christ. Colored. Size, 2 ft. 8 in. by 2 ft. 2 in.,	1 00
Map of Illinois, with Population for 1840 and '50, and Plans of the Cities of Chicago and St. Louis, and much valuable Statistical Information. Colored in Counties. Size, 2 ft. 4 in. by 3 ft.	1 00
Map of Illinois, with Population for 1840 and '50, and a Plan of the City of Chicago. Colored in Counties. Size, 1 ft. 10 in. by 2 ft. 2.,	0 75
Map of Missouri, with Population for 1840 and '50, and a Plan of the City of St. Louis. Colored in Counties. Size, 2 ft. 2 in. by 1 ft. 10 in.,	0 75
Map of Wisconsin, with Population for 1840 and '50, and a Plan of the City of Milwaukee. Colored in Counties. Size, 1 ft. 10 in. by 2 ft. 2 in.	0 75
Map of Iowa, with Population for 1840 and '50. Colored in Counties. Size, 2 ft. 2 in. by 1 ft. 10 in.,	0 88
Township Map of Pennsylvania, with Population of 1840 and '50. Colored in Counties. Size, 2 ft. 7 in. by 2 ft.	0 75
Map of the Empire State, with Population of 1840 and '50. Colored in Counties. Size, 2 ft. 7 in. by 2 ft.,	0 75
Township Map of Ohio, with Population of 1840 and '50. Colored in Counties. Size, 2 ft. by 2 ft. 7 in.,	0 75
Township Map of Massachusetts, Connecticut, and Rhode-Island. Colored in Counties. Size, 2 ft. 7 by 2 ft.	0 75

	Retail Prices.
Map of the City of New-York, with Portions of Brooklyn, Williamsburgh, and Jersey City. Size, 2 ft. 1 in. by 1 ft. 9 in.,	0 62½
Map of Thirty Miles around New-York, with Bird's-eye View of the City. Size, 2 ft. by 2 ft. 7 in.,	0 75
FANNING'S Map of New-York City, showing the Streets Seven Miles from the Battery. Size, 2 ft. by 2 ft. 7 in.,	0 75
Do. Do. Do. showing the entire Island, with Brooklyn and Williamsburgh. Size, 2 ft. by 2 ft. 7 in.,	1 00
New Railroad Map, showing all the completed and projected Railroads in the United States and Canadas,	1 25
Europe and her Sovereigns,	1 25
War in Europe,	0 75
RANNEY'S United States,	0 75
Ireland,	0 62
MORSE'S World,	0 75
World's Progress,	0 50
United States at one View,	0 50
World at one View.	0 50
JOHNSON'S Philosophical Charts for Schools,	12 50

FOREIGN PAPERS.

Bell's Life,	25	$10 00
Dublin Freeman's Journal,	25	10 00
Dublin Nation,	25	10 00
London Art Journal,	75	9 00
" Athenæum,	12½	
" Illustrated News,	25	10 00
" Weekly Times,	12½	6 00
" Pictorial Times,	12½	
" Punch,	12½	
" Picture News,	12½	
" Sunday Dispatch,	25	
Wilmer & Smith's Times,	25	
News of the World,	12½	
London Journal,	5	
Reynolds' Miscellany	5	
Family Herald,	5	
Cassell's Illustrated Family Paper,	8	
Atlas,	25	
Literary Gazette,	12½	
Home Companion,	8	

Address

O. F. PARSONS,

140 *Nassau Street.*

www.ingramcontent.com/pod-product-compliance
Lightning Source LLC
LaVergne TN
LVHW010201110826
845151LV00002B/578

9781425535919